MW00761100

THE

SALVATION

OF THE

WORLD

THE

SALVATION

OF THE

WORLD

"All Ages Will Call Me Blessed" (Lk 1:48)

A gift of love for you from Mary!

Gerard B. Tall, Jr., T. O. Carm

Published by San Michel's Alcove, 29576, USA
International publication by arrangement with San Michel's Alcove

Library of Congress Cataloging-in-Publication Data

Tall, Gerard B., Jr.
...FOR THE SALVATION OF THE WORLD; *All Ages Will Call Me Blessed* | Her mission over the past one-hundred and eighty-eight years | Pope John Paul II | Intense spiritual battle | final confrontation between the Church, the anti-church and the antichrist | confrontation lies within the plans of divine Providence |

Includes Index

Catalog Card Number: TXu 1-798-786
Catalog Card Date: 2012-02-29
ISBN-13: 978-0-692-96633-4

First Publication	May, 2012
Second Printing	June, 2012
Third Printing	July, 2012
Fourth Printing	October, 2012
Fifth Printing	January, 2013
Sixth Printing	July, 2013
Second Publication	March, 2014
Eighth Printing	June, 2014
Ninth Printing	October, 2014
Tenth Printing	September, 2015
Third Publication	October 13, 2017

Covers by Michel
Cover pix – Anon.

20 19 18 17 16 15 14 13 12

San Michel's Alcove
Murrells Inlet, SC 29576
https://www.sanmichelsalcove.com

DEDICATION

To Two Hearts

Perpetual Eucharistic Adoration Chapel

- *Adoration Chapel, St. Michael's Church*
- *Assumption of the Blessed Virgin Mary, 2012*
- *Updated Publication, October 13, 2017*

· On June 13, 1917, Our Lady told Sr. Lúcia: *"Jesus wishes to make use of you to make me known and loved. He wishes to establish in the world devotion to my Immaculate Heart."*
- On May 18, 1936, Christ told her: *"I want My whole Church to acknowledge that consecration as a triumph of the Immaculate Heart of Mary…and put the devotion to the Immaculate Heart beside the devotion to My Sacred Heart."*

PRIVATE REVELATIONS

The Church teaches that "Christ, the Son of God made man, is the Father's one, perfect, and unsurpassable Word. In Him, He has said everything; there will be no other word than this one" (CCC n. 65). "Yet, even if Revelation is already complete, it has not been made completely explicit; it remains for Christian faith gradually to grasp its full significance over the course of the centuries" (CCC n. 66). "Throughout the ages, there have been so-called 'private' revelations, some of which have been recognized by the authority of the Church. They do not belong, however, to the deposit of faith. It is not their role to improve or complete Christ's definitive Revelation, but to help live more fully by it in a certain period of history. Guided by the magisterium of the Church, the sensus fidelium knows how to discern and welcome in these revelations whatever constitutes an authentic call of Christ, or His saints, to the Church. Christian faith cannot accept 'revelations' that claim to surpass or correct the Revelation of which Christ is the fulfillment, as is the case in certain non-Christian religions and also in certain recent sects which base themselves on such 'revelations'" (CCC n. 67).

"The judgment of the Church is essential because apparitions add nothing to the Creed, nor to the Gospel. They are a reminder for an age that has a tendency to forget them; they are indeed, a prophetic visitation to our world. God does not want us focusing on the wonderful or the extraordinary; but, through the apparitions, He gives us a sign that we should return to the Gospel which is the Word of His Son, the Word of Life. Faithfulness to the message of the Gospel, the authenticity of one's life of witness, and the results of holiness which flow out from it for the people of God are the criteria of an authentic apparition in the Church. The Church is not deceived in these matters."

- https://en.Lourdes-France.org

"The Nihil Obstat and Imprimatur are not required for publications dealing with private revelations, providing they contain nothing contrary to faith or morals" (A.A.S., 58, 1186). The author states unequivocally that he will adhere to the final disposition of the writings contained herein, and the unresolved apparitions in this book, as judged by the Magisterium of the Church.

In the event any of the apparitions currently under investigation are eventually deemed to be unworthy of belief, they would not discredit the other apparitions, nor would the eventual outcome of Our Lady's mission for *"the salvation of the human race"* be compromised in the slightest. Since her appearances in Fatima, in 1917, she has continued to give us greater insight about the future in order to help us understand our present day situation, and the consequences if we fail to heed her advice!

TABLE OF CONTENTS

A NOTE TO THE READER

This is a true story. It is about love, albeit tough love at times but love nonetheless. It is about the unwavering love a mother has for her children. She laughs with them, pleads with them, and cries for them whenever she sees them going astray. She teaches them about life and love, and its boundaries. She tells them about the future and cautions them about the consequences if they fail to heed her advice.

The words and pictures were carefully selected to appeal to all people – *believer* and *unbeliever* – pre-teen to old, while portions remain challenging to the most learned among us. It may be difficult to accept because it tells us about ourselves and our present day world in a clear and concise manner: what we did yesterday; where we are today, and what awaits us in the near future. However, once you comprehend her mission it may profoundly change your life: how you see the world, yourself, and the people around you. Unfortunately, many will not accept her words because, to do so, one may be required to change a part of their life, perhaps even give up some of the attachments to the things one has accumulated. Here, we would do well to reflect on the words of Christ: *"No one can serve two masters. He will either hate one and love the other, or be devoted to one and despise the other. You cannot serve God and mammon [money]"* (Mt 6:24).

We are driven by two distinct forces throughout our lifetime: we know them as *good* and *evil*. They begin in our childhood as *like* and *dislike* [*pleasure* and *pain*]; then, as we mature, they become better understood as *love* and *hate*. We choose which path to follow in our youth and, eventually, find that choice follows us throughout this life, on into the next one - eternity.

None are immune to this great struggle: *"...I have set before you life and death, the blessing and the curse. Choose life, then, that you and your descendants may live, by loving the Lord, your God, heeding his voice, and holding fast to him. For that will mean life for you..."* (Dt 30:19:20).

Psychiatry in the twentieth century generally acknowledged that the average person attains what is termed *spiritual maturity* by the time one reaches 30 to 35 years of age. Christ was just 30 years old when His public ministry began. What happens, then, to those who have not reached that spiritually mature age, those who have neither found nor developed a love for their Creator?

This story is also about difficult times that lay ahead, consisting of an immense conflict between those forces of good and evil. This trial is directed against Christianity itself, resulting in a worldwide apostasy by entities who, perhaps unknowingly, have enjoined the trial Pope Leo XIII foresaw in 1884.

These events were further clarified when Our Lady appeared in Fatima, in 1917. Now, additional information concerning the apparitions since Fatima has been added.

On December 2, 1983, one century after the vision of Pope Leo XIII, the pastor in Medjugorje sent a letter to Pope John Paul II concerning an apparition wherein Our Lady told Mirjana, a visionary in Medjugorje, *"You must realize that Satan exists...he appeared before the throne of God and asked permission to submit the Church to a period of trial. God gave him permission to try the Church for one century."*

Our Lady appeared many times since leaving the Rue du Bac in 1830. Her mission, *"the salvation of the human race"* is an attempt to save mankind from total annihilation. In 1983, Sr. Lúcia sent a letter to Cardinal Caffarra which noted *the decisive battle* is well underway. Pope John Paul II advises us that the battle will be intense: "We are now facing the final confrontation between Christ and the antichrist...It is a trial which the Church must face courageously."

A new chapter has been added to the book. Chapter 19, *The Decisive Battle,* is the next logical step in the unfolding of the Divine plan; a plan specifically chosen for Our Lady to bring about a triumphant conclusion to the events that began in 1830. It includes additional information regarding the more recent events in Fatima, Garabandal, Akita and Medjugorje, including the messages that are termed secrets.

While portions of several of the secrets are speculative at this time, the first three of the above noted apparition sites provide similar secrets that are applicable to the ten secrets given to Mirjana in Medjugorje. We finally have a glimpse of that part of the future. They are fully enjoined in the new chapter.

The known statements about the secrets, provided via various interviews of Mirjana and Ivan, are duly noted. One should not read the secrets with a morbid curiosity but, rather, in a wholesome manner. The secrets are, after all, part of the original messages which Our Lady did not hesitate to give to the seers. Hopefully, those listed herein will help to dispel some of the sensational claims made by the media.

St. Paul exhorts us: *"...work out your salvation in fear and trembling"* (Ph 2:12). Scripture also teaches us: *"The fear of the Lord is the beginning of wisdom"* (Ps 111:10). This *"holy fear"* is understood as the fear of the loss of a relationship with God and is one of the seven gifts of the Holy Spirit (CCC 1831). *"Do you not know that your body is a temple of the Holy Spirit within you"* (1 Cor 6:19) Thus, we are admonished: *"...Beloved, let us cleanse ourselves from every defilement of flesh and spirit, making holiness perfect in the fear of the Lord"* (2 Cor 7:1).

If we bide our time to wait and hear what Our Lady has to say tomorrow, then we have misunderstood her: she has already told us what must be done. It is through understanding Mary during the times to come that we will learn to fully appreciate her words and be drawn inexorably closer to her Son.

Our Lady advised us over the years that many changes are in the offing: *"...good for some; bad for others!"* The messages given by Mary are a call for mankind to return to God. On April 25, 1983, in Medjugorje, Our Lady said: *"Be converted! It will be too late when the Sign comes. Beforehand, several warnings will be given to the world. Have people become converted. I need your prayers and your penance."*

"After the third secret is fulfilled and the Sign is acknowledged by all, we will be *'either for God, or against Him!'"*

· This update was completed on October 13, 2017, exactly one century after Our Lady's final appearance in Fatima, Portugal. The new covers better reflect Our Lady's mission as it is currently unfolding. The sub-title *"All Ages Will Call Me Blessed"* (Lk 1:48) acknowledges the gratitude we should have for this lady who is so concerned about her children that she spends an extraordinary amount of time with them.

AUTHOR

G erard Beacham Tall, Jr. was born into one of the oldest traditional Roman Catholic families in the state of Maryland on August 14, 1932. His ancestors initially settled on its Eastern shore in 1670. After attending parochial grade schools he furthered his education in engineering at Severn Prep, Calvert Hall College, Johns Hopkins University and the University of Maryland. An adventurer at heart he even-tually married and, shelving his global sailing plans, fathered five children who remained faithful to the tenets of the Holy Roman Catholic Church despite the confusion that arose during the transitional period following the close of the Second Vatican Council [Vatican II].

In the early 1970s, he held the chair of the Spiritual Committee of the Shrine Guild at the Basilica of the National Shrine of the Immaculate Conception in Washington, DC. In 1972, he received an award from Patrick Cardinal O'Boyle and Archbishop Fulton J. Sheen for that endeavor. He was also the director of a Marian Center for the dissemination of information concerning Our Lady at many of the churches throughout the Archdioceses of Baltimore and Washington, and the Arlington Diocese in Northern Virginia.

On October 6, 1991, after twenty-five years as a Capuchin Franciscan Tertiary, he made his profession as a Third Order Carmelite and will remain in that order throughout the rest of his life. During a sojourn of four trips to Europe over a thirty year period prior to the close of the millennium, he resided for several months in many of the Marian Shrines noted herein.

He has retained his belief that the Holy Roman Catholic [universal] Church is the Church founded by Christ when He gave Peter the keys to the Kingdom: *"And so I say to you, you are Peter [Petros], and upon this rock [Petra] I will build my Church, and the gates of the netherworld shall not prevail against it"* (Mt 16:18). *"Whose sins you forgive are forgiven them, and whose sins you retain are retained"* (Jn 20:23).

Until his retirement in the mid-1980s, he was the captain of a government, oceanographic, research vessel, stationed in Annapolis, Maryland. His field of expertise was hydrographic engineering. While routine assignments consisted of the study of aquatic organisms and the determination of water quality standards by an onboard crew of marine biologists and chemists, numerous experiments were conducted in cooperation with industry and advanced research institutes.

In 1961, he was in charge of communications for a team assigned to trace nuclear radiation in the State of Maryland and vicinity. He was personally responsible for the city of Annapolis. Ongoing nuclear studies were routinely conducted throughout the 1970s and well into the 1980s. [1]

In the mid-1970s, the prototype of the 3-dimension, side-scanning, sonar imaging unit successfully passed the initial sea trials near Solomon's Island. Later, the equipment was placed in the unmanned submarine, Argo, and on September 1, 1985 – following several failed missions – the hull of the British passenger vessel RMS Titanic was finally located at a depth of almost 13,000 feet. The Titanic sank on April 15, 1912 after a fatal collision with an iceberg on her maiden, trans-Atlantic voyage from Southampton, England to New York City, USA.

---

[1] - pp. 188-191

ACKNOWLEDGEMENT

I express my sincerest gratitude to Rt. Rev. Stanislaus Gumula, O.C.S.O., abbot of Mepkin Abbey – a Trappist monastery in Moncks Corner, South Carolina – whose blessing afforded the courage to begin this book. I express my sincerest thanks to the Most Reverend Victor B. Galeone, Bishop Emeritus of St. Augustine, Florida, for his encouragement, correction of errors and suggesting a more legible font for the later editions. I am most grateful to Robert E. Guglielmone, Bishop of Charleston, SC, for his referral to Rev. Fr. Christopher Smith for revisions, and to Robert J, Baker, Bishop of the Diocese of Birmingham, Alabama for his personal words of encouragement.

In Memoriam

I offer my sincerest gratitude to Patrick Cardinal O'Boyle whose leadership in the Washington Archdiocese was so enlightening; to Lawrence Cardinal Shehan for his gracious permission to lecture in the Baltimore Archdiocese; to Archbishop Fulton Sheen for the example of his great love for Our Lady; to Bishop Nicholas D'Antonio, O.F.M., a fellow Baltimorean, for his personal blessing and encouragement; to Rt. Rev. Edward McCorkell, O.C.S.O., abbot of Our Lady of the Holy Cross Abbey in Berryville, Virginia, who guided me through several private retreats; to Msgr. William McDonough, sixth director of the Basilica of the National Shrine of the Immaculate Conception in Washington, D.C., for his guidance over a number of years; to Rev. Joseph A. Pelletier, A.A. for his enlightenment about Mary during a weekend visit to our home in Maryland; and finally, to Rev. Joseph Leo Lilly, C.M., S.T.D., S.S.L., both a cousin and wise mentor, noted for his tremendous contribution to the new translation of the Roman Catholic Bible [Confraternity of Christian Doctrine Edition] quoted throughout this manuscript.

I offer my thanks to Msgr. Walter R. Rossi, Rector, and Dr. Geraldine M. Rohling, Archivist-Curator of the Basilica of the National Shrine of the Immaculate Conception in Washington, DC for information regarding the chapter *The Immaculate Conception*; to Rev. John J. Nicola, former assistant director of that shrine, who guided my family in our knowledge of Mary at both the shrine and our home; to Rt. Rev. Edmund F. McCaffrey, O.S.B., a former abbot of Belmont Abbey in North Carolina, whose inspiring homilies about Mary helped me see the world in a brighter light. He remains a true patron of Our Lady;

I thank Rev. William Hearne, Rev. Ronald J. Farrell and members of the clergy who have reviewed or made suggestions to improve the accuracy and quality of this work. My gratitude additionally to Deacon Donald Efkin for his valued suggestions; to Deacon Charles Fiore for his splendid example of courage; and to James Kulway, a seminarian, for his probing questions which caused me to rewrite one chapter.

I am indebted to Dr. Stacy M. Cretzmeyer whose initial suggestions inspired me to begin this manuscript; this work would never have been attempted without her encouragement. I am additionally grateful to Caroline S. Banfield for her seasoned thoughts and input.

Most of all, I offer my fondest gratitude to five children: Gerard III, Loretta Marie, Karen Theresa, Michael Howard, and Mary Helen who taught me much about life, and to their mother, Alice Theresa, who did a magnificent job of raising and inspiring them, especially in their faith. It is my earnest desire that they heed the words contained herein, using them as guidelines during the remainder of the time allotted them by their Eternal Father.

Finally, I extend my thanks to the innumerable *man in the street* – the *Great Unwashed* – whom I have had the pleasure of meeting in my sojourn throughout the world over the course of a long life. They and the friends I grew up with knew literally nothing about Mary, seeing her only occasionally in the seasonal greeting cards and the store window Christmas displays so prevalent in our youth. Today, only a few outside the Church mention her by name; to many, she has become a remnant of Christmas past. This, then, is for their instruction and for all those who come after them.

PROLOGUE

The salvation of souls is Christ's mission. Mary, the Mother of God, assists her Son in this work by her prayers and, in difficult times, by her direct intervention into our present day lives as she attempts to save our world from destruction, salvaging many souls in the process. In 1983, Sr. Lúcia of Fátima noted that Our Lady was engaged *"in a decisive battle with Satan for the salvation of mankind."* Now, Mary tells us for the first time: *"Prayer is the only way to save the human race!"*

If one were to read a mystery novel and find the last chapter missing, how is it possible to understand the entire story, especially after the author went to great lengths to convince the reader that the butler didn't actually do it? In a similar manner one would have a difficult time understanding Christ if all they knew were the *Beatitudes* from His Sermon on the Mount (Mt 5;2-11), but never knew that Jesus said: *"I know your works...So, because you are lukewarm, neither hot nor cold, I will spit you out of my mouth"* (Rv 3:15-16).

Much like assembling a large jigsaw puzzle, wherein each piece provides only a glimpse of the picture, it is only after all the pieces are in place that one is able to gaze upon the beauty of the entire panorama. In a similar manner, when each apparition is seen in its proper context, one begins to comprehend the totality of her mission: her plan for *"the salvation of the world."* When one finally grasps the overall meaning, one will also understand why the Mother of God spends such extraordinarily longer times at each site, even shedding tears for us.

The author wishes to convey to the reader a deeper understanding of Our Lady's mission over these last 187 years, not by concentrating on any specific apparition site, albeit each one is demonstrably meaningful in itself, but rather, to emphasize their cumulative effect as the dates for the fulfillment of the final events of her mission grow ever nearer.

This total cumulative meaning of the unspoken message of all the sites appears to have been generally overlooked in the past. Oftentimes, the correct interpretation of the original language, and its translation into English, make it difficult to phrase their exact meaning.

I intend to be as explicit as possible regarding the wording of the messages, neither adding to, nor subtracting from what was actually said or implied. Insofar as changing the meaning of words, surely most of you are acutely aware of the recent changes in the translation of a number of prayers recited by the laity during the Mass, for the better I believe.

I well remember that time when they were originally changed. In the late 1960s, shortly after the closing of Vatican II, ICEL began reinterpreting the biblical words and phrases used in the Liturgy, subjecting many of them to what is called a *dynamic* [thought-for-thought] translation. As a result, much of their poetic beauty and true meaning was consigned to the dustbin of history, fortunately, to return in recent years! The 1960s and 1970s were also a time of dissent and rebellion. Many of the university campuses were in absolute chaos, reaching a peak on May 4, 1970 when thirteen students at Kent State University were shot by the National Guard who were summoned in an attempt to squelch the riots. Four students died, nine others were wounded, and one was paralyzed. Earlier, during the summer of 1969, over 500,000 counterculture *flower children* attended a three-day concert at Woodstock, New York. *Kumbaya* was one of the favorite songs of the guitar genre. The so called *sexual revolution* was in full swing: *"If it feels good, do it"; "Make love, not war!"* was another of the infamous slogans. Sex was confused with love, becoming one and the same. It is no wonder so many of the clergy and laity were perplexed!

The children of those times are coming of age now, assuming the reins of industry, education, and government. Unlike those of previous generations, many were denied contact with religion for the most part of their lives. They are the first generation in memory raised without the *Ten Commandments* or a prayer in their classrooms. To this day, it is illegal to say a prayer or bring a Bible into the public schools.

At the same time, many of the Catholic schools either shuttered their windows or denied religious instruction to the pupils, many under the mistaken guise they would receive government funds for books and public transportation if they didn't teach religion. The religious principal of the Catholic school where my children were enrolled told me that they would teach religion after receiving the grants! We didn't have the luxury of waiting so we enrolled them in public school the following year. Sadly, CCD was of little help so we turned to the famous old *Baltimore Catechism* which, fortunately, reinforces their faith to this day.

I can further attest to that same time when devotion to the Mother of God fell out of vogue. The rosary, her scapular and statues, as well as many of those of the angels and saints, were often discarded as being from a superstitious era, no longer relevant. They were literally thrown out of many of the churches. These events will be clarified in the ensuing chapters.

It was at this time that a stalwart of the Catholic Church, Patrick Cardinal O'Boyle, the archbishop of Washington, D.C., championed the teaching of Pope Paul VI's *Humanae Vitae.* Unfortunately, however, so many of his own priests publically objected to his insistence on its values – which merely reaffirmed the traditional teaching of the Catholic Church regarding married love and responsible parenthood – that the Cardinal had to warn the dissident priests against "false ideas." He eventually placed sanctions against the rebelling priests; some were not allowed to hear confessions; others were forbidden to preach or teach.

At the semi-annual USCCB conference held in Washington in 1968, 235 bishops became the target of a bizarre series of demonstrations by 3,500 dissident laymen who rallied at the Mayflower hotel in support of the 41 local priests who were being disciplined by the Cardinal for their public criticism of Pope Paul VI's encyclical. Later, 130 priests burst into another meeting held at Washington's Hilton hotel. A number of priests affixed their signatures to an advertisement in the local newspaper in a public show of support for the dissident priests. Eventually, most recanted their objections but, sadly, 25 actually left the priesthood!

Inasmuch as the USCCB meeting was held in Washington that year, the Archdiocese of Baltimore was spared such notoriety. Baltimore, the largest city in Maryland, is known in America as the *Cradle of Catholicism.* There, the old Baltimore Cathedral, the first metropolitan Cathedral constructed in America after the adoption of the Constitution, still proudly stands; it is now a Basilica. The *Baltimore Catechism* was promulgated there. Baltimore is also the home of St. Mary's Seminary, and now University; it is the first major seminary established for priests in the United States. It is not to be confused with Mount St. Mary's Seminary located in a mountainous area 50 miles to the west.

Baltimore achieved international fame during the War of 1812. After pillaging the city of Washington the British fleet began bombarding Fort McHenry early on the morning of September 13, 1814. By dawn the following morning, despite sustaining a twenty-five hour continuous bombardment, the British fleet had to abandon the battle and was forced to withdraw. A lawyer, trapped on board a vessel near the  British fleet, noticed that flying over the fort, "the flag was still there."

Inspired, he immediately composed a poem on an envelope he had retrieved from his pocket. That poem was later entitled *The Star Spangled Banner* and, in 1931, it became our National Anthem. The lawyer's name was Francis Scott Key.

I was privileged to serve in the Naval Reserve at Ft. McHenry In the summer of 1949, and was discharged after several years. Ten years later, on July 2, 1961 – shortly before the global dissension of the 1960s was in full swing – Our Lady began a series of appearances to four children in San Sebastian de Garabandal, a remote village in Spain. Her appearances there started about a year prior to the opening of Vatican II and ended one month before its closing.

Unfortunately, many of the reformists and the secular media, who misunderstood the true meaning and intent of Vatican II, gave impetus to a rampant rebellion within the Church. It became known as *the spirit of Vatican II.* Many of its adherents had not even taken the time to read all sixteen documents promulgated by the council, especially the longest document which extolled the role of Mary in the Church.

According to the view of Pope Benedict XVI, certain changes made in the name of *the spirit of Vatican II* are contrary, not only to canon law and Church tradition, but also to the actual teachings of the Council and its official interpretations. "The correct view of the Council is that which interprets it 'within the context of tradition, not as a rupture with tradition, and the false view is that which only accepted as authentic the *spirit* or progressive thrust of the documents, and rejected any elements of the older tradition found in the texts, which were regarded as compromises and not binding.'"

As a result of the unwillingness of many of the laity and hierarchy in the Church to unanimously adhere to the teaching of *Humanae Vitae* – and, here, we must admit we have not been completely honest about its implementation – we are paying the price for that folly today! It was indeed unfortunate that so few could foresee those impending evils of abortion and euthanasia that would soon be unleashed upon the world: two of the most atrocious misdeeds ever committed by mankind.

Pope Paul VI was truly a prophet for our times when on June 30, 1972 – seven years after the false implementation of the true wishes and teaching of Vatican II – he remarked: "The smoke of Satan has entered the very heart of the Church!"

HISTORY

History teaches us much about ourselves and what is expected of us. By studying who we are and what we did, we can deduce what works and what leads to failure. The information can be of tremendous assistance to those who wish to prepare for the future. Winston Churchill said it well: "Those who fail to learn from history are doomed to repeat it." So, as we begin this story, I shall beg your indulgence over the next several pages for a very brief sojourn through a period of time from the Garden of Eden until 1830, the year Mary's mission began!

The Bible is the most well-read of all the historical books; however, the secular world doesn't readily accept sacred Scripture verbatim. Most professional genealogists will not readily accept names and dates in printed Scripture; however, information which progenitors wrote in the margins or on pages reserved for family information are generally accepted as fact. The Bible contains lessons for the rule of life and, if we harken well to those admonitions, God will bestow numerous blessings upon us and our descendants. It is beyond dispute that over a long period of time, when men forgot and turned away from those teachings in order to pursue their own fashions, indulging instead in ideas that are offensive to Him, the wrath of their heavenly Father eventually fell upon them.

In about [c.] 1926 B.C., long after Adam and Eve proved to be a disappointment to their Creator, God selected Abram whom He severely tested, telling him: *"...your name shall be Abraham, for I am making you the father of a host of nations"* (Ex 17:5-6). Abram became the progenitor of a nation peculiarly God's own, promising him and his descendants special favors if they remained faithful to His teachings. We know them today as the Israelites; they are the direct descendants of Abraham, Isaac and Jacob. Then, c. 1625 B.C., Abraham's great-grandson, Joseph, found much favor with Pharaoh. Owing to the famine that was devastating the land of Canaan, Abraham and his family arranged to move to Goshen, Egypt where they escaped the seven-year famine that eventually ravaged most of the livestock and crops in that part of the world.

However, over a period of hundreds of years, the ensuing Pharaohs became concerned about the increase of the Jewish population. Fearing they might eventually rebel, they were bent to the rule of Pharaoh, enslaved by their Egyptian masters. They labored in this manner for hundreds of years, making bricks with mud and straw. Finally, they began to plead with their heavenly Father, praying for relief.

In 1230 B.C., God answered their pleas by calling upon an exiled Egyptian prince known as Moses to ascend Mount Sinai. *"There an angel of the Lord appeared to him in fire flaming out of a bush. As he looked on, he was surprised to see that the bush, though on fire, was not consumed. So Moses decided, 'I must go over to look at this remarkable sight and see why the bush is not burned. When the Lord saw him coming over to look at it more closely, God called to him from the bush, 'Moses! Moses!' He answered, 'Here I am.' God said, 'Come no nearer! Remove your sandals from your feet, for the place where you stand is holy ground. I am the God of your father; the God of Abraham; the God of Issac...'"* (Ex 3:2-6). Then, He told Moses: *"Come now! I will send you to Pharaoh to lead my people, the Israelites, out of Egypt"* (Ex 3:10). Moses said: *"If they ask me What is his name?"* God replied: *"I am who am...tell the Israelites: I am sent me to you"* (Ex 3:13-14).

Now, Pharaoh was a hard-hearted man and it was only after ten severe plagues were sent upon the Egyptians, made worse because they came directly from God, that he finally relented, telling the Israelites to go, to leave Egypt. The plagues were so terrifying that, with the blessing of all the Egyptians, Ramses II sent them off with gold and cattle; food and clothing; anything to be rid of these people and their plagues.

Journeying through the desert the Israelites finally made camp at the base of Mount Sinai. There, Moses began his ascent to the top of the mountain where he remained for forty days and nights. However, because the area was spouting smoke and flames similar to that of a volcano, the Israelites erroneously believed Moses perished in the flames. In their fear and anger they foolishly made a golden gilded image of their god, Baal, in the form of a bull. They began to worship it and did much unbridled revelry in the process.

God said: *"I see how stiff-necked this people is"* (Ex 32:9). So, He sent Moses down from the mountain to put a stop to their carousing. In his anger Moses smashed both the tablets given to him by God; then, he had the revelers who opted to return to slavery, all those who rejected God, put to the sword.

Moses ascended the mountaintop where he received a second set of the *Ten Commandments* on two tablets of stone *"inscribed by God's own finger"* (Ex 31:18).  He was given 613 Statutes (Dt; Nm), details of the law prescribing how these people were to live in a manner that would be acceptable and pleasing to God. Then, He told Moses: *"Therefore, if you harken to my voice and keep my covenant, you shall be my special possession; dearer to me than all other people. You shall be to me a kingdom of priests, a holy nation"* (Ex 19:5-6).

"When Moses came down from Mount Sinai with the two tablets of the Commandments in his hands, he did not know that the skin of his face had become radiant while he conversed with the Lord...they were afraid to come near him...he put a veil over his face" (Ex 34:29-30; 33).

Owing to the ingratitude and doubts of these people who had just been freed from slavery, God forced all of them to wander in that unforgiving desert for forty years before reaching the *Promised Land:* the area that stretched from the River of Egypt to the Euphrates River. All the original Israelites perished during this time; save one, Joshua, who was Moses' trusted right hand man. Only their descendants were permitted to go into that *Promised Land* with Joshua. Even Moses was not permitted to enter. He died and was buried within sight of the *Promised Land*: a land where it rained; a *"land flowing with milk and honey"* (Ex 33:3).

We must remember that the Israelites were especially chosen by God: *"For you are a people sacred to the Lord, your God, who has chosen you from all the nations on the face of the Earth to be a people peculiarly his own"* (Dt 14:2). Yet we are all God's children. These Commandments were given for mankind out of love, not punishment; rather, for their guidance and the future of all mankind. The Creator knew that ignoring them would eventually harm those nations who didn't adhere to them.

After many generations adhering to the admonitions given by God to Moses on Mount Sinai, the Israelites built their first temple in Jerusalem. It was finished in 968 B.C. during the reign of King Solomon. When the temple was consecrated, God sternly warned him: *"But if you and your descendants ever withdraw from me, fail to keep the commandments and statutes which I set before you, and proceed to venerate and worship strange gods, I will cut off Israel from the land I gave them...and this temple shall become a heap of ruins"* (1 Kg 9:6-8).

Still, over the course of several centuries, people forgot and completely ignored those warnings; others began to partake in idolatrous revelry, pursuing gods made of stone.

God, the Eternal Father, rarely intervenes directly [physically] in human history. Therefore, we should not be surprised when He sends His angels to guide us back to the *narrow road!*

About 775 B.C., God chose Jonah – a farmer from Gath Hepher, in Israel - to go to Nineveh, a city in Iraq. There, he was to warn the people to repent of their evil ways. Basically, God said: *"Go";* Jonah said: *"No!"* And God responded: *"Oh!"* What transpired next is one whale of a story! When this reluctant prophet was finally deposited on the shore he began his journey through the streets of Nineveh proclaiming: *"Forty days more and Nineveh shall be destroyed"* (Jon 3:4). Then, sitting down, he eagerly awaited the city's destruction.

However, much to Jonah's surprise, King Jeroboam II issued an edict to the populace and they began to fast. Many rent their clothing, donned sackcloth and poured ashes on their heads. As a result, God accepted their penance and spared both the people and the city.

We, ourselves, may not be as fortunate as the inhabitants of Nineveh. Certainly, not for the people in Noah's time, nor those in Sodom and Gomorrah; not everyone is eager to adapt to torn clothing and unkempt faces drawn thin from fasting.

Then, in 626 B.C. God sent the prophet, Jeremiah, to warn the people to discontinue their widespread idolatrous practices. His words went unheeded so God sent the Babylonian king, Nebuchadnezzar, to invade the nation of Israel. They completely destroyed the temple and took the survivors into captivity as slaves. Slavery is an abomination; yet, out of that misery great events can transpire, often having a huge impact upon history.

During their captivity in Babylon, there was genuine concern that the oral traditions of the Chosen People would be lost under slavery. Hoping to preserve their faith for all future generations, the sages began recording the *Torah.* The first book, *Genesis,* was written on parchment by these priestly scribes and, eventually, all the *Old Testament* was put into writing for their future generations. [1]

When the specified time of the prophet's captivity in Babylon ended, God directly intervened again in the affairs of His people to lead them out of slavery. We read that *"King Belshazzar, the son of Nebuchadnezzar, gave a great banquet for a thousand of his nobles and drank wine with them. While drinking from the gold and silver goblets that had been taken from the temple in Jerusalem, they praised the gods of gold and silver. Suddenly, the fingers of a human hand appeared, writing on the plaster of the wall in the king's palace. When the king saw the wrist and hand that wrote, his face blanched; his thoughts terrified him"* (Dn 5:1-6).

A common expression, *The Writing On the Wall,* actually comes from scripture: *"...writing on the plaster of the wall of the king's palace"* (Dn 5:5). The writing: *"Mene, Tekel, and Parsin [Upharsin]"* is translated: *"God has numbered the days of your kingdom and brought it to an*  end; you have been weighed in the balances and found wanting; your kingdom is divided and given to the Medes and Persians"* (Dn 5:25-26). That very night, in 539 B.C., Belshazzar was slain and Darius, the Mede, a nephew of Cyrus, succeeded to the throne at the age of 62. His father, Nebuchadnezzar, died earlier in 562 B.C.

In 525 B.C., Cyrus the Persian, recalling the fate of King Belshazzar, issued an edict permitting the Israelites who wished to do so to return home. He actually assisted them in their efforts to relocate there. He also returned the vessels of silver and gold that had been looted.

Cyrus even ordered the rebuilding of their temple and committed funds from his treasury to accomplish it. This second temple was finally completed in 516 B.C. Centuries later, c. 19 B.C., King Herod the Great, modernized and enlarged the temple. He died in the springtime c. March 13, 4 B.C.

---

[1] - "The Annals of the World," James Ussher, Master Books, pp. 779, 4000a AM, 4709 WP, 5 BC

Jesus, the Christ, was born during the final years of Herod's life, most likely about 5 B.C. This Messiah (Redeemer) that the Father had promised mankind, begotten of the Holy Spirit and born of a virgin named Mary – a Jewish woman betrothed to Joseph – fulfilled that which was foretold in the Scriptures: *"And the Word became flesh and made his dwelling among us"* (Jn 1:14). He was descended from the ancestral tribe of David. During His public ministry, encompassing His last three years on Earth, Jesus gave us a *Second [Everlasting] Covenant* which complemented the *First Covenant.* Near the end of His ministry He wept over Jerusalem because His own people did not accept Him as the promised Savior. He described the fate of those people and the temple: *"...there shall not be one stone left upon another that will not be thrown down"* (Mk 13:2).

He was 33 years old when He was crucified and buried. He rose from the dead on the third day. He remained with His apostles and friends for 40 days, then, ascended into Heaven, witnessed by His apostles. Thus, He fulfilled all the prophecies concerning Him in the Old Testament.

Jerusalem, the main city and site of the temple, was a hotbed of anarchy with numerous rebellious groups attempting to overthrow the shackles of the invaders. By A.D. 70, the Romans invaded the city and slaying everyone in their way, burning the buildings in the process. As the temple burned, the fine gold melted and ran down between the joints in the stones. In order to retrieve this precious metal, the invaders dismantled each stone so there was literally *"...not...one stone left upon another"* (Mk 13:2). Eventually, an edict was passed making it a serious crime for anyone of Jewish descent to remain there. Those found later were either put to death or taken into slavery, effectively scattering the Jews throughout the world for almost two millennium.

Then, we read, *"With a mighty hand and outstretched arm, with poured-out wrath, I will bring you out from the nations and gather you from the countries over which you are scattered"* (Ez 20:34). This was fulfilled when Israel was established as an independent nation by the United Nations on May 14, 1948. Worldwide, many an elderly Israelite shed tears on that day, never thinking they would live to see that prophesy fulfilled in their lifetime. This also fulfilled the prophesy: *"Can a country be brought forth in one day, or a nation be born in a single moment...Shall I bring a mother to the point of birth, and yet not let her child be born? says the Lord; or shall I who allow her to conceive, yet close her womb? says your God"* (Is 66:8-9).

Finally, in the late 1960s, after almost two thousand years in exile, the Israelites began returning to their homeland. By 2010 the population of Israel increased to more than 7,624,600. Over time, even to this day, perhaps no race of people has been mistreated more than they; yet, they held onto their faith for they know they are a chosen people very special to Him. As Christians we so easily forget that Christ was a Jew, born of a Jewish mother, Mary. Inasmuch as the Jews rejected Christ as their Redeemer, the Church was opened for the Gentiles. We are all God's children and, if we choose to follow Him, we can also be special to Him.

We learn from history that God is a *jealous* God who wants no one to take His place. We are often reminded of this love God has for us and, especially over the last 45 years, it seems to have been all about love: how much we must love God and love our neighbor; but, what are the consequences if we aren't able to do that? Holy Scripture reminds us that: *"The beginning of wisdom is the fear of the Lord"* (Pr 9:10); we are also told: *"This is the one whom I approve: the lowly and afflicted man who trembles at my word"* (Is 66:2).

During an earlier meeting of the National Conference of Catholic Bishops in the previous millennium, one of the bishops rose to declare: "I apologize for the fact that we taught about love, but we neglected to teach the other side [of the equation]." This would not be acceptable in mathematics or science: both sides of an equation must contain equal values; it must be balanced. Unfortunately, he sat down when no one took up his challenge!

As we read on we will learn that Our Lady does not hesitate to point out what needs to be done. There is no timidity when she presents us with both sides of the equation. Our Lady comes from Heaven to assist her children in these perilous times. She does so without apology; rather, with genuine concern for all while, at the same time, showing her sincere love for each one of her children. She does not hesitate to remind us of the consequences if we fail!

In her Magnificat, Mary tells us, *"His mercy is from age to age to those who fear him"* (Lk 1:50); however, Jesus cautions us: *"Not everyone who says to me, 'Lord, Lord,' will enter the kingdom of Heaven, but only the one who does the will of my Father in Heaven"* (Mt 7:21). *"Many will say to me on that day, 'Lord, Lord, did we not prophesy in your name? Did we not drive out demons in your name? Did we not do mighty deeds in your name?' Then I will declare to them solemnly, I never knew you. Depart from me, you evildoers"* (Mt 7:22-23).

The Church and Holy Scripture clearly instruct that our bodies are temples of the Holy Spirit. St. Paul tells us, *"Do you not know that your body is a temple of the Holy Spirit within you, whom you have from God, and that you are not your own? For you have been purchased at a price. Therefore glorify God in your body"* (1 Cor 6:19-20); *"If anyone destroys God's temple, God will destroy that person; for the temple of God which you are, is holy"* (1 Cor 3:17). As temples of the Holy Spirit we must keep ourselves holy and pure for Him. We do that by obeying His *Commandments* and *Statutes*. That includes loving our neighbor and doing good, even to those who hurt us!

As Christ was dying on the cross, *"...he said to his mother, 'Woman, behold, your son"* (Jn 19:26). In uttering these words, Jesus established a relationship of love between Mary, the disciples and, ultimately, all of us. The Bible reminds us, the Israelites were a *"...stiff necked...people"* (Ex 32:9). Now, in 1982 in Medjugorje, we are told: "God is at the end of His patience" and, later, "God cannot take it anymore!" and retribution is inevitable! Obviously, then, the burden is upon us.

Earlier, referring to La Salette, Pope Pius IX reminded us: "In this place, Mary, the loving Mother appeared manifesting her pain for the moral evil caused by humanity. Her tears help us to understand the seriousness of sin and the rejection of God and, at the same time, it is a manifestation of the passionate fidelity that her Son has for each person, even though His redemptive love is marked by the wounds of treason and abandonment by men. The Shrine of La Salette is of great authenticity and is destined to have a future. I love this devotion and shall be glad to see it spread."

In 1997, John Paul II stated: "The universal motherhood of Mary, the 'Woman' of the wedding at Cana and of Calvary, recalls, *'The man called his wife Eve, because she became the mother of all the living'"* (Gn 3:20). Yet while the first [Eve] helped to bring sin into the world, the new Eve, Mary, co-operates in the saving event of Redemption.

On November 11, 2013, Archbishop Carlo Vigano, Apostolic Nuncio to the United States, addressed the opening session of the USCCB Fall General Assembly in Baltimore, Maryland with the following statement: "At this point, I would like to call your attention to the words the then [Karol] Cardinal Wojtyla is reported to have given in an address during the Eucharistic Congress [in Philadelphia] in 1976, for the Bicentennial celebration of the signing of the *Declaration of Independence.* It seems to be so profoundly prophetic:

"'We are now standing in the face of the greatest historical confrontation humanity has ever experienced. I do not think that the wide circle of the American Society or the whole wide circle of the Christian Community realizes this fully. We are now facing the final confrontation between the Church and the anti-church, between the Gospel and the anti-Gospel, between Christ and the antichrist. The confrontation lies within the plans of divine Providence. It is, therefore, in God's Plan and it must be a trial which the Church must take up, and face courageously.'" [1]

That timely prophesy of John Paul II is being fulfilled throughout the world these days. Our Lady advises us what needs to be done now and in the future. As you read through this book you will understand that, since the death of John Paul II in 2005, we are now living in a new era, albeit a tumultuous one, that era disclosed by Our Lady in 1961.

In the early 1960s, Our Lady advised Conchita, a visionary in Garabandal, that: *"...after Pope Paul VI there would be two more popes and that would be the end of an era, but not the end of the world!"* On October 16, 1978, John Paul II became that second pope.

Mary, the Mother of God, has been appearing at various places throughout the world over the past 187 years to help us understand that God is again very angry with us. She tells us what we must do in order to restore His trust in us. The history of the events she prophesied during those past apparitions was for us, fortunately or not, quite accurate.

It follows then that whatever else she has predicted may well come to fruition. What happens next will depend largely upon our responses to her. However, this must not be the old cliché about *gloom and doom* because we have a choice. Sure, we may have to endure some difficult times and many a hardship, maybe a bruise here and there; yet, to a great extent, which way we go now depends on us.

That choice is truly ours yet, regardless of what we do, we must accept Christ's words to Sr. Lúcia concerning the timeframe for the conversion of Russia: *"...it will be late."*

As was stated earlier, this is a true story! It is about hope for the world. It is a story that looks forward to the time when we will see the fulfillment of that promise given by Our Lady of Fátima, words that echo down from one-hundred years ago, *"...In the end, My Immaculate Heart will triumph. The Holy Father will consecrate Russia to Me, and she will be converted, and a period of peace will be granted to the world."*

This is also a love story about Mary, your mother, who is doing all she can to be of help to you. She loves you very much and is truly concerned about what you are doing. She cares about you even more than your own mother for, truly, she is our heavenly mother, our spiritual mother! What she has to say to you is very, very important.

As proof of this, I will note what she has done for you in the past, what she is doing now, and what she is doing about your future! Then, in consideration of her love and concern for our welfare, I will try to help you understand what must be done in gratitude to her, for our future and for our salvation.

Will we turn away from her, continually ignoring her pleas, or will we finally begin to heed her advice? Perhaps recalling one of the basic tenants of the Baltimore Catechism will help: *"God made me to know Him, to love Him, and to serve Him in this world, and to be happy with Him forever in the next!"*

---

[1] Karol Cardinal Wojtyla's speech made in 1976, two years prior to his election as pope.

- *The Wanderer*, Volume 145, No. 47, November 21, 2013

- Reference to this speech was also noted by George Weigel in his biography of John Paul II, *Witness to Hope*: "These remarks are cited on the editorial page of the Wall Street Journal, November 9, 1978, and attributed to Wojtyla's 'last speech in the U.S. in September, 1976, as quoted in the New York City News.'"

THE STORY

T his story actually has its beginning in Rome, in A.D. 312; then, by 1689, the focus is on France, a country often referred to as the *Eldest Daughter of the Church*. At the height of the reign of King Louis XIV, France was enjoying the longest, most prosperous reign in European history, Christ sought specific favors from this *Sun King;* after all, when he was born in 1638 he was known as the miracle child, the son of Louis XIII, of France and Anne Hapsburg, of Austria.

Palace of Versailles, France

Unfortunately, Louis XIV was unable to accomplish what Our Lord requested of him through St. Margaret Mary. France, as a nation, never regained her former status. Hence, over the next one-hundred and eight years, following that golden era of the Palace at Versailles, France was to lose her crown and suffer constant revolutions and wars, continuing down through the present day.

Inasmuch as France had originally been so favored, she was especially chosen by Our Lady in 1830 for the beginning of her mission for *"the salvation of mankind."* However, when her requests went unheeded over the next forty-nine years, she expanded her mission to include other nations throughout much of Europe.

Thus began a series of appearances of the Mother of God in various places throughout the world. Her favors graced Ireland, Portugal, Belgium, Spain and finally, Yugoslavia – a nation behind the *iron curtain* upon whom Communism (atheistic Socialism) had been imposed by its dictatorial devotees – culminating in a rather remote village in a Communist country in 1981, a nation behind the *iron curtain*. As we shall see, Pope John Paul II had been praying to Our Lady, hoping she would appear where her voice might be heard.

In 1936, Christ told Sr. Lúcia of Fátima that: *"...the salvation...has been entrusted to Mary, and she alone can save it!"* Sixty-four years later at Fátima, on May, 13, 2000, mindful of the angel's actions after Adam and Eve were cast out of the Garden of Eden, Pope John Paul II revealed the long-awaited third and final secret of Fátima:

"An angel, with a flaming sword in his left hand..." threatened to destroy a large part of the Earth by casting fire upon it from Heaven; however, Our Lady intervened and he paused what he was about to do.

We do not know how long the angel will delay this chastisement. We do know the angel then pointed to the Earth with his right hand and cried out in a loud voice: *"Penance; Penance; Penance."* Will we heed the angel's warning and perform that penance? We might; we might not!

PART I

Past

Mary, the Mother of God, has become increasingly involved in the affairs of mankind, especially over the last several centuries as she attempts to warn her children about the godless path on which they are treading. God advises us through His word, the Bible: *"The fear of the Lord is the beginning of wisdom"* (Ps 111:10) and *"His mercy is from age to age to those who fear him"* (Lk 1:50).

Does fear of the Lord eventually result in love for Him? And, why does Mary shed tears during so many of her appearances? What does it mean to us: the end of the world as we know it? It might; after all, Heaven has warned us so many times in the past. However, before we continue further to understand what the correct path is, we must first go back in time – almost two millennium.

The Bible reminds us that Mary, the Mother of Christ, will be honored by every nation throughout history: *"All ages will call me blessed"* (Lk 1:48).

CHAPTER 1

Constantine, Rome, Italy

"A great sign appeared in the sky, a woman clothed with the sun, with the moon under her feet, and on her head was a crown of twelve stars...Then another sign appeared in the sky..." (Rev 12.1).

A great battle was about to be waged that would have tremendous historical consequences upon the world in general, and Christianity in particular. The place was Rome, the capital of an empire that ruled most of the known world; the year A.D. 312; the battle, October 28.

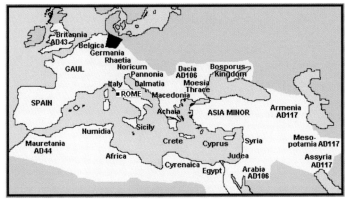

The Roman Empire

By July, 306, the Roman Empire was split into two parts, governed by two co-Emperors. These men were rulers who had similar backgrounds and were very close in age. In fact, they were in-laws. They should have been allies or, at the least, friends; instead, they became the bitterest of enemies. One of them, Constantine, dissatisfied with the manner in which the capital was being governed by Emperor Maxentius, chose to do battle with him. The winner would become sole Emperor of Rome!

After marching all day Constantine's troops arrived at a location just outside the city, stopping overnight to rest prior to crossing the Tiber River from whence the battle would begin the following morning. It was now October 27th.

Constantine

Maxentius

Later that day, Constantine experienced quite an extraordinary event. While looking up just above the sun, he saw a cross of light and he clearly heard the Greek words *Εv Τούτω Νίκα* which, translated into Latin, are *In Hoc Signo Vinces!* (By this [sign] win!) [1]

The Sign

Constantine immediately commanded his troops to adorn their shields and banners with that Christian symbol, much to the chagrin of many of these battle-hardened soldiers. Try to imagine their thoughts as they affixed these signs onto their shields, asking themselves just what did they signify, for they knew full well they would have to face a formidable enemy in the morning.

Maxentius was worried: although he had almost four times as many troops they were not as battle hardened as Constantine's, nor as well disciplined. He could have fought him from the heavily fortified Roman city itself, but the citizens were restless. So, on that fateful October 28th, his army left the city and crossed over to the right bank of the Tiber River.

The Milvian Bridge

A ferocious confrontation began and, when the fighting neared the Milvian Bridge, another bridge of pontoon boats was constructed to facilitate the additional troops crossing the river. However, when Constantine's army forced his opponent's army back onto the pontoon bridge, it collapsed under the strain. In the ensuing melee, Maxentius himself drowned along with many of his soldiers. When Constantine's soldiers recovered his body they paraded his head through Rome on a pike.

Following the battle, the sole Emperor, Constantine *the Great*, ignored the altars to the gods prepared on the Capitoline. He did not perform the customary sacrifices to celebrate a general's victorious entry into Rome. Instead, he headed directly to the imperial palace. He fully understood that the *sign of the cross* he saw in the heavens meant Rome would not survive without the Church.

From that time on, persecution of the Christians ceased! In fact, owing to that sign, Constantine took over the role as patron for the Christian faith by supporting the Church financially. He built an extraordinary number of basilicas, granted privileges to members of the clergy and promoted Christians to high-ranking offices. He returned property that was confiscated during the *Great Persecution* of Diocletian and endowed the Church with land and great wealth.

The Heavenly Sign

In 330, Constantine built a new imperial capital at Byzantium, known as the great city of Constantinople. He was finally baptized as a Christian on his deathbed. It is likely he chose to delay this inasmuch as, in the early Church, confession was only permitted once in a lifetime. Since then, that privilege has been relaxed and one may receive the sacrament as often as desired.

---

[i] This *Sign of the Cross* Constantine saw in the heavens is an important theme throughout this story! You will read more about this in several of the ensuing chapters.

CHAPTER 2

Our Lady of Guadalupe, Mexico

—†———†——
312   1531

"...All those who sincerely ask my help in their work, and in their sorrows, will know my Mother's Heart in this place. Here I will see their tears; I will console them and they will be at peace..."

Twelve centuries later, in 1531, Our Lady appeared in the Americas, atop a small hill in the Tepayac hill country of the Mexican desert, to a simple Aztec Indian named, Juan Diego. He was 57, a recent convert to Christianity. This beautiful lady, '*...surrounded by a ball of light as bright as the sun'* told him: *"My dear little son, I love you. I desire you to know who I am. I am the ever-virgin Mary, Mother of the true God who gives life and maintains its existence. He created all things. He is in all places. He is Lord of Heaven and Earth."*

She added: *"I desire a church in this place where your people may experience my compassion. All those who sincerely ask my help in their work, and in their sorrows, will know my Mother's Heart in this place. Here I will see their tears; I will console them and they will be at peace. So run now and tell the bishop all that you have seen and heard."*

Juan hurried as fast as he could and upon arriving at Bishop Juan de Zumárraga's house, he asked to see the bishop; however, the servants were suspicious of this rural peasant and they kept him waiting for hours. Finally, he was escorted to see the bishop where Juan told him the whole story.

The bishop advised Juan that he would consider the Lady's request and suggested meeting Juan again if he wished. Naturally, Juan was very disappointed by the response and felt unworthy to persuade someone so important as a bishop.

Returning to the hill where he had first seen Mary, he found her waiting for him. He implored her to send someone else but she responded: *"My little son, there are many I could send. But you are the one I have chosen."*

She told him to return the next day and repeat the same request to the bishop. So, next Sunday, after waiting several hours, he again talked to the bishop. This time, though, the bishop told him to ask the Lady to provide a sign as a proof of who she was.

Juan & Our Lady of Guadalupe

Juan dutifully returned to the hill where Our Lady was again waiting for him. When he told her what the bishop said, she responded: *"My little son, am I not your Mother? Do not fear. The bishop shall have his sign. Come back to this place tomorrow. Only peace, my little son."*

Upon reaching home Juan discovered that his uncle, Bernardino, whom he dearly loved as a father, was extremely ill. He was much worse by daybreak, so Juan set out to obtain medicine from a doctor. Yet, the following morning found him near death so Juan left his side to find the priest. Passing near Tepayac Hill Juan realized he had not done as Our Lady asked; however, fearing his uncle would die, he took another road. Not to be outdone, Mary appeared in front of him on the path. He was frightened and falling to his knees informed her he was hurrying to find a priest for his uncle.

Mary replied: *"Do not be distressed, my littlest son. Am I not here with you who am your Mother? Are you not under my shadow and protection? Your uncle will not die at this time. There is no reason for you to engage a priest, for his health is restored at this moment. He is quite well. Go to the top of the hill and cut the flowers that are growing there. Bring them then to me."*

Juan obeyed Mary's instructions and went to the top of the hill. There, despite the fact that it was freezing, he found a full bloom of Castilian roses. Removing his tilma, a poncho-like cape made of cactus fiber, he cut the roses and carried them back to Mary. She rearranged the roses

and told him: *"My little son, this is the sign I am sending to the bishop. Tell him that with this sign I request his greatest efforts to complete the church I desire in this place. Show these flowers to no one else but the bishop. You are my trusted ambassador. This time the bishop will believe all you tell him."*

At the palace, Juan retold his story to the bishop. Then, on opening the tilma, he let the flowers fall out. But it wasn't the beautiful roses which bloomed in winter that caused the bishop and his advisors to fall to their knees in wonder and awe! It was the tilma, for emblazoned on it was a picture of the Blessed Virgin Mary precisely as Juan had described her. The next day, after showing the tilma at the Cathedral, Juan took the bishop to the place where he first encountered Mary.

Later that day, he returned to his village where he met his uncle. He had been completely cured. His uncle relayed to him that he met a young woman, surrounded by a soft light, who told him that she had just sent his nephew to the bishop with a picture of herself. She told his uncle: *"Call me, and call my image, Santa Maria de Guadalupe."*

Santa Maria de Guadalupe

The picture on the tilma is similar to an icon with precise meanings for each symbol to the native population, one of which shows Mary as the God-bearer who is pregnant with her Divine Son.

Since the time the tilma was first impressed with a picture of the Mother of God, and over the first six years, six million Aztecs were converted to Catholicism.

The tilma has been subjected to a variety of environmental hazards, including smoke from fires and candles, water from floods, and torrential downpours. In 1921, anti-clerical forces planted a bomb which exploded, but the tilma was untouched and no one in the church was injured. However, a cast-iron cross next to the tilma was twisted out of shape and the marble altar rail was heavily damaged.

New and Old Basilicas of Our Lady of Guadalupe

The image, inexplicable in its longevity and method of production, is a miracle in itself and can be seen today in Mexico City, Mexico, in a large Cathedral built to accommodate up to ten thousand people. It is by far the most popular religious pilgrimage site in the Western Hemisphere.

Epilogue, Guadalupe

In 1977, the tilma was thoroughly examined using infrared photography and digital enhancement techniques. Unlike other paintings, the tilma shows no sketching or any sign of outline drawn to permit an artist to produce a painting. Furthermore, the very method used to create the image is still unknown.

One of the most common attributions and reported discoveries lie with the Virgin's eyes in the image. Recently, with advanced electronic photographic magnification, it was discovered that Mary's eyes reflected the face of the bishop, as well as that of Juan Diego.

Dr. Jose Alte Tonsmann, a Peruvian ophthalmologist, conducted a study. One of his tests involved examining the eyes at 2,500 times magnification. With the images of her magnified eyes, the scientist was able to identify as many as 13 individuals in both eyes at different proportions, just as the human eye would reflect an image. It appeared to be a snapshot of the very moment Juan Diego unfurled his tilma before the archbishop.

CHAPTER 3

Paray-le-Monial, France

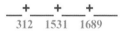

$$\frac{+ \quad + \quad +}{312 \quad 1531 \quad 1689}$$

"My Heart wants to reign in his palace, to be painted on his banners, engraved on his coat of arms, to make them victorious so he will triumph over all the enemies of the Church."

One-hundred, fifty-eight years later, in 1689, Our Lord appeared to Sr. Margaret Mary Alacoque, a Visitation nun residing in a convent in Paray-le-Monial, France, a town several hundred miles from Paris.

Christ **Margaret Mary**

He appeared to her many times and, during one of those visits, He told her that for those who receive the Eucharist [Holy Communion] on nine consecutive First Fridays: *"I promise you, in the excess of the mercy of My Heart, that Its all-powerful love will grant to all those who will receive Communion on the first Friday of nine consecutive months, the grace of final repentance; they will not die under My displeasure nor without receiving the Sacraments, My Divine Heart becoming their assured refuge at that last hour."*

In 1689, Sr. Margaret Mary received a message from Christ in the Chapel of the Visitation. It was for King Louis XIV and it contained four very specific requests. The king was to:

1) *"...engrave the Sacred Heart of Jesus on the royal flags.*

2) *"...build a temple in His honor where He would receive the homage of the court.*

3) *"...make his consecration to the Sacred Heart.*

4) *"...pledge his authority before the Holy See to obtain a Mass in honor of the Sacred Heart of Jesus."*

King Louis XIV

Do you remember the supernatural sign Emperor Constantine saw above the sun before the famous battle at the Milvian Bridge? He immediately painted that sign on all his banners and was victorious. Sadly, despite her best efforts to advise Louis XIV, nothing was achieved. It is unknown whether the king ignored it out-of-hand or, as is quite possible, it never even came to his attention.

Unfortunately, from that time on, the kingdom of Louis XIV was plagued with difficulties and defeats. Political and national disasters, in addition to ongoing religious conflicts, saw to it that this elegant *Eldest [First] Daughter of the Church* would never again bask in her previous glory. Ever since that time, France and England have remained highly competitive, even enemies.

"Storming of the Bastille"

On July 14, 1789, exactly one century after ignoring the requests of Christ, the celebrated *Storming of the Bastille* occurred, marking the beginning of the French Revolution. Its infamous slogan *Liberté, Égalité, Fraternité* (Liberty, Equality, Fraternity) became the national motto of France. It had also become a nation without God! [1]

Those who were not dispatched to the guillotine faced a major economic crisis, ironically due in part to its financial agreement to assist the colonists in America in their fight against England. Benjamin Franklin had negotiated a loan for between seven to eleven million dollars to finance the War of Independence in 1776. This later became known as the American Revolution. Unfortunately America completely reneged on the loan and, due in part to this added burden, France eventually had to declare bankruptcy. These events became a major factor for the justification of the French Revolution which began to sweep through France in 1789.

Three years later, in 1792 – one-hundred and three years after Christ first requested those four specific favors from Louis XIV – his great-great-great grandson, Louis XVI, made that consecration. He promised to fulfill the other three requests as soon as he was able.

In March, 1824, Leo XII pronounced Sr. Margaret Mary Venerable and on September 18, 1864, Pius IX declared her Blessed. When her tomb was canonically opened in July, 1830, two instantaneous cures took place.

In 1919, two-hundred and thirty years after Christ requested Louis XIV to build the temple, it was finally completed. Known as the Sacré Cœur (Basilica of the Sacred Heart), this white-domed temple was erected on the famous *Montmartre* (mountain of the martyr) in Paris, which owes its name to the martyrdom of St. Denis, the bishop of Paris, and patron saint of France.

Margaret Mary was canonized by Benedict XV in 1920. Her body rests under the altar in the chapel at Paray-le-Monial. Many favors have been obtained by pilgrims attracted there from all parts of the world. Her feast day is celebrated on October 17.

---

1 - The year 1870 would mark the end of the second empire and the beginning of the third republic for France.

PART II

Present

Ⓑy 1830, one-hundred, forty-one years after Christ appeared to St. Margaret Mary – a time which gave the Church the *Feast of the Sacred Heart* and impetus to the *Devotion of the Nine First Fridays* – the Eternal Father entrusted a mission to His most beloved Daughter. It was in a non-descript convent in Paris, France that Our Lady began the countdown for *"the salvation of mankind."*

Starting with her most notable appearance in France in 1830, through the mid-twentieth century – a time which led up to *World War II* – on into the third millennium, Our Lady has appeared in many places, warning of the turbulent times that lay ahead for her children if they continued to stray further from God's *Commandments* and *Statutes*.

Thus began a series of appearances of the Mother of God in various places throughout the world, culminating in a rather remote village in a Communist country – a nation behind the *iron curtain*. As we shall see, Pope John Paul II had been praying to Our Lady, pleading with her to appear in a Communist nation where her voice could be heard!

CHAPTER 4

Rue du Bac – Paris, France

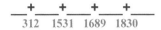

312   1531   1689   1830

"Have a Medal struck after this model. All who wear it will receive great graces; they should wear it around the neck. Graces will abound for persons who wear it with confidence."

The Mission

Our Lady's present mission began as the 19th of July ushered in an eerie, foreboding evening. An era of peace reigned over most of France for the first half of 1830. Now, however, whispers of revolution were filling the dark corners in the streets of Paris. In eight days, revolution will run rampant throughout the city!

As is their custom, the nuns in the Sisters of Charity convent at 140 Rue du Bac retired very early. Suddenly, just before midnight, one of the nuns was awakened from a deep sleep by a child's voice urgently calling her: *"Sister; Sister; Sister!"*

Chapel, Rue du Bac

Rubbing the sleep from her eyes, Catherine Labouré turned toward the voice and was amazed to see a young child, a small angel. He was pleading with her insistently: *"Come to the chapel. Get up quickly and come to the chapel; the Blessed Virgin is waiting for you there!"*

Perplexed, she instinctively arose and dressed; then, was quickly escorted to the chapel by the little angel. Upon their arrival she noticed that all the candles were lighted as though for a midnight Mass, yet the chapel appeared to be empty. However, as soon as they entered, the angel said: *"Here is the Blessed Virgin. Here she is!"*

Hearing the rustle of a dress, Catherine glanced in that direction and was startled to see the Blessed Virgin walking toward the spiritual director's chair in front of the altar. The moment she sat down the little angel whispered: *"The Blessed Mother wishes to speak with you."*

Catherine immediately went over to the chair and, kneeling on an altar step, placed her hands in Mary's lap. She remained there, talking with Mary for the next two hours. Then, Our Lady said God wishes to charge her with a mission. Thus began a series of appearances of the Mother of God in various places throughout the world, culminating in a rather remote village in a Communist country.

Mary told her of the great difficulties that were to come; however, she promised to give help and graces to those who prayed. Mary told her a religious persecution would break out in Paris later in the century. She also told of the coming events in Paris, the capital. She specifically told Catherine that she would have many trials to bear.

Mary went on to say: *"There will be bad times to come. Misfortunes will come crashing down on France. The throne will be toppled. The whole world will be turned upside-down by misfortunes of all kinds...But, come to the foot of this altar. There, graces will be poured out on all those, small, or great, who ask for them with confidence and fervor. Graces will be poured out especially on those who ask for them."*

Mary then returned to the theme of the sorrows coming upon France and the whole world, telling her not to be afraid, since she would always be protected and granted many graces. However, she said that other communities and individuals would have to suffer. In fact, a moment would come when everything would seem to be lost but that, since God was with her, she should continue to have confidence.

Mary continued with tears in her eyes: *"There will be victims...There will be victims among the clergy of Paris; Monsignor, the archbishop, will die...My child, the cross will be held in contempt. It will be thrown to the ground...Our Savior's side will be opened anew. The streets will run with blood...My child, the whole world will be plunged into sadness."*

Four months later, on November 27, Mary appeared to her again. She wore a white veil which covered her head, falling on either side to her feet. This time she was standing upon a white globe inside an oval frame, rays of light came out of her hands in the direction of a globe. Her hands held a golden ball which represented the world. It was surmounted with a little golden cross.

There were rings on her fingers – three rings to each finger – set with gems which emitted rays of light. The rays bursting from all sides flooded the base so that she could no longer see Mary's feet.

Mary said: *"The ball which you see represents the whole world, especially France, and each person in particular. These rays symbolize the graces I shed upon those who ask for them. The gems from which rays do not fall are the graces for which souls forget to ask."*

Then, Mary showed her an oval frame with gold lettering. She told her: *"Have a Medal struck after this model. All who wear it will receive great graces; they should wear it around the neck. Graces will abound for persons who wear it with confidence."*

On the back of the medal are two hearts. The Immaculate heart of Mary is shown elevated alongside the Sacred Heart of Jesus. It is a visual prophetic fulfillment of the request Christ will make over a century later, in 1936, to Lúcia of Fátima. [1]

Medal of the Immaculate Conception [i]

A sword is piercing Mary's immaculate heart recalling the Biblical story about the presentation of Jesus in the temple. A holy man, Simeon, had been told by the Holy Spirit that he would not die until he had seen the Messiah. So, he took the Child into his arms and blessing Him, said to Mary: *"Behold, this child is destined for the fall and rise of many in Israel, and to be a sign that will be contradicted [and you yourself a sword will pierce] so that the thoughts of many hearts may be revealed"* (Lk 2:33-35).

Owing to the numerous miracles attributed to it, the Medal of the Immaculate Conception became known as the Miraculous Medal. To this day no one knows how many millions have been distributed.

---

[i] – During the apparitions at Rue du Bac, the back of the medal shown to St. Catherine displayed the Immaculate Heart of Mary alongside the Sacred Heart of Jesus. This confirms the request Jesus made in 1936: *"I want My whole Church to acknowledge that consecration as a triumph of the Immaculate Heart of Mary...and put the devotion to the Immaculate Heart beside the devotion to My Sacred Heart."*

A rather amusing incident occurred in the chapel when I was there in the early 1970s. I was asked to assist a young man, Stephen Feld, into the chapel. Unfortunately, he was blind in both eyes – quite likely due to diabetes – and required thrice daily injections of insulin in order to maintain his health. As if these problems weren't enough he also had a wooden (plastic) leg and relied heavily upon two crutches to maintain his balance.

Stephen and I entered the chapel through a side aisle. In order to view the sarcophagus that enclosed the body of St. Catherine, we had to cross the main isle from this side aisle we were currently navigating. This meant we would pass in front of the Tabernacle and, naturally, as a Catholic Christian, this meant genuflecting on one knee. Yes, people, a genuflection it still requested although only a bow is given out of respect for the altar itself!

Well, there we were, ambling along, his arm on my shoulder; I stopped and genuflected, completely forgetting to tell him, and he performed the proverbial head over teacups act! As you can imagine, everyone was watching *the blind leading the blind* as Stephen fell over on top of me. The noise in this usually quiet chapel was just horrendous; the artificial leg only amplified the din.

The obvious pity in the form of *"oohs"* and *"aahs"* emanating from the pews merely added to the drama occurring in front of poor St. Catherine. Fortunately, as soon as my knee hit the floor, I realized my mistake and was able to grab him as he fell onto my back. Although this appeared to be extremely clumsy it turned out to be a rather easy landing for both of us.

A bit earlier, just prior to the drama going on in this revered chapel, our assorted group requested permission to celebrate Mass in the chapel. However, it was denied! Even though the spiritual adviser who accompanied us was a priest, we were advised by one of the ever present nuns that, other than the regular times assigned for Mass, it was: "Impossible, it just wasn't permitted."

Now, however, owing to the dubious entertainment my friend and I provided, one of the nuns closely watching our antics apparently felt great empathy for us. Very quietly, she hastened over to the priest and told him he could celebrate Mass, *"immediately."* Perhaps she felt this would provide the additional graces we obviously needed to be on our way without further mishap.

It was welcome news, but it came with an unexpected condition. Inasmuch as my shenanigans were the cause of the commotion, it was requested that I read the epistle during Mass. I felt honored but I couldn't do that! You must understand: when I was in the third grade, I was asked to perform a solo in the high school operetta; yet, all I felt capable of doing was to join in with the chorus.

I tried but, after sufficient snickers and laughter, I was left quite incapable of speaking in front of a small class, let alone a chapel half full of people. It just wasn't possible! I was petrified at this suggestion and began a quiet litany of prayers. What should I do; how could anyone refuse when we had been granted special permission to celebrate Mass? Then, immediately, a grace I had never felt before flowed over me; it was a favor from Our Lady, granted to me while I prayed on the steps at "...the foot of this altar."

There I rediscovered a voice that was previously lost and, for the first time since the third grade, I was able to speak in front of a crowd. Because of that gift I have, until recently, been able to speak fairly well publicly; however, I limit it strictly to religious matters, especially those pertaining to Mary.

Catherine died on December 31, 1876, certain she was going directly to Heaven. She believed she had earned that privilege. And, fifty-seven years later, as part of the process of canonization, her body was exhumed and found to be completely incorrupt. She was canonized on July 27, 1947. Her body is perfectly preserved in a glass sarcophagus, just above the main steps of the sanctuary in Rue du Bac, to the right of the tabernacle. Near the end of her life, she stated that, if her "...bishop had given his permission, the events that occurred in Lourdes could have happened earlier in Paris."

CHAPTER 5

Our Lady of La Salette, France

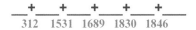

"...How long I have suffered for you...No matter how well you pray in the future, no matter how well you act, you will never be able to make up to me what I have endured for your sake."

Sixteen years later, on the afternoon of September 19, 1846, two children, Melanie Calvat, 15, and Maximin Giraud, 11, were grazing their cows in a field above the small village of La Salette, a place very, very high up in the French Alps.

La Salette, the French Alps

Suddenly, the children saw a globe of light coming down from the sky, settling in the valley below. They were absolutely fascinated at this light as it was much brighter than the sun. Then, as the globe opened, Melanie saw a very beautiful woman within it. She was seated with her face in her hands in an attitude of sorrow; she was weeping. The children thought she was crying for the loss of her child so they went over to console her.

The lady then stood up and said; *"Come nearer, children, do not be afraid; I am here to tell you something of the greatest importance."*

Our Lady of La Salette

The children described her as wearing a white cloak with a bright yellow apron and white shoes, decorated with roses of many colors. Roses were also clearly visible on her crown. Around her neck she wore a chain with a large cross; a hammer and pliers were hanging from the cross bar.

They described the crucifix on Mary's breast as more radiant than anything else in the apparition. The hammer which hung on one side represents sin, which nailed Jesus to the Cross. Just as the pliers on the other side were used to remove the nails, penance and prayer help us reconcile the world to God. The Cross of La Salette is known world-wide as a symbol of Mary's message: for us to be reconciled with God.

The Cross of La Salette

As she began to speak, she shed tears, saying: *"If my people will not obey, I shall be compelled to loose my Son's arm. It is so heavy, so pressing, that I can no longer restrain it. How long I have suffered for you! If my Son is not to cast you off, I am obliged to entreat Him without ceasing. But you take no notice of that. No matter how well you pray in the future, no matter how well you act, you will never be able to make up to me what I have endured for your sake.*

"I have appointed you six days for working; the seventh I have re-served for myself. And, no one will give it to me. This is what causes the weight of my Son's Arm to be so crushing. The cart drivers cannot swear without bringing in my Son's name. These are the two things which make my Son's arm so burdensome."

"If the harvest is spoiled, it is your own fault. I warned you last year by means of the potatoes. You paid no heed. Quite the reverse, when you discovered that the potatoes had rotted, you swore; you abused my Son's name. They will continue to rot and, by Christmas this year, there will be none left. If you have grain, it will do no good to sow it, for what you sow the beasts will devour, and any part of it that springs up will crumble into dust when you thresh it. A great famine is coming; but, before that happens, the children under seven will die in their parents' arms. The grownups will pay for their sins by hunger. The grapes will rot and the walnuts will turn bad."

Our Lady of La Salette

Mary gave an individual secret to each child that was unknown to the other, then, continued: *"If people are converted, the rocks will become piles of wheat, and it will be found the potatoes have sown themselves."* She added: *"Only a few rather old women go to Mass in the summer; all the rest work every Sunday throughout the summer. And, in winter, when they don't know what to do with themselves, they go to Mass only to poke fun at religion. During Lent they flock to the butcher shops like dogs."*

Mary looked earnestly at Melanie and Maximin, and said: *"My children, you will make this known to all my people."* She turned and repeated the same command: *"My children, you will make this known to all my people."* Then, rising into the air, she faded into the sky.

Our Lady ascending

La Salette is perhaps considered the granddaddy of apparitions because the messages given to Melanie and Maximum were of such an apocalyptic description. They told of the chastisements that would be visited upon a sinful world. One year earlier, in 1845, an American ship carrying the potato bug landed in Ireland; shortly afterward the potato crops were infected. The seed for the great Irish potato famine had already been sown!

Although reluctant to do so, both children penned their secrets for the edification of the Holy Father. He said a summary of the secrets given to each child would state: "Maximum's secret announced mercy and the rehabilitation of things, whereas Melanie's secret would announce great chastisements."

Two representatives, Frs. Pierre Joseph Roussilot and Jean-Baptiste Gérin, were sent to Rome where they handed the sealed envelopes to Pope Pius IX on July 18, 1851. Upon reading them he summed up the messages by declaring: *"If we do not pray we shall all perish!"* On the very next day, July 19, 1851, less than five years after Our Lady first appeared, the apparition under the title of *Our Lady of La Salette* was officially approved in a pastoral letter sent by the diocesan bishop.

Neither of the visionaries led particularly saintly lives afterward. Maximin Giraud fell under the spell of unscrupulous people who used him for his notoriety. He led an unhappy and wandering life, taking a variety of odd jobs. Returning to Corps, he died on March 1, 1875 at 39 years of age. Melanie Calvat attempted living as a Carmelite nun several times but eventually returned to the secular world. She began to espouse her own prophecies and mystical dogmas and unsuccessfully tried to develop a personal following. She died at Altamura, Italy on December 15, 1904, having lived for 74 years.

La Salette, 2000

As the crow flies, La Salette is not far from Grenoble where the Winter Olympics were held in 1968. It is so desolate, so high in the French Alps, that you would not imagine driving up such a steep, dangerous mountainside. In late May, 1970, before many of the present day amenities were added, I spent one very long, cold night at the site of the apparitions. There were still five foot deep snow drifts on the ground; yet, as there were no clouds in the sky, the afternoon sunshine warmed us somewhat. However, the cloudless skies permitted the temperature to plummet that night. It became so bitter cold in the little unheated dormitory with its crude double-deck bunk beds that, despite using two sleeping bags and applying an extra set of clothing, one could not sleep for fear one might literally freeze to death!

Needless to say, the piping hot coffee shop became the favored place to gather early the following morning. I remained at the site for two days and only one night although I learned that some hardy younger individuals stayed for weeks at a time. As a parent, I had the impression their guardians imposed some sort of penance on them to atone for a previous misadventure.

CHAPTER 6

Our Lady of Lourdes, France

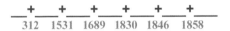

$$\underline{\quad +\quad +\quad +\quad +\quad +\quad +\quad}$$
312 1531 1689 1830 1846 1858

'She lifted up her eyes to Heaven, joined her hands as though in prayer that were held out and open towards the ground, and said to me: "Que soy era Immaculada Councepciou."'

Twelve years after her apparitions in La Salette Our Lady appeared to Bernadette Soubirouis in Lourdes, a village in southern France, located in the foothills of the Pyrenees mountains near the Spanish border. It was February 11, 1858. Earlier that day, Bernadette – a poor sickly child of 14 – accompanied her sister and a friend to Massabielle, a place near town to collect firewood. At that time the grotto area was an old garbage dump on the side of the Gave River and, although it  had a bad reputation, the area around it contained firewood.

Two of the girls crossed the river ahead of Bernadette but, as the water was so cold, they told her to stay where she was. Nevertheless, she decided to follow them anyway. She said: "I was taking off my stocking when I heard a noise like the sound of a storm. I looked at the trees near the river, but nothing was moving. I was frightened, and I stood up straight. Bewildered, I looked across the mill-stream to a niche above a cave in the rock of Massabielle. A rosebush on the edge of the niche was swaying in the wind. It was all that moved.

 "A golden cloud came out of the cave and flooded the niche with radiance. Then a lady, young and beautiful – exceedingly beautiful – the like of whom I had never seen, stood on the edge of the niche. She smiled at me, beckoning me to come closer as though she were my mother, and she gave me to understand in my soul that I was not mistaken."

"The Lady was dressed in white, with a white veil on her head, and a blue sash at her waist. A rosary of white beads on a golden chain was on her right arm. On that cold winter's day, her feet were bare, but on each foot was a golden rose radiant with the warmth of summer.

The Grotto, Massabielle

"Thinking that I was faced with an illusion, I rubbed my eyes, but in vain. I looked again and I could still see the same lady. I fell upon my knees. Then, I put my hand into my pocket and took out my rosary. I wanted to make the Sign of the Cross, but in vain. I could not raise my hand to my forehead, it kept on dropping.

"The Lady took the rosary that she held in her hands and made a beautiful Sign of the Cross; then, I could do the same. The Lady let me pray the rosary on my own. She passed the beads through her fingers; she did not say the words. The lady made a sign for me to approach, but I was seized with fear and did not dare. She smiled at me, she bowed to me. She disappeared into the niche, the golden cloud faded, and I was all alone."

Meanwhile, the other two finished gathering wood and upon returning to the grotto noticed Bernadette acting rather strangely. She wasn't moving; they thought she might have died! When they asked her again she finally told them what was happening; but, only on the condition they wouldn't tell anyone else! They agreed; however, as soon as they arrived home, her sister told their mother all about the events at the grotto. She was scolded severely by her mother for making up such stories, so harshly that her mother eventually broke a broom over her back. Louise Casterot Soubirouis' children do not lie!

However, this was just the beginning of her difficulties. Although her parents had forbidden her to return to that garbage dump again, she felt an interior force three days later drawing her back to the grotto. Finally, owing to Bernadette's insistence accompanied with uncontrollable crying, her mother eventually relented. Away she went to the grotto and as soon as she arrived she knelt down to say the rosary. Just after finishing the first decade, the lady appeared. This time Bernadette sprinkled holy water in her direction; but, the lady only smiled and inclined her head downward. When they finished the rosary, the lady again disappeared.

Four days later, on the 18th, the lady spoke for the first time. Bernadette held out a pen and paper and asked her to write her name. The lady replied: *"It is not necessary"* adding, *"I do not promise to make you happy in this world, but in the other. Would you be kind enough to come here for a fortnight?"* Bernadette agreed, telling her she would. Over the next nine days the lady appeared to her seven times; however, at the end of this time, the local judge threatened to put her in prison because of all the commotion she was causing. During that same time, the lady revealed a secret to her, only for her alone. On the following day the lady said: *"Penance; Penance; Penance! Pray to God for sinners. Kiss the ground as an act of penance for sinners!"*

Meanwhile the crowds were continuing to increase in size. During one apparition with many people present, Bernadette related; "She told me to go *'...drink of the spring.'* I only found a little muddy water. At the fourth attempt I was able to drink. She also made me eat the bitter herbs that were found near the spring. She also told me to wash myself in the spring which, at first, was only mud, then, the vision left and went away." The crowd was incredulous at this scene! When they asked: "Do you think that she is mad doing things like that?" Bernadette replied: "It is for sinners."

However, shortly after she humbled herself by digging in the mud, a spring emerged, and the water flowing from it began to produce miraculous healings. By March 1st, over fifteen hundred people gathered and, for the first time, a priest was among them. During that night a friend of Bernadette's from Lourdes, Catherine Latapie, went to the grotto. Plunging her dislocated arm into the water of the spring, both her arm and her hand regained their strength immediately.

By the next day the crowd grew even larger. The lady told her: *"Go, tell the priests to come here in procession and to build a chapel here."* Bernadette immediately told this to Father Peyramale, the parish priest in Lourdes. He wanted to know only one thing: "What was the lady's name?" Then, he also demanded a test. Inasmuch as he was a fancier of roses, he asked: "to see the wild rosebush flower at the grotto in the middle of winter." Perhaps the dean was thinking about the miraculous blooming of the roses in Guadalupe, Mexico when he demanded a similar miracle from Our Lady in Lourdes.

On the following day, at seven in the morning, about three thousand people had gathered. Bernadette came to the grotto, but the lady did not appear! After school, she heard the interior invitation of the lady and returned to the grotto. When she appeared this time Bernadette again asked for her name. but the lady's only response was a smile. When she relayed this to the parish priest, he insisted: "If the lady really wishes that a chapel be built, then, she must tell us her name and make the rose bush bloom at the grotto." By the next day, the crowd grew to about eight thousand people, all waiting for a miracle. Apparently, Our Lady was not one to be told what she must do in order for us to believe in her for her appearance was silent; no miracle occurred.

Still, Father Peyramale stuck to his original position. Bernadette stayed away from the grotto for twenty days as she no longer felt the irresistible invitation of the lady. During these days, many inspected the site for a hint of budding flowers, but there was none.

Finally, on March the 25th, Our Lady revealed her name. Bernadette vividly recalled: "She lifted up her eyes to Heaven, joined her hands as though in prayer that were held out and open towards the ground, and said to me: *'Que soy era Immaculada Councepciou.'"* Bernadette left hurriedly, running all the way to tell Father Peyramale, meanwhile, repeating over and over those words she did not understand. When she finally relayed them to the priest it troubled him for he knew Bernadette was ignorant of their meaning.

She was completely unaware of the fact that, just four years earlier, on December 8, 1854, this theological expression had been assigned to the Blessed Virgin when Pope Pius IX declared this to be a dogma of the Catholic Church. Interestingly, even though Father Peyramale commanded that the lady: "...must tell us her name and make the rose bush bloom at the grotto," the wild rose bush on which she stood during the apparitions never bloomed.

During an apparition on the 7th of April, Bernadette kept her candle lighted and, although her fingers and hand were directly in the flame for some time, she was not harmed in the slightest. Dr. Douzous, the local medical doctor, noticed this very carefully and recorded it.

On the 16th of July, she received the mysterious interior call to the grotto but, this time, her way was blocked; it had been closed off by a barrier. Instead, she went to the other side of the Gave River, just across from the grotto. She said: "I felt that I was in front of the grotto, at the same distance as before; I saw only the Blessed Virgin, and she was more beautiful than ever!" That was the eighteenth and final apparition of Our Lady. As the sun was setting, the lady who called herself *L'Immaculada Councepciou* took her leave of the child. Just as she was disappearing she cast one final smile to Bernadette. Never again in this life would she see the Lady; now, she could only wait for her to keep the promise she had made during her second appearance: *"I do not promise to make you happy in this world, but in the other."*

Later, Bernadette would declare: "The Blessed Virgin is so beautiful that when one has seen her once, one would gladly wish to die so as to see her again." That feeling was to flower within the heart and soul of this faithful child and remain with her for the rest of her life.

Bernadette gave a classic response to the question: "What is a sinner?" Without hesitation, she answered: "A sinner is one who loves evil." It was a simple and sincere answer; she did not say one who does evil; rather, "...one who loves evil."

When Bernadette was 22 years of age, she went to the hospice school run by the Sisters of Charity of Nevers. There she finally learned to read and write. She eventually joined the Sisters at their motherhouse in Nevers and spent the rest of her brief life working as an assistant in the infirmary there. She was given the name, Marie Bernard. After the first night there, telling all the nuns about the events that transpired at Lourdes, she was ordered to never speak to them again about the apparitions.

She died of her long-term illness at the age of 35. She died at the convent in Nevers on April 16, 1879. Her last words after the conclusion of the Hail Mary: "Holy Mary, Mother of God, pray for us sinners...sinners..."

In 1911, the Church began an investigation into Bernadette's cause for canonization. As part of the formal proceedings, her coffin was opened and it was found that, after thirty-two years, her body was found to be incorrupt, except for a slight facial discoloration. A crystal coffin was made for Bernadette's body and placed in the convent in Nevers. She has remained undisturbed and on view in this chapel since August 3, 1925.

On December 8, 1933, Pope Pius XI declared that Bernadette was a saint and her feast day would be on February 18th. A church was erected later at the site of the spring. The Sisters of Charity in Nevers welcome visitors and encourage others to learn about the life, example, and messages of their sister saint.

Saint Bernadette

People come to Lourdes for the curative waters and the great candlelight procession held every evening. During the entire evening the song, *Ave, Ave, Ave, Maria* is sung in as many languages as there are people who represent their nations throughout the world. To this day, whenever

I reminisce about Lourdes, those beautiful sounds still clearly resonate in my ears! My eyes moisten whenever the words are sung in church.

Pilgrims continue to visit the shrine where the water still flows from a spring at the same spot where it was uncovered by Bernadette. It has produced thousands of healings. While many of the visitors fully immerse themselves in the waters in cubicles provided for that purpose, others take samples of the water home to those who are unable to make the pilgrimage.

While most people believe the waters are the source of the numerous miracles reported there, it is generally unknown that most of the miracles that occur in Lourdes take place during the procession of the Blessed Sacrament. Every afternoon at 4:30, during the closing Benediction, either the Bishop or a priest carries a monstrance containing the Blessed Sacrament to bless the sick who are present. The monstrance is usually sheltered from the elements with a mobile awning carried by four assistants.

Although miracles still grace the grotto in Lourdes the Church does not readily accept miracles! Of the thousands of miraculous events that are reported, only sixty-five have met these strictures to date and been officially approved by the Church. The Church insists a miracle must be like a lightning bolt – a complete, instantaneous cure from one millisecond to another – and have adequate documentation to prove it. It would be well for us to also remember that true miracles are something that cannot be explained by natural means and that coincidences are not necessarily miracles.

While recalling the description of the apparitions, the bishop explained the reason for the caution the Church exhibits in examining supernatural events. The Church demands definite proof before admitting them and proclaiming they are of a divine nature; even the devil can lead people astray by taking on the form of an angel. The bishop stated: "We are inspired by the Commission comprising of wise, holy, learned and experienced priests who questioned the child, studied the facts, examined everything and weighed all the evidence.

"We have also called on science, and we remain convinced that the Apparitions are supernatural and divine, and that by consequence what Bernadette saw was the Most Blessed Virgin. Our convictions are based on the testimony of Bernadette, but above all on the things that have happened, things which can be nothing other than divine intervention."

Epilogue, Lourdes

Europe had been torn asunder by violence and revolution during the years before and after Mary appeared in France. It was hoped that Heaven would bestow benevolence upon the entire continent due to the apparitions; perhaps her appearances might eventually present France and all of Europe time to heal.

Franz Werfel

Franz Werfel was a Jewish playwright caught up in the frenzy of the Nazi regime that lead up to *World War II*. He tried to flee from Czechoslovakia into Spain which, along with Portugal, remained neutral during the war; however, unable to do so, he eventually found himself in Lourdes, France. As with so many other Jews who were especially targeted by the Gestapo during those times, Werfel went through the constant fear of being captured, knowing full well what awaited him if he was captured.

Additionally, he knew he was putting the lives of all those who had any part in hiding him at risk! Yet, in spite of this threat, many of the families in Lourdes alternately took turns concealing him. While there, he learned firsthand about the appearances of Our Lady to Bernadette and of the ensuing miracles. He made a solemn promise to Our Lady that if he survived the war he would somehow publicize those events.

In late 1940, Franz managed to escape to the United States via the port of Marseilles, France. He fulfilled his promise the following year with the publication of his book *The Song of Bernadette*. It was eventually made into an inspiring movie of the same name.

One of the more interesting statements in the movie was attributed to Fr. Pomian. He was attending a terminally ill child when the mother took the child and immersed him in the water at the new spring. He was immediately cured. After personally witnessing this Fr. Pomian remarked when leaving the next morning: "Last night when I came here, it was very dark. It's much lighter now!"

CHAPTER 7

Our Lady of Pont Main, France

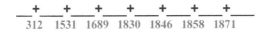

+   +   +   +   +   +   +
312 1531 1689 1830 1846 1858 1871

"But pray, my children, God will soon answer you. My Son permits Himself to be moved."

Thirteen years later, on the cold winter evening of January 17, 1871, Our Lady appeared to several children in Pont Main, a small village in France. At the time almost all of France was engulfed in the Franco-Prussian War which had continued unabated since July 19, 1870. On this particular day, however, Paris itself was under siege.

Prussian troops were on the outskirts of Laval, a nearby town where people were being vaccinated because of an outbreak of typhoid fever. Smallpox was spreading rapidly! Everything was going wrong! Some commentators wrote that even the elements seemed disturbed.

Six days earlier, an aurora borealis had occurred that made a deep impression on those who witnessed it. Some saw in it the masts of a phantom ship; others saw the steeples of the Cathedral. Then, to top it off, at about half past twelve, there was an earthquake in Pont Main. Fear was widespread. Many of those in the town were saying: "No use praying. God doesn't hear us."

The Barbedettes

However, one family in Pont Main, the Barbedettes, remained busy with their household chores despite the fact they could hear the roar of the cannons from the nearby village.

The Barbedettes were simple, hardworking, devout country people from one of the oldest families in the region. Two of the boys, Eugène, 12, and Joseph, 10, were working in the barn with their father when Eugène began thinking about his older brother who, earlier, was drafted into the army. He decided to walk over toward the barn door to gaze up at the clear sky. He was looking above the roof of a neighboring house about seventy feet away from him when, suddenly, he noticed that one area – about five feet above the roof – was completely free of stars.

Our Lady of Pont Main

As the stars melted away he saw "a beautiful lady dressed in a flowing robe of deep, radiant blue, studded with gold stars. Her sleeves were full, extending down to the hands. She was wearing blue slippers, tied with a golden ribbon in the shape of a rosette. Her hair was completely covered with a black veil over her shoulders, reaching down to the level of her elbow. There was a golden crown on her head that rose slightly to a peak. It had no ornament in front except a red band circling the center. Her hands were extended like those on the Miraculous Medal, but without the rays of light." And the lady was smiling at Eugène.

When Eugène heard his sister, Jeanette, he pointed to the sky where he wanted her to look; however, she didn't see anything. He then called his brother, Joseph, and when he came over he said he could see her. Yet, when his father and a neighbor looked, they could only see a starry sky.

As it was now about a quarter past six, the boys were called inside for supper. They were allowed to go out again as soon as they finished a hurried meal and, when they did, the lady was still there. Later on, their mother joined them, but she didn't see anything unusual. By now, she was quite puzzled because her boys were usually very truthful. She suggested that it might be the Blessed Virgin and that they should say five Our Fathers and Hail Marys in her honor.

They decided to call the two nuns of the village school, Sr. Vitaline and Sr. Marie Edward. Sr. Vitaline came over but saw nothing of the heavenly vision so she decided to fetch three young children from the school to test their reactions: Frances Richer, 11, Jeanne Marie Lebosse, 9, and a third child. Both the older girls immediately saw the smiling beautiful lady and expressed their delight at the apparition, describing it exactly as the two boys had. However, the third child could not.

Sr. Vitaline then came over with Sr. Marie Edward, but, neither of them saw anything unusual. Another quite sickly child, Eugène Friteau, 6-1/2, also saw the lady. Then a neighbor, Madame Boitin, brought her baby who was only 2 years old. In her childish way, Augustine, the baby, showing signs of great joy, reached out with her little arms towards the lady in the sky. As the neighbors became aware of the commotion the parents tried to distract the attention of the boys, but to no avail. By now, the crowd had grown to about sixty and they gathered around the two small boys.

They summoned Abbé Michel Guerin who had been their pastor for 35 years and, when he arrived, they all began a prayer vigil to the lady. While the people prayed in the snow, the children exclaimed that something new was happening: "The lady increased in size and became more beautiful; she became both covered with and surrounded by the stars. Those which spangled her robe multiplied and the dark blue color of the robe brightened."

"A blue oval that formed around the vision expanded in size as the stars surrounding the apparition moved aside to make way for the oval, arranging themselves two by two at the feet of the lady."

"The large blue oval forming around the lady contained four candles, two at the level of her shoulders and two near her knees; then, a short red cross appeared over her heart."

Sr. Marie Edward, kneeling at the open doorway of the barn, was leading the rosary. As the rosary progressed the figure and its frame grew larger, until it was twice life size. The stars around her began to multiply and attach themselves to her dress until it was covered with them. During the Magnificat the four children cried out: "Something else is happening!"

A broad streamer, on which letters were appearing, unrolled beneath the feet of the lady, so that eventually the phrase: *"But pray, my children"* could be seen.

"But pray, my children, God will soon answer you.
My Son permits Himself to be moved."

Abbé Michel Guérin then ordered that the Litany of Our Lady should be sung and, as this progressed, new letters appeared forming the message: *"God will soon answer you."* As they continued to sing, another message formed, one that removed any doubt that it was the Blessed Virgin who was appearing to the children: *"My Son permits [allows] Himself to be moved."*

At this, the children were beside themselves with joy at the beauty of the Lady and her smile. Suddenly, however, they noticed, "Our Lady's expression changed to one of extreme sadness as a large red crucifix appeared before her.

The color of the cross itself took on a much darker shade of red than previously. It had a figure of Jesus on it, surmounted by a placard bearing in beautiful red letters the name *'Jesus Christ.'"* As the Virgin presented the crucifix to the children, the sadness that appeared on the face of Our Lady was reflected onto the children. Then, as the crucifix vanished, one of the stars proceeded to light the four candles that surrounded the figure.

Our Lady of Pont Main

The message produced a strong emotional reaction in the crowd. After a momentary silence the pastor suggested they sing the hymn, *Mother of Hope.* The children leapt for joy and clapped their hands while repeating: "See how she smiles! Oh, how beautiful she is!" At the end of the hymn the banner bearing the inscription vanished. The children reported that a white veil was rising slowly from the Lady's feet, gradually blotting her out. Finally, by nine o'clock, she had completely disappeared.

On the evening of that memorable night on the 17th, the Commander of the Prussian forces took up his quarters at the archiepiscopal palace of Le Mans where he informed the bishop of that diocese, Msgr. Fillion: "By this time my troops are at Laval."

It was inevitable that Pont Main would be overrun by morning. In fact, the Prussian forces were already in sight of Laval. They had stopped all forward progress at half-past five o'clock in the afternoon to rest before the next day's battle. However, late that same night, General Von Schmidt of the Prussian Army received orders from his Commander to not take the city.

Their retirement early the next morning signaled the end of the war in that part of France. The invasion of Pont Main and Laval never occurred. Brittany and France would soon be at peace.

Signing the Peace Treaty

Twelve days later, on January 23, 1871, the long-hoped for Armistice was signed at Versailles. The promise of Our Lady of Hope had been fulfilled: *"But pray, my children, God will soon answer you. My Son permits Himself to be moved."* Soon all thirty-eight of the conscripted men and boys from that area returned home, unscathed by the fighting.

Following this event, the devotion to the Blessed Virgin under the title of *Notre Dame d' Esperance de Pont Main* [Our Lady of Hope of Pont Main] was authorized by the ecclesiastical authorities. The confraternity of that name has since been extended all over the world. Many signal graces, both spiritual and temporal, have been granted by Heaven because of it.

After the apparition of Our Lady of Hope on January 17, 1871, pilgrims – made up of both clergy and the laity – flocked to Pont Main. The following March, 1871, a canonical inquiry into the apparition was held and, in May, the local bishop questioned the children. The inquiry continued later in the year, with further questioning by theologians, then, a medical examination. The bishop was satisfied by these investigations and, by February 1872, declared his belief that it was the Blessed Virgin who had appeared to the children.

Finally, on the Feast of the Purification, February 2, 1872, Msgr. Wicart, the bishop of Laval, issued a pastoral letter giving a canonical judgment on the apparition. Thus, the veneration of *Our Lady of Hope of Pont Main* was given official Church recognition and approval. Pope Pius XI gave a final decision regarding the Mass and office in her honor.

A final papal honor was given to Our Lady of Hope on July 16, 1932 by Cardinal Pacelli, who would later become Pope Pius XII, by passing a decree from the Chapter of St. Peter's Basilica that the statue of the *Blessed Lady, Mother of Hope* be solemnly honored with a crown of gold. On July 24, 1934, the Lady was crowned by Cardinal Verdier, the archbishop of Paris, in the presence of all the bishops, priests and laity.

The sadness that was seen on Our Lady's face during the apparition made an especially deep impression on Joseph, the youngest son. He would later write: "Her sadness was more than anyone can imagine. I saw my mother overwhelmed with grief when, some months later, my father died. You know what such grief in a mother's face does to the heart of a child. But, as I remember, what instinctively came to mind was the sadness of the Most Blessed Virgin, which must have been the sadness of the Mother of Jesus at the foot of the Cross that bore her dying Son."

Joseph Barbedette became an OMI priest, a member of the Congregation of the Oblates of Mary Immaculate. His brother, Eugène, became a secular priest. Jeanne-Marie Lebossé became a nun and one of the other girls with her who had seen Mary, became Eugène's housekeeper.

A large basilica was built in Pont Main and consecrated in 1900. Later, one of the chapels at the *Basilica of the National Shrine of the Immaculate Conception,* in Washington, D.C. was donated by Bob and Delores Hope, dedicated to *Our Lady of Hope of Pont Main.*

Pont Main Basilica

In Pont Main, as in La Salette, Our Lady again shows us that, if we heed her requests, she can restrain the arm of her Son. We will also note this in a later apparition of Our Lady wherein she reminds us: *"You have forgotten that, through prayer and fasting, you can avert wars and suspend the laws of nature!"*

CHAPTER 8

Our Lady of Knock, Ireland

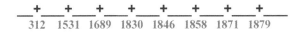

+	+	+	+	+	+	+	+
312	1531	1689	1830	1846	1858	1871	1879

"Look at the beautiful figures. They're not statues, it's the Blessed Virgin!"

Eight years later, on the evening of August 21st, 1879, Our Lady appeared again. This time it was in the village of Knock, a remote hamlet in the west of Ireland. Father Cavanagh's housekeeper, Mary McLoughlin, was on her way to visit a friend. At about 8:30 in the evening, as she passed the church of St. John the Baptist, she was astonished to see the exterior south wall of the church bathed in a mysterious light. She noticed three figures were standing atop an altar in front of the wall, outside the church.

Mary thought the local priest had purchased additional statues, as was his habit, and placed them there for storage. Even though it seemed a bit strange, she continued on her way to see her friend, Margaret Byrne. It was only later that she would find two other parishioners noticed the same thing, remarking: "Another collection; God help us!"

Then, shortly after talking to Margaret, Mary decided to leave. Margaret's sister, Mary Byrne, agreed to walk home with her so they both left together in the rain. As they neared the church, Mary cried out: "Look at the beautiful figures. When did the priest put those statues at the gable?" As they got closer they saw that the mysterious light was now extraordinarily brilliant and surrounded both the gable wall and the figures standing there. One stated: "They're not statues, they're moving; it's the Blessed Virgin!"

On the altar were a cross and a Lamb, a traditional image of Jesus. All the figures were to the left of the Lamb; Mary was between St. Joseph and St. John, the Evangelist. The figure of the Blessed Virgin was life-size and a bit larger than the other two. They all stood several feet above the ground and a little away from the gable wall. It was the most amazing thing they had ever seen.

The Blessed Virgin was very beautiful: "She wore a white cloak which hung in full folds that were fastened at the neck. The crown on her head appeared brilliant; it was a golden brightness, but with a deeper hue than the brilliant whiteness of the robe she wore. The upper parts of the crown appeared to be a series of sparkles, or glittering crosses." Also, she was described as being deep in prayer, with her eyes raised to Heaven. Her hands were raised to the shoulders or a little higher, with the palms inclined slightly to the shoulders.

Shrine of Our Lady of Knock

St. Joseph was wearing white robes; he stood on the Virgin's right with his head bent forward from the shoulders, towards the Blessed Virgin. St. John, the Evangelist, was dressed in a long robe and wore a miter. He was to the left of the Blessed Virgin, partly turned away from the other figures. He appeared to be preaching while holding a large open book in his left hand. To the left of St. John was the altar with a lamb on it. There was a cross standing on the altar behind the lamb.

When the apparition began, there was good light but, even when it became very dark, those gathered there could still see the figures quite clearly. They appeared to be the color of a bright whitish light. The apparition did not flicker or appear to move in any way.

While Mary McLoughlin gazed at the apparition, Mary Byrne ran to tell her family. Soon, a crowd gathered and everyone who stayed saw the apparition. They stood in the pouring rain for up to two hours, reciting the rosary. They reported that, even though the wind was blowing from the south, the ground around the figures remained completely dry during the apparition; yet, they noticed that the ground at the gable was very wet. The vision lasted for about three hours, then faded, and was gone.

Our Lady of Knock

One of the witnesses, Bridget Trench, said: "I went in immediately to kiss the feet of the Blessed Virgin; but I felt nothing in the embrace but the wall, and I wondered why I could not feel the figures which I had so plainly and so distinctly seen."

For whatever reason, Father Cavanaugh, the parish priest, did not come out to see the apparition; his absence was a disappointment to the villagers. The following day a group of them went to see the priest. He accepted their report as genuine and he dutifully reported the events to the diocesan bishop of Tuam. The Church then set up a commission to interview a number of the people who claimed to witness the apparition.

Among the original witnesses was Patrick Hill, who described the scene: "The figures were fully rounded, as if they had a body and life. They did not speak but, as we drew near, they retreated a little towards the wall." Patrick reported that he got close enough to make out the words in the book held by the figure of St. John.

Others out in the fields, some distance away, saw the strange light around the church. Two years later, Archbishop John Joseph Lynch, of Toronto, made a visit to the parish and claimed he had been healed by the Virgin of Knock.

In due course many of the witnesses died. Mary Byrne married, raised six children, and lived her entire life in Knock. In 1936, shortly before her death at age 86, she was interviewed again. Her account did not vary from the first report she gave in 1879. She declared: "I am going before my God. I saw the Blessed Virgin, St. Joseph and St, John. I can see it as plain as can be." Even though the Church approved the apparition as being quite probable by 1971, it has never been formally acknowledged by the Church.

Our Lady of Knock Shrine

The village of Knock was transformed by the thousands who came to commemorate the vision; they also came to ask for healing for themselves and for others. The local church was too small to accommodate the crowds and, in 1976, a new church, Our Lady, Queen of Ireland, was erected; it holds over two thousand people.

In 1979, on the centenary of the apparition, the personal pilgrimage of Saint John Paul II gave Our Lady of Knock the indelible seal of the Vatican's approval. This inspired an even greater devotion to the shrine. Then, in June, 1993, Mother Teresa of Calcutta visited the shrine. Each year, approximately one and a half million pilgrims visit the shrine to pay their respects to the Blessed Virgin.

CHAPTER 9

Saint Michael, France

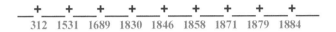

"St. Michael, the Archangel, defend us in battle. Be our defense against the wickedness and snares of the devil. May God rebuke him we humbly pray..."

Five years after the events in Knock, Ireland, Pope Leo XIII was conferring with several cardinals who were attending a Mass of thanksgiving in his private chamber. It was October 13, 1884. He was staring at the area above where the celebrant's head had been. The look on Leo's face changed rapidly and he fell into a mystical ecstasy. When his color faded and no pulse was detected, a doctor was immediately summoned! Within a short time, however, he regained consciousness and stated: "What a horrible picture I was permitted to see!"

He then described a frightful conversation in a vision he had just witnessed. It consisted of two voices he clearly understood to be that of Christ and Satan, wherein the latter boasted he could destroy the Church if he were granted approximately one century to carry out his plan. Satan also asked for *"...a greater influence over those who will give themselves to my service";* to which Christ said: *"You will be given the time and the power."*

Deeply shaken by this vision, Pope Leo XIII went into another room where he immediately composed the *Prayer to St. Michael, the Archangel.* Returning to his private chamber he ordered the prayer to "be recited after all the [Low] Masses as a protection for the Church against the attacks from Hell."

Presumably, Satan chose the twentieth century, an approximately one-hundred year period from the time Mary affirmed the existence of Hell at Fatima in 1917, through the early part of the twenty-first century.

This is the prayer Pope St. Leo XIII composed: *"St. Michael the Archangel, defend us in battle. Be our defense against the wickedness and snares of the Devil. May God rebuke him, we humbly pray, and do thou, O Prince of the heavenly hosts, by the power of God, thrust into Hell, Satan, and all the evil spirits who prowl about the world seeking the ruin of souls."*

St. Michael, the Archangel

Pope Leo XIII died in Rome on July 20, 1903 at the age of 93. He was the oldest reigning pope in history. The prayer Leo XIII composed to St. Michael was said at the end of every Mass until 1970.

Unfortunately, it was forgotten during the promulgation of the Mass of Pope Paul VI, even though there was no provision in the documents that stated it should not continue to be said. Paul VI, clearly understood the value of the prayer as he cautioned on June 30, 1972: "The smoke of Satan has entered the very heart of the Church!"

Eleven years later, on December 2, 1983, Fr. Vlasic, pastor of St. James Church in Medjugorje, sent a letter to Pope John Paul II stating: "Mirjana had an apparition in 1982, wherein the Blessed Virgin told her: *'...you must realize that Satan exists. One day he appeared before the throne of God and asked permission to submit the Church to a period of trial. God gave him permission to try the Church for one century. This century is under the power of the devil; but when the secrets confided to you come to pass, his power will be destroyed.*

"Even now he is beginning to lose his power and has become aggressive. He is destroying marriages, creating divisions among priests, and is responsible for obsessions and murder.'"

Then, on April 24, 1994, at the end of his Angelus message given in St. Peter's Square, Pope John Paul II urged Catholics to begin once again to recite the prayer to St. Michael. In recent times, it has found renewed favor and is now being recited in many of the churches at the dismissal time following the end of Mass.

In 590, the Bubonic plague struck Rome, killing Pope Pelagius II. He was immediately succeeded by Pope Gregory I. Born in Rome about 540, he eventually exercised a momentous influence on the Catholic Church. He is certainly one of the most notable figures in Ecclesiastical History.

When this great plague that killed so many throughout the world finally reached its breaking point, Pope Gregory I rallied the people from the seven corners of Rome. He led a procession through the streets. He carried a miraculous image of Mary as an act of penance and prayed for the forgiveness of sins. Many of the sick, moved by their faith, left their beds and homes to join in the procession.

Upon arriving at the bridge of St. Peter's where the tomb of the Emperor Hadrian is located, Gregory was given a vision of St. Michael the Archangel over the tomb of Hadrian, putting his sword back into its sheave. It was taken as a sign that the plague was over; and, so it was!

Castle of Sant' Angelo

Later, in memory of this vision, the statue of St. Michael was raised on top of that structure which stands today at the gate to St. Peter's. It is known as the Castle of Sant' Angelo. A chapel was eventually built at the top of the tomb along with a large marble angel, which remained there for centuries until Pope Benedict XIV replaced the statue with a bronze one. Pope Gregory I, the Great, died on March 12, 604. and was eventually declared a Saint and Doctor of the Church.

St. Michael, the Archangel, figured quite prominently during several of the appearances of Our Lady. In 1915, an angel, quite likely Michael, told the children in Fatima that he was the guardian angel of Portugal. He is known as the guardian of nations and heads of state. His task was to prepare the children for the appearances of the Mother of God. You will notice a great similarity of this vision of St. Michael with his sword, to the angel depicted in the third secret of Fatima.

Of all the shrines and places in the world that honor St. Michael, the Archangel, there is one very special place that honors him more than any other. *Mont Saint-Michel*, a wonder of the western world, forms a tower in the heart of an immense bay invaded by the highest tides in Europe. It is located in Normandy, France, approximately one-half mile offshore from the country's Northwestern coast.

Mont Saint-Michel

On October 19, 709, a bit further inland from the present Mont, St. Michael, the Archangel, appeared to Bishop Aubert of Avranches, wherein he requested the bishop to build and consecrate a small church on a rocky islet. When the bishop repeatedly ignored the angel's instruction, St. Michael burned a hole in the bishop's skull with his finger. Needless to say, construction began shortly thereafter.

At the same time the abbey was developing, a village sprung up during the Middle Ages. It flourished on the southeast side of the rock surrounded by walls, dating for the most part during the *Hundred Years War,* from 1337 to 1453. The *French Revolution* waged from 1787 to 1799 and reached its height in 1789, when the Abbey was turned into a prison. It was finally restored near the end of the nineteenth century.

On the monastic's 1000th anniversary, celebrated in 1966, a religious community returned and restored the original vocation there with the goal of perpetuating prayer. Friars and sisters from *Les Fraternités Monastiques de Jerusalem* have been ensuring a spiritual presence since the year 2001. This village has always had numerous shops to serve the visitors; yet, by 2006, it had a population of only 41.

I mentioned that "St. Michael burned a hole in the bishop's skull with his finger...construction began shortly thereafter." Lest you have any doubts about that altercation, I suggest you pay a visit to the Saint-Gervais Basilica in Avranches. Once there, you may closely inspect the hole in the bishop's skull to decide for yourself!

In 1848, Friedrich Engels, a German social scientist residing in England, issued the founding documents of Communism entitled the *Communist Manifesto*. It was co-authored by Karl Marx. By 1910, Portugal itself had been overrun by a people's Socialist Republic revolution whose purpose was to establish a police-state similar to that which Vladimir Lenin had proposed for Russia in 1895. Once in power they began an anti-religious policy against the Church; all religious orders were suppressed.

This led to the exile of the majority of the countries' bishops and the imprisonment of many priests. Dr. Alfonso Costa, chief organizer of the revolution, stated: "Thanks to this law of separation, in two generations Catholicism will be completely eliminated in Portugal."

St. Michael, the Archangel

On April 3, 1917, Vladimir Lenin, returned to Russia to further the revolution there where he said: "We need the real, nation-wide terror which reinvigorates the country and through which the Great French Revolution achieved glory."

Fortunately, as we shall see in the ensuing chapters, Our Lady had a different plan in mind, a plan from Heaven destined to radically change the world as we know it.

In 1981, Our Lady said: *"I am the Blessed Virgin Mary...I am your Mother, the Queen of Peace...I love you...I come on a mission from God the Father. God has chosen each one of you to use you in a great plan for the salvation of mankind. I wish to be with you to reconcile the world through prayer, fasting, faith, conversion and peace."*

The following year, on May 22nd, Our Lady told the children that this series of her appearances will be her last one on Earth: *"I have come to call the world to conversion for the last time. I will never again appear on Earth [in this way]."*

The breakup of the Soviet Union occurred in 1989. It was dissolved on December 26, 1991. On the previous day, Soviet President, Mikhail Gorbachev, resigned, declared his office extinct, and handed over its powers to Russian President Boris Yeltsin. That evening at 7:32, the Soviet flag was lowered from the Kremlin for the last time and replaced with the pre-evolutionary Russian flag. So it would seem that the cold war was finally over!

Epilogue, St. Michael

There is much speculation about the "century" afforded Satan by Christ in his attempt to destroy the Church, an approximate one-hundred year period. It has been suggested to be the century between 1884 – the date the prayer to St. Michael was composed – and 1984, when Pope John Paul II made the Consecration that Lúcia later confirmed was "accepted by Heaven."

Recently, however, it has been updated to be the time Our Lady affirmed the existence of Hell in the vision in Fatima in 1917, until the first secret in Medjugorje has been fulfilled.

CHAPTER 10

Our Lady of Fátima, Portugal

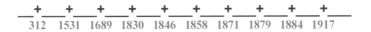

__+___+___+___+___+___+___+___+___+___+___

| 312 | 1531 | 1689 | 1830 | 1846 | 1858 | 1871 | 1879 | 1884 | 1917 |

"If my requests are heeded, Russia will be converted, and there will be peace. If not...The good will be martyred ...various nations will be annihilated...In the end, my Immaculate Heart will triumph...and a period of peace will be granted to the world."

Thirty-three years after Pope Leo XIII composed the prayer to St. Michael, the Archangel, Europe was in turmoil. *World War I* had ravished most of Europe since July 28, 1914. After raging for almost three years, Pope Benedict XV pleaded for the intercession of the Mother of God during his public prayer on May 5, 1917. He invited the world to perform a nine-day novena of prayer, asking Mary for peace and a quick end to the war. On the ninth day, in a direct response to those pleas, Our Lady appeared to three children at the Cova da Ira in Fatima, Portugal. It was May 13, 1917.

Several years prior to this, in the summer of 1915, the children were in the fields near the village, caring for their flocks. They were shepherds from poor peasant families: the eldest being Lúcia Dos Santos, 9, her cousins, Francisco Marto, 8, and his sister, Jacinta, 6. One afternoon that summer the children noticed a nearby cloud in the shape of a human form. It seemed strange but, inasmuch as they couldn't make it out, they put the thought aside. Then, during spring of the following year they again saw a globe of dazzlingly bright light, like a miniature sun; this time it was in the form of an angel, about 14 years old, gliding slowly toward them.

The angel appeared, "...more brilliant than crystal pierced by the rays of the sun!" He said to them: *"Do not be afraid! I am the Angel of Peace. Pray with me."* Kneeling down, the angel invited the children to pray and, bowing so low that his forehead touched the ground, began to recite a prayer with great fervor: *"My God, I believe, I adore, I hope and I love You! I ask pardon of You for those who do not believe, do not adore, do not hope and do not love You."* He repeated this twice, then rising, the angel said: *"Pray thus. The Hearts of Jesus and Mary are attentive to the voice of your supplications."* Then, he disappeared.

The Angel of Peace

Somewhat later that same year – while the children were playing near the family well – the angel appeared to them again. He sternly questioned them: *"What are you doing? Pray! You must pray very much! The Hearts of Jesus and Mary have designs of mercy on you. Offer prayers and sacrifices constantly to the Most High."*

When Lúcia asked him how they were to make sacrifices, he told them: *"Make of everything you can a sacrifice, and offer it to God as an act of reparation for the sins by which He is offended, and in supplication for the conversion of sinners. You will thus draw peace upon your country. I am its Angel Guardian, the Angel of Portugal. Above all, accept and bear with submission, the suffering which the Lord will send you."*

Lúcia said he was preparing us for the appearances of Our Lady, adding: "The angel's words were impressed upon our souls like a light that made us understand who God is, how much He loves us and wishes to be loved, the value of sacrifice and how it pleases God, and how He converts sinners because of it."

Later, in September of the same year, the angel appeared to them for a third time "holding a chalice in his hands. A host was directly above it; some drops of blood were falling from the host into the sacred vessel. Leaving the chalice and the host suspended in the air, the angel prostrated himself on the ground and repeated this prayer three times:'

"Most Holy Trinity, Father, Son and Holy Spirit, I adore You profoundly, and I offer You the most precious Body, Blood, Soul and Divinity of Jesus Christ, present in all the tabernacles of the world, in reparation for the outrages, sacrileges and indifference with which He Himself is offended. And, through the infinite merits of His most Sacred Heart and the Immaculate Heart of Mary, I beg of You the conversion of poor sinners."

Then, rising, he once more took the chalice and the host in his hands. He gave the host to me and the contents of the chalice to Francisco and Jacinta, saying, *"Take and drink the Body and Blood of Jesus Christ, horribly outraged by ungrateful men. Repair their crimes and console your God."*

On May 13, 1917, the children were tending their flocks when they saw what they thought was a flash of lightning. Thinking it was about to rain they hurried toward home. Suddenly, there was another flash of light. Directly in front of them on a small holm oak they saw "a lady all dressed in white."

The children were only a few feet from her and were bathed in the light which surrounded her. The light radiated from her. Lúcia said: "She was more brilliant then the sun, and radiated a light more clear and intense than a crystal glass filled with sparkling water, when the rays of the burning sun shine through it." She spoke to us: *"Do not be afraid. I will do you no harm."* Lúcia inquired: "Where are you from? *'I am from Heaven.'* What do you want of me?'" Our Lady replied: *"I have come to ask you to come here for six months in succession, on the 13th day, at the same hour. Later on I will tell you who I am and what I want. Afterwards, I will return here yet a seventh time."*

Lúcia asked: "Shall I go to Heaven too? *'Yes, you will.'* And Jacinta? *'She will go also.'* And, Francisco? *'He will go there too, but he must say many rosaries.'"*

Remembering an older teenage friend named Amelia who died recently, Lúcia asked about her. Our Lady responded: *"She will be in Purgatory until the end of the world."* Then, she asked Lúcia: *"Are you willing to offer yourselves to God and bear all the sufferings He wills to send you, as an act of reparation for the sins by which He is offended, and of supplication for the conversion of sinners?"* Lúcia answered: "Yes, we are willing," to which Our Lady responded: *"Then you will have much to suffer, but the grace of God will be your comfort."*

Lúcia said: "Our Lady opened her hands for the first time, communicating to us a light so intense that, as it streamed from her hands, its rays penetrated our hearts and the innermost depths of our souls, making us see ourselves in God – Who was that light – more clearly than we see ourselves in the best of mirrors.

"Then, moved by an interior impulse that was also communicated to us, we fell on our knees, repeating in our hearts, *'O most Holy Trinity, I adore You! My God, my God, I love You in the most Blessed Sacrament.'"* After a few moments, Our Lady spoke again: *"Pray the rosary every day, in order to obtain peace in the world, and the end of the war.'"* Lúcia said: "Then, she began to rise serenely, going up towards the East until she disappeared in the immensity of space.

"The light that surrounded her seemed to open up a path before her in the firmament, and for this reason we sometimes said that we saw Heaven opening. The door to Heaven closed so fast we thought her feet would be caught outside."

Lúcia reminisced about this feeling: "The peace and happiness we felt were great, but intimate, as our souls were entirely concentrated on God. The physical weariness that overwhelmed us was also great. I do not know why, but the fact is that the apparitions of Our Lady had a very different effect on us. There was the same intimate gladness, the same peace and happiness. But instead of physical weariness, we felt a certain expansive liveliness, a sense of glee instead of that annihilation in the Divine Presence, a certain communicative enthusiasm instead of that difficulty in speaking."

The following month, on the 13th of June, the children went to the Cova da Iria. This time they were accompanied by several hundred people. After praying for a while, Mary appeared to the children and Lúcia told her: "I would like to ask you to take us to Heaven." Mary told them: *"Yes, I will take Francisco and Jacinta soon. But you are to stay here for some time longer. Jesus wishes to make use of you to make me known and loved. He wishes to establish in the world devotion to my Immaculate Heart."*

Our Lady told Lúcia: *"I promise salvation to those who embrace it and these souls will be loved by God, like flowers placed by me to adorn His throne."* Lúcia asked: "Am I to stay here alone?" And, Our Lady responded: *"Are you suffering a great deal? Don't lose heart. I will never forsake you. My Immaculate Heart will be your refuge and the way that will lead you to God."*

"As Our Lady spoke these last words, she opened her hands for the second time; she communicated to us the rays of that same intense light. We saw ourselves in this light, as it were, immersed in God. Jacinta and Francisco seemed to be in that part of the light which rose toward Heaven, and I in that which was poured out on the Earth."

Lúcia continued: "In front of the palm of Our Lady's right hand was a heart encircled by thorns, which pierced it. We understood that this was the Immaculate Heart of Mary, outraged by the sins of humanity and seeking reparation."

By the 13th of July, approximately four-thousand people were present at the Cova. They observed strange occurrences such as flashes of light and a halo. After this display Our Lady appeared to the three children, and Lúcia asked her: "What do you want of me?" She told Lúcia: *"I want you to continue to come here on the 13th of next month, to pray the rosary every day in honor of Our Lady of the rosary, in order to obtain peace for the world and the end of the war, because only she can help you. Continue to come here every month. In October, I will tell you who I am and what I want, and I will perform a miracle for all to see and believe. Sacrifice yourselves for sinners, and say many times, especially whenever you make some sacrifice: O Jesus, it is for love of You, for the conversion of sinners, and in reparation for the sins committed against the Immaculate Heart of Mary."*

Then, Our Lady entrusted the children with a very somber message. It consisted of three parts. The first two parts would remain a secret until October 7, 1941, at which time Lúcia was asked by her bishop to write them down. Sr. Lúcia describes how Our Lady communicated these secrets to them that July, 1917: "As she spoke these words, she opened her hands once more as she had done during the two previous months. The rays of light seemed to penetrate the Earth, and we saw as it were a sea of fire. Plunged in this fire were demons and souls in human form like transparent burning embers, all blackened or burnished bronze, floating about in the conflagration, now raised into the air by the flames that issued from within themselves together with great clouds of smoke, now falling back on every side like sparks in huge fires, without weight or equilibrium, amid shrieks and groans of pain and despair which horrified us and made us tremble with fear. The demons could be distinguished by their terrifying and repulsive likeness to frightful and unknown animals, black and transparent like burning coals."

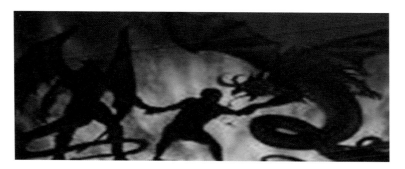

"Terrified and as if to plead for succor, we looked up at Our Lady, who said to us so kindly and so sadly: *'You have seen Hell where the souls of poor sinners go. To save them, God wishes to establish in the world devotion to my Immaculate Heart. If what I say to you is done, many souls will be saved and there will be peace. The war is going to end; but, if people do not cease offending God, a worse one will break out during the Pontificate of Pius XI. When you see a night illumined by an unknown light, know that this is the great sign given you by God that he is about to punish the world for its crimes, by means of war, famine, and persecutions of the Church and of the Holy Father.'*

"To prevent this, I shall come to ask for the Consecration of Russia to my Immaculate Heart, and the Communion of reparation on the First Saturdays. If my requests are heeded, Russia will be converted, and there will be peace. If not, she will spread her errors throughout the world, causing wars and persecutions of the Church. The good will be martyred; the Holy Father will have much to suffer; various nations will be annihilated. In the end, my Immaculate Heart will triumph.

"The Holy Father will consecrate Russia to me, and she will be converted, and a period of peace will be granted to the world. In Portugal, the dogma of the faith will always be preserved; etc.* [third secret of the message]. *Do not tell this to anybody. 'Francisco?' Francisco, yes, you may tell him. When you pray the rosary, say after each mystery: O my Jesus, forgive us, save us from the fire of Hell. Lead all souls to Heaven, especially those who are most in need."*

Lúcia noted: "This vision lasted but an instant. How can we ever be grateful enough to our kind heavenly Mother who had already prepared us by promising, in the first apparition, to take us to Heaven? Otherwise, I think we would have died of fright."

The following month, on the 13th of August, about 18,000 people were at the Cova, They saw the usual phenomena of thunder and lightning that was encountered previously; however, Our Lady did not appear. The children were nowhere to be seen! The administrator, Mayor Artur de Oliveira Santos, kidnapped them! Claiming they were a disturbance to public order, he took them to Ourém where he threatened them with death by "boiling them in oil" if they would not reveal the secret; however, they did not reveal it, nor would they deny seeing Our Lady. Because of their stubbornness, they were placed in the local jail with the common criminals but, eventually, were released after several days.

On Sunday, the 19th of August, the Virgin appeared to the children for the fourth time, asking them to continue to pray and promising them that at her last apparition at the Cova she would accomplish a Miracle "...for all to see and believe." Looking very sad, Our Lady said: "Pray, pray very much, and make sacrifices for sinners, for many souls go to Hell because there are none to sacrifice themselves and to pray for them."

On the 13th of September there were about 30,000 people present; some were begging the three children to implore their succor to heal the sick. During this appearance, Mary told Lúcia that on the following month the Holy Family would appear and bless the crowd, followed by Our Lady of Sorrows, then, as Our Lady of Mt. Carmel. Our Lady added: "Continue to pray the rosary in order to obtain the end of the war."

The roads into Fátima began filling with people all through the afternoon and throughout the night on the 12th of October; by the morning of the 13th a crowd of about seventy thousand had gathered. The rains pounded the Cova da Iria, turning the ground into mud; it was everywhere. Then, just about noon, Lúcia told the crowd to close their umbrellas despite the fact it was still raining.

When Mary appeared at the appointed time, she said: "I want to tell you that a chapel is to be built here in my honor. I am the Lady of the rosary. Continue always to say the rosary every day. The war is going to end and the soldiers will soon return to their homes."

Lúcia asked her to heal several of the sick and convert sinners. Our Lady responded: "Some, yes, but not others. They must amend their lives and ask forgiveness for their sins."

Looking very sad, she added: *"Do not offend the Lord our God anymore, because He is already too much offended."*

Opening her hands, Our Lady made them reflect on the sun and, as she ascended near the sun, the reflection of her own light continued to be projected onto the sun itself. Lúcia then commanded the people: "Look at the sun!" At that exact moment the rain stopped completely and, as the clouds parted, the sky cleared directly overhead.

Let Dr. Almedia Garrett, a professor from the University of Coimbra, describe the event. "The sun...was shining clearly and intensely...It  was possible for us to look at the sun – a blaze of light and burning heat – without any pain to the eyes or blinding of the retina. This lasted...about ten minutes. The sun...was rotating upon itself with exceedingly great speed. Suddenly, the people broke out with a cry of extreme anguish. The sun, still rotating, had loosened itself from the skies and came hurtling towards Earth. This huge, fiery millstone threatened to crush us with its weight. It was a dreadful sensation."

It repeated this action three times, causing many of the people to fall onto their knees, certain the sun would crash into Earth each time. Believing they were going to die, the people began to beg for mercy, screaming out in terror and beseeching Heaven: "God, forgive me; don't let me die in my sins!"

Lúcia would later relate: "After Our Lady had disappeared into the immense distance of the firmament we beheld St. Joseph with the Child Jesus, and Our Lady robed in white with a blue mantle, beside the sun. Saint Joseph and the Child Jesus appeared to bless the world, for they traced the sign of the cross with their hands. When, a little later, this apparition disappeared, I saw Our Lord and Our Lady; it seemed to me that it was Our Lady of Dolores (Sorrows). Our Lord appeared to bless the world in the same manner as St. Joseph had done. This apparition also vanished, and I saw Our Lady once more, this time resembling Our Lady of [Mt.] Carmel."

After these visions witnessed by the three children ended, the sun returned to its proper place in the heavens. Then, the people noticed for the first time that their clothes, which had previously been soaking wet and muddy, were completely dry.

Portugal and Spain were both spared participation in World War II; however, by July 13, 1917, the scourge of atheistic Socialism [Communism] that Our Lady warned about as a punishment for sin, was now on the march. Its prime objective was to expand out from Portugal and Russia, meeting in the middle of Europe; then, on toward world domination. However, owing to a renewal of the faith in Portugal since the miracle of the sun, it never progressed northward of the capitol. Yet, to this day, some evidence of Communism remains further south of Lisbon.

Eight years later, on December 10, 1925, Our Lady appeared again to Sr. Lúcia in the convent in Pontevedra, Spain. This time, Mary was elevated on a luminous cloud; by her side was a Child. Mary rested her hand on Lúcia's shoulder, then, showed her a heart, encircled by thorns, which she was holding in her other hand. At the same time, the Child said: *"Have compassion on the Heart of your most holy Mother, covered with thorns, with which ungrateful men pierce It at every moment and there is no one to make an act of reparation to remove them."*

Then, Our Lady said, *"Look, my daughter, at my Heart, surrounded with thorns, with which ungrateful men pierce me at every moment by their blasphemies and ingratitude. You, at least, try to console me and say that I promise to assist at the hour of death with the graces necessary for salvation all those who on the first Saturday of five consecutive months will confess, receive Holy Communion, recite five decades of the rosary, and keep me company for fifteen minutes while meditating on the fifteen mysteries of the rosary with the intention of making reparation to me."*

On February 25, 1926, Jesus again appeared to Lúcia as a Child and further clarified that anyone who missed confession within the required time could do that at their first opportunity. Also, if the intention of making reparation to the Immaculate Heart of Mary was forgotten, one could mention that in their next confession.

Two years later, in 1928, Lúcia Dos Santos took her vows as a Carmelite nun. The following year, on June 13th, she received an additional apparition of Our Lady in the chapel in Tuy, Spain. Lúcia wrote: "I had sought and obtained permission from my superiors and confessor to make a Holy Hour from 11:00 o'clock until midnight, every Thursday to Friday night. Being alone one night, I knelt near the altar rails in the middle of the chapel and, prostrate, I prayed the prayers of the angel. Feeling tired, I then stood up and continued to say the prayers with my arms in the form of a cross."

"Suddenly the whole chapel was illuminated by a supernatural light, and above the altar appeared a cross of light, reaching to the ceiling. In a brighter light on the upper part of the cross, could be seen the face of a man and his body as far as the waist; upon his breast was a dove of light; nailed to the cross was the body of another man."

"A little below the waist, I could see a chalice and a large host sus-pended in the air, onto which drops of blood were falling from the face of Jesus Crucified and from the wound in his side. These drops ran down onto the host and fell into the chalice. Beneath the right arm of the cross was Our Lady, and in her hand was her Immaculate Heart.

"It was Our Lady of Fátima with her Immaculate Heart in her left hand, without sword or roses, but with a crown of thorns and flames. Under the left arm of the cross, large letters – as if of crystal clear water which ran down upon the altar – formed these words: **Gratia et Misericordia** *[Grace and Mercy]. I understood that it was the mystery of the Most Holy Trinity which was shown to me, and I received lights about this mystery which I am not permitted to reveal."*

Then, Our Lady said: *"The moment has come in which God asks the Holy Father, in union with all the bishops of the world, to make the consecration of Russia to My Immaculate Heart, promising to save it by this means. There are so many souls whom the Justice of God condemns for sins committed against me, that I have come to ask reparation: sacrifice yourself for this intention and pray."*

Later, in August, 1931, during an intimate conversation with Our Lord in Rianjo, Spain, He complained to Sr. Lúcia: *"They did not wish to heed My request! ...Like the King of France [Louis XIV], in delaying the execution of My command, they will repent and do it, but it will be late. Russia will have already spread her errors throughout the world, provoking wars, and persecutions of the Church; the Holy Father will have much to suffer."*

In a letter dated May 18, 1936, Lúcia noted she asked Our Lord why He would not convert Russia without the Church and, specifically, the Holy Father saying the consecration. Christ replied: *"Because I want My whole Church to acknowledge that consecration as a triumph of the Immaculate Heart of Mary, so that it may extend its cult later on and put the devotion to the Immaculate Heart beside the devotion to My Sacred Heart."*

When Lúcia again asked if the pope personally had to do the consecration of Russia to the Immaculate Heart of Mary, Christ advised her: *"The Holy Father! Pray very much for the Holy Father. He will do it but it will be late. Nevertheless, the Immaculate Heart of Mary will save Russia. It has been entrusted to her."*

Those first two parts of the secret would become publicly known on October 7, 1941. Two months later, on December 8, the entire world would be at war.

It was that *Second Great War* Our Lady predicted would occur if certain conditions were not met. On January 3, 1944, Lúcia wrote the third part of the secret "by order of His Excellency, the bishop of Leiria, and the Most Holy Mother." It was then placed in an envelope. The sealed envelope was given to the bishop of Leiria; however, he informed Sr. Lúcia he did not read it. Thirteen years later, on April 4, 1957, the envelope was placed in the Archives of the Holy Office at the Vatican.

On August 17, 1959, Alfredo Cardinal Ottaviani brought the envelope to Pope St. John XXIII. After some hesitation, His Holiness said: "We will wait. I shall pray. I shall let you know what I decide." Later, the pope returned the sealed envelope to the Holy Office, choosing not to reveal it at that time.

John Paul II   Sr. Lúcia

Lúcia had previously stated that the secret could be revealed either upon her death, or after 1960, whichever occurred first. Many of the faithful who had waited for so long misunderstood, for they believed it *must* be revealed in 1960. Yet, this did not happen and many people were quite dismayed that nothing further was forthcoming

However, following the attempt to assassinate John Paul II on May 13, 1981, the pope, convinced it was the Blessed Virgin who had saved his life, asked for the envelope containing the secret. After reading it, he returned it to the Archives of the Holy Office. Soon, thereafter he composed a prayer for what he called an *Act of Entrustment* which was to be celebrated in the Basilica of Saint Mary Major on June 7, 1981, the Solemnity of Pentecost.

John Paul II attempted to fulfill Our Lady's request in 1982 by making a formal consecration of the world, especially Russia, to her Immaculate Heart. However, in response to the pope's inquiry, Sr. Lúcia informed him that the consecration had not been accepted by Heaven.

Then she reminded him that Our Lady previously said: *"The moment has come in which God asks the Holy Father, in union with all the bishops of the world."* The pope then performed another consecration on March 25, 1984 "...in spiritual union with the bishops of the world who had been convoked beforehand, entrusting men and women and all peoples to the Immaculate Heart of Mary."

Later, Sr. Lúcia personally confirmed that this solemn and universal act of consecration corresponded to what Our Lady requested, writing: "Yes, it has been done, just as Our Lady asked, on March 25, 1984."[1]

Shortly before his death, Francisco told Lúcia: "I am going to Heaven soon, but you must stay here to make known God's wish to establish in the world devotion to the Immaculate Heart of Mary. Do not be afraid to tell it. Tell everyone that God gives us all graces through the Immaculate Heart of Mary, so that everyone may ask her. Make it known that the Sacred Heart of Jesus wishes that the Immaculate Heart of Mary be honored with Him. People must ask for peace through the Immaculate Heart of Mary, for God has confided the peace of the world to her." As Our Lady predicted, Francisco died in 1919; Jacinta, in 1920.

In 1917, Our Lady of Fátima had stated with great clarity that, if men did not cease offending her Son, the world would be punished, *"by means of war, famine, and persecutions of the Church and of the Holy Father."* Indeed, all too soon – from 1917 through the beginning of *World War II* – the elements for these scenarios were being fulfilled. Communism, under the theories of Marx, Engels, and Lenin raised its ugly head: first in Portugal, then in Russia. When economic depression began to engulf the world, Hitler began his meteoric ascent to power in Germany.

On October 13, 1942, Cardinal Cerejeira, Patriarch of Lisbon, stated: "The mystery is now becoming clear. Fatima now speaks not only to Portugal, but to the whole world. We believe that the apparitions of Fatima are the beginning of a new epoch, that of the Immaculate Heart of Mary. What has happened in Portugal proclaims the miracle. It is the presage of what the Immaculate Heart of the Mother of God has prepared for the world."

By 1953, about eight years after the war's end, much discussion began in the media about the possible revelation in 1960 of the third part of the secret of Fátima. Cardinal Ottaviani said he had talked to Sr. Lúcia in Coimbra in 1955, asking her why it could not be disclosed before the date she previously specified and she answered: "Because then it will appear clearer." Still, some members of the Church doubted it would be revealed by then, if ever. Unfortunately, many individuals begun to speculate on the contents of the message; many of their pronouncements ranged from the banal to the far-out fringe.

Sr. Lúcia stated she understood that, "prior to God's chastising the world – after He had offered us every means to save us – He gave us His mother." Lúcia added: "Our Lady is our last hope and it is through devotion to the Immaculate Heart of Mary and the rosary that this can be accomplished." Lúcia had stated earlier that "only a limited portion would be saved." Later, she confirmed that, saying Our Lady told her: *"...many, many are lost!"* She said that "Mary was sad because so few heeded her words," adding that, "Our Lady was engaged in a decisive battle with Satan for the salvation of the world and, at the end of this present era, one would be, *'...either of God, or of the evil one.'"* There would be no more straddling fences in the future. Recall Jesus' stern warning: *"I know your works; I know that you are neither cold nor hot. I wish you were either cold or hot. So, because you are lukewarm, neither hot nor cold, I will spit you out of my mouth"* (Rv 3:15-16).

On May 12-13, 2000, eighty-three years after the miracle of the sun at Fatima, the Beatification of Francisco and Jacinta took place. With Lúcia at his side at the site of the apparitions, Pope St. John Paul II finally permitted the third part of the message to be revealed, the secret she had written a half-century earlier!

He read as follows: *"'A woman, clothed with the sun...'* (Rv 12:1) came down from Heaven to this Earth to visit these privileged children of the Father...Francisco exclaimed earlier that, *'We were burning in that light which is God and we were not consumed. What is God like?"*

"It is impossible to say. In fact we will never be able to tell people."

"What most impressed and entirely absorbed Blessed Francisco was God in that immense light which penetrated the inmost depths of the three children. But God told only Francisco *'how sad'* He was...One night his father heard him sobbing and asked him why he was crying; his son answered: 'I was thinking of Jesus who is so sad because of the sins that are committed against Him.' He was motivated by one desire – so expressive of how children think – to console Jesus and make Him happy. He died on April 4, 1919.

"Little Jacinta personally felt and personally experienced Our Lady's anguish, offering herself heroically as a victim for sinners. One day, when she and Francisco had already contracted the illness that forced them to bed, the Virgin Mary came to visit them at home, as the little one recounts: 'Our Lady came to see us and said that soon she would come and take Francisco to Heaven. And she asked me if I still wanted to convert more sinners. I told her, "Yes." And when the time came for Francisco to leave, the little girl tells him: 'Give my greetings to Our Lord and to Our Lady and tell them that I am enduring everything they want for the conversion of sinners.' Jacinta had been so deeply moved by the vision of Hell during the apparition of July 13 that no mortification or penance seemed too great to save sinners. She could well exclaim with St. Paul: *'Now, I rejoice in my sufferings for your sake, and in my flesh I am filling up what is lacking in the afflictions of Christ on behalf of his body, which is the Church'* (Col 1:24)."

Less than a year before her death on February 20, 1920, Jacinta received many revelations from Our Lady regarding morality and the future. On April 4, 1919, Our Lady told her: *"Certain fads [fashions] will be introduced that will offend Our Lord very much; many marriages are not good; they do not please Our Lord and are not of God; most people go to Hell because of sins of the flesh."* She died on February 20, 1920.

Lúcia learned to read and write and went on to author several books about the apparitions. Seventy-five years later, after a full lifetime of service to Our Lord and Our Lady, Sr. Lúcia died on February 14, 2005. She was 97 years old.

---

i - Due to the impact of the third part of the secret, and its continuing consequences upon the world, a separate Chapter entitled *Revealed Secrets* will deal more fully with this matter.

CHAPTER 11

Our Lady of Beauraing, Belgium

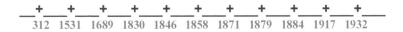

__+___+___+___+___+___+___+___+___+___+___+__
312 1531 1689 1830 1846 1858 1871 1879 1884 1917 1932

"I will convert sinners...I am the Mother of God, the Queen of Heaven. Pray always... sacrifice yourself for me."

Fifteen years after her appearances in Fátima Our Lady appeared to five young children of varying ages, between nine and fifteen, in Beauraing, a small town of French speaking people in the southern area of Belgium. Early in the evening of November 29, 1932, several children passed a small Lourdes' grotto in front of a railway embankment on their way to the local convent school, then, entered the grounds that skirted the convent garden.

The Visionaries

While waiting for someone to answer the door, one of them, Albert, 11, looked towards the embankment over the grotto and cried aloud: "Look! The Blessed Virgin, dressed in white, is walking above the bridge!" The girls looked and could see the luminous figure of a lady dressed in white.

She was walking in midair, her feet hidden by a little cloud. The Sister who answered the door could see nothing, but when Gilberte, 13, reached the door she, too, saw the figure.

Over the next few evenings a pattern gradually developed in which the children would see Mary by a hawthorn tree near the grotto, but from outside the convent grounds. The children simultaneously dropped to their knees on the cobble-stoned street with a force that made by-standers wince; yet they suffered no injury. The people also knelt down in the street, looking through the railings from the outside of the convent gate. They were astonished with the high-pitched quality of the children's voices as they prayed. The children later described how they saw a beautiful Lady wearing a white gown with rays of light surrounding her head. She was holding her hands together as if in prayer. On the 2nd of December, Albert asked her if she was the Immaculate Virgin, to which she smiled and nodded her head; then, in answer to what she wanted, Our Lady simply said: *"Always be good."*

On December the 8th, the feast of the Immaculate Conception, a crowd of about fifteen thousand assembled expecting a great miracle; but, they only saw the children in ecstasy. Testing the children while they were in ecstasy, they were found to be impervious to lighted matches held underneath their hands. Lights shone in their eyes and pin pricks did not bother them in the slightest. Meanwhile, the local priest, Father Lambert, and the Church authorities were taking a very prudent attitude towards events in Beauraing. They refused to get involved and the local bishop ordered his priests not to go to the site.

Although the children assembled and said the rosary every night, the apparitions did not occur each time; however, if Mary did appear they would fall to their knees in unison. They were closely watched to ensure they could not talk to each other and, when the apparition was over, they were questioned separately. On the 28th of December, the children said Our Lady told them: *"My last apparition will take place soon."*

The next day, the 30th, Fernande, 15, saw the Blessed Virgin with a heart of gold surrounded by rays. This was seen by two of the children as Mary repeated the phrase: *"Pray, pray very much."*

Yet, only Fernande heard her say this. On New Year's Eve, all the children saw Mary's golden heart. On New Year's Day, Mary asked Gilberte to *"Pray, always"* with the emphasis on always. The next day she told the children that on January the 3rd, the date of the final apparition, she would speak to each of them separately.

A very large crowd of about thirty-five thousand people assembled that evening as the children began their rosary. After saying only two decades, four of them said they could see her and fell to their knees, leaving the oldest, Fernande, in tears because she could see nothing. Mary spoke to Gilberte, imparting to her what was seen as the main message in Beauraing: *"I will convert sinners"* and, then, *"Goodbye!"* Just before disappearing, Our Lady said to Andree: *"I am the Mother of God, the Queen of Heaven. Pray, always."*

Our Lady of Beauraing

While the other children went inside for questioning, Fernande remained kneeling. Suddenly, along with many in the crowd, she heard a loud noise like thunder. She then saw a ball of fire on the hawthorn tree. Mary appeared from within this ball and, speaking to Fernande, asked if she loved her Son, and herself. When Fernande said she did, Our Lady responded: *"Then sacrifice yourself for me!"*

Upon saying this, the Blessed Virgin glowed with extraordinary brilliance and, extending her arms, Fernande could see her golden heart. She then said, *"Goodbye"* and disappeared.

Epilogue, Beauraing

The bishop appointed a commission of inquiry in 1935. By that time, opposition to Beauraing had practically ceased. The investigation resumed under his successor. In February, 1943, Bishop Charue authorized public devotions to Mary in Beauraing; however, it was not until July 1949, four years after the end of *World War II*, that the shrine was officially recognized and two important documents issued.

The first dealt with two of the many cures that had taken place in Beauraing. They were declared to be miraculous. The second document was a letter to the clergy in which the bishop said, "We are able in all serenity and prudence to affirm that the Queen of Heaven appeared to the children of Beauraing during the winter of 1932-1933, especially to show us in her maternal Heart, the anxious appeal for prayer, and the promise of her powerful mediation for the conversion of sinners."

CHAPTER 12

Our Lady of Banneux, Belgium

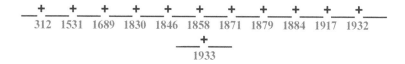

$$\underline{\quad\overset{+}{312}\quad\overset{+}{1531}\quad\overset{+}{1689}\quad\overset{+}{1830}\quad\overset{+}{1846}\quad\overset{+}{1858}\quad\overset{+}{1871}\quad\overset{+}{1879}\quad\overset{+}{1884}\quad\overset{+}{1917}\quad\overset{+}{1932}\quad}$$

$$\underline{\quad\overset{+}{1933}\quad}$$

"I am the Virgin of the Poor...I am the Mother of the Savior, Mother of God...I come to alleviate suffering."

Less than two weeks after the last appearance in Beauraing, the Blessed Virgin appeared to an 11 year old girl named Mariette Beco, who came from a poor, lapsed Catholic family in Banneux, a town about fifty miles north of Beauraing. Shortly before suppertime, on the evening of January 15, 1933, Mariette was looking out her kitchen window and noticed a glowing figure standing motionless near the vegetable garden.

Mariette Beco and Child

The figure "was enveloped in a great oval light, wearing a long white gown with a sash of an unforgettable blue, with a white transparent veil covering her head and shoulders. Her right foot was visible and crowned with a golden rose between the toes. She had a rosary on her right arm with diamond-like beads and a golden chain and cross."

She stood on a cloud with her head and shoulders bent slightly to the left. She was smiling at Mariette. The young girl asked to go outside, but her mother feared the girl might be seeing a ghost and refused to let her go; however, when Mariette returned to the window, the lady had vanished.

Three days later, Mariette knelt on the frozen ground where she had seen the figure and began praying the rosary. A figure appeared in the distant sky, coming closer and closer until she was only a few feet away. The lady led Mariette to a spring, then spoke for the first time, saying: *"Plunge your hands into the water. This spring is reserved for me."* Then, Our Lady left, promising to return.

Our Lady of Banneux

The next day, the lady appeared for a third time. Mariette asked her who she was, and she replied, *"I am the Virgin of the Poor."* Mary led Mariette to the spring again, saying, *"This is reserved for all nations, for the sick."* The following day, Mariette asked, "What do you want, beautiful Lady?" The Virgin told her that she would like to have a little chapel built. Our Lady then made the sign of the cross.

On February the 11th, the Virgin took Mariette to the spring again and said, *"I come to alleviate suffering."* Four days later, the Virgin said, *"Believe in me, I will believe in you."* Five days after that, Mary told her to: *"Pray hard."* The last apparition occurred on the 2nd of March. The Virgin said, *"I am the Mother of the Savior, Mother of God"* then, she repeated, *"Pray hard."*

The Shrine of the Virgin of the Poor

Although the Virgin spoke only briefly during her apparitions, she encouraged the girl to pray, then, led her to a spring with miraculous healing powers. After the apparitions, many miracles that were associated with the spring were reported.

In 1949, the site of the apparitions in Banneux was officially approved by the Church. The Shrine of Our Lady of Banneux is now a Marian shrine, known for the healing of the many pilgrims who go there.

Epilogue, Banneux

Banneux was investigated from 1935 until 1937 by an Episcopal commission, after which the evidence collected was submitted to Rome. Meanwhile growing numbers of pilgrims came to the shrine, and in May 1942 Bishop Kerkhofs of Liege approved the cult of the Virgin of the Poor.

In 1947 the apparitions themselves received preliminary approval, with this becoming definite in 1949. Like the children at Beauraing, Mariette married and had a family, being, like them, content to remain in the background.

PART III

Future

Thus difficult times for the world continued! War upon war – seemingly without end – began early in the twentieth century. Since World War I most of us have never known a time when the world was at peace. Now, even in our own country, we seem to be at war with our neighbors. It would appear we are living in that time which Fulton Sheen noted in the 1960s: "We don't need hair-shirts today; our neighbors are our hair-shirts!" The *feminist movement* is causing a great rift in family life, given its ensuing proclamations endorsing birth control, abortion, euthanasia and divorce. When will we come to our senses?

Will we perform that penance Our Lady has requested over the past 185 years; the same *"Penance"* the angel thrice warned us about in the third secret of Fátima? God gave to the *"woman clothed with the sun"* the power to use the sun to perform a great miracle in 1917.

Therefore, it seems quite logical to assume the sun may once again be used in order to bring mankind to its knees! Even then, will we listen, or must we suffer the consequence? Must it take a direct intervention of God to show us the correct path?

This mission given to Our Lady is further clarified by several of her appearances, two of which are still under investigation. In due time, the Church will either accept them as genuine, else dismiss them as unworthy of belief. While they are not absolutely necessary to fulfill Mary's mission these sites predict numerous future events that will affect us all.

Of particular interest are the reported apparitions of Our Lady in Garabandal in 1961, and Medjugorje in 1981, both of which are still under investigation by the Church. Each of these apparitions are of intense interest to the author. He personally experienced an event in his life shortly after the onset of each of the apparitions, either of which could have resulted in global thermonuclear war. The events came with a "nuclear hair-trigger" that could go out of control in a moment's notice, beyond man's ability to stop them!. One cannot fully comprehend the gravity of those situations without being personally involved, or fully aware of the consequences.

It is these events that resulted in the author's interest and, years later, writing this manuscript so that others may understand their significance, Mary's mission and her role in combating them. They are further clarified on pp. 188-191.

The outcome of all these events may well be determined by what we do now! How will we handle the future once we have discovered the correct path? The answer lies in understanding Mary's mission over the last 185 years.

CHAPTER 13

Divine Mercy, Poland

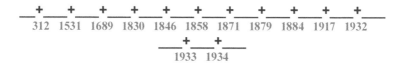

___+___+___+___+___+___+___+___+___+___+___+___
312 1531 1689 1830 1846 1858 1871 1879 1884 1917 1932
___+___+___
1933 1934

"You have to speak to the world about His great mercy and prepare the world for the Second Coming of Him who will come, not as a merciful Savior, but as a just Judge. Oh, how terrible is that day! Determined is the day of justice, the day of divine wrath. The angels tremble before it. Speak to souls about this great mercy while it is still the time for mercy...."

A year later, following Our Lady's appearance in Banneux, Christ entrusted a message of great importance to a young woman named Helena Kowalska. The third of ten children, she was born in Poland on August 25, 1905. At the age of 20 she received her habit in the Congregation of the Sisters of Our Lady of Mercy, taking the name *Maria Faustina of the Blessed Sacrament.*

St. Faustina Kowalska

During the course of her short lifetime she experienced numerous visions of both Christ and His Mother. Sr. Faustina wrote in her diary that on the night of February 22, 1931, while she was in her cell (room) in the convent, Jesus appeared to her as the *King of Divine Mercy.* He was wearing a white garment with rays of white and red lights emanating from near His heart.

He said to her: *"Paint an image according to the pattern you see, with the signature: Jesus, I trust in You. I desire that this image be venerated, first in your chapel, and [then] throughout the world. I promise that the soul that will venerate this image will not perish. I also promise victory over [its] enemies already here on Earth, especially at the hour of death. I, Myself, will defend it as My own glory"* (Diary, 47-48). *"The two rays denote blood and water...These rays shield souls from the wrath of My Father. Happy is the one who will dwell in their shelter"* (Diary, 299).

Jesus I Trust in You!

"I desire that there be a Feast of Mercy, I want this image...to be solemnly blessed on the first Sunday after Easter; that Sunday is to be the Feast of Mercy" (Diary, 49). Then, He added: *"At the hour of their death, I defend as My own glory every soul that will say this chaplet; or when others say it for a dying person, the indulgence is the same. When this chaplet is said by the bedside of a dying person, God's anger is placated, unfathomable mercy envelops the soul, and the very depths of My tender mercy ore moved for the sake of the sorrowful Passion of My Son"* (Diary, 811).

Sr. Faustina approached some of the other nuns at the convent but received no assistance concerning the painting of the image. Three years later she was assigned to Vilnius where the first artistic rendering of the image was performed under her direction.

In the summer of 1934, Sr. Faustina made a most important entry in her diary wherein Christ told her: *"Write this: before I come as the Just Judge, I am coming first as the King of Mercy. Before the day of justice arrives, there will be given to people a sign in the heavens of this sort: All light in the heavens will be extinguished, and there will be great darkness over the whole Earth. Then, the sign of the cross will be seen in the sky and, from the openings where the hands and the feet of the Savior were nailed, will come forth great lights which will light up the Earth for a period of time. This will take place shortly before the last day"* (Diary, 42).

On March 25, 1936, Our Lady appeared to her and said: *"Oh, how pleasing to God is the soul that follows faithfully the inspirations of His grace! I gave the Savior to the world; as for you, you have to speak to the world about His great mercy and prepare the world for the Second Coming of Him who will come, not as a merciful Savior, but as a just Judge. Oh, how terrible is that day! Determined is the day of justice, the day of divine wrath. The angels tremble before it. Speak to souls about this great mercy while it is still the time for [granting] mercy...Fear nothing. Be faithful to the end. I sympathize with you"* (Diary, 635).

On Good Friday March 26, 1937, Christ appeared to Sr. Faustina and asked her to recite a chaplet for nine days. The following prayer was to be recited on the large beads: *"Holy God, Holy Mighty One, Holy Immortal One, have mercy on us and on the whole world"* and, on the smaller beads, *"For the sake of His sorrowful Passion have mercy on us and on the whole world"* (Diary, 476).

Shortly before her death, Sr. Faustina predicted: "There will be a war, a terrible, terrible war." She then asked the nuns to pray for Poland. By 1939, the year following Faustina's death, aware that her predictions about the war had taken place, the archbishop allowed public access to the *Divine Mercy* image. This resulted in large crowds which hastened the spread of the Divine Mercy devotion. It became a source of strength and inspiration for many people in Poland who would have much to endure through the horrendous occupations by both the Nazis and Russians. By 1941, the devotion reached the shores of the United States.

Thirteen years after entering the convent, Faustina made her final confession. She died in Krakow on October 5, 1938 and was canonized by Pope John Paul II on April 30, 2000 – the first saint of the 21st century.

A year later, on April 22, 2001, John Paul II said: "It is a great joy for me to be able to join all of you...to commemorate, after one year, the canonization of Sr. Faustina Kowalska...Indeed the message she brought is the appropriate and incisive answer that God wanted to offer to the questions and expectations of human beings in our time, marked by terrible tragedies. Jesus told Sr. Faustina one day: *'Mankind will not have peace until it turns with trust to My mercy'* (Diary, 699)."

Epilogue, Divine Mercy

At this time we venture into an area wherein Our Lady's apparitions are still ongoing. Inasmuch as the Church has not, as yet, made a definitive judgment as to their authenticity, one must carefully study those under investigation and remain open to the Church's wisdom regarding these matters. Should any of these apparitions eventually prove to be erroneous, that would not discredit the other places Our Lady has graced with her visits and it would not affect the eventual outcome of her plans for the salvation of the world.

In order to help us understand the present day situation and its consequences, she has provided us with additional details since her appearances in Beauraing and Banneux. None of the statements made at these later appearances are contrary to Church teaching. Should they ever prove to be erroneous, we may be certain the Church will not hesitate to condemn them as unworthy of belief.

If they are truly from Heaven, and do not conflict with Church teaching, we best heed what she is trying so earnestly to tell us. We would do well to recall those words spoken by Pope Pius IX on July 18, 1851, upon reading the secrets of La Salette. He summed up the messages by declaring: "If we do not pray we shall all perish!"

CHAPTER 14

Our Lady of Garabandal, Spain

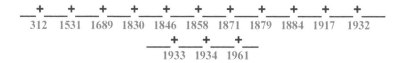

+	+	+	+	+	+	+	+	+	+	+
312	1531	1689	1830	1846	1858	1871	1879	1884	1917	1932

+	+	+
1933	1934	1961

"Before, the chalice was filling up. Now it is flowing over. I, your mother, ask you to amend your lives. You are now receiving the last warnings. I love you much and do not want your condemnation."

Twenty-eight years later in the tiny village of San Sebastian de Garabandal – high up in the Cantabrian mountains of Northern Spain - four girls were playing a game. Conchita Gonzalez, Maria Dolores (Mari-Loli) Mazon and Jacinta Gonzalez were 12 years of age; Maria Cruz Gonzalez was only 11. Although not related, several of the children had similar last names.

San Sebastian de Garabandal

It was about 8:30 in the evening of Sunday, June 18, 1961. The children were playing in a small rocky lane, pretending to hide behind a stone wall next to whence they had just "pinched" several rather bitter, crab apples. They thought the owner of the apple trees really wouldn't mind, but in case he did...

Suddenly, they heard a loud noise similar to a clap of thunder. Then, directly in front of them, they saw the bright figure of an angel. The children ran to the village church. Pale and visibly shaken, their only comment was: "We've seen an angel." Later they would learn that he is an Archangel named Michael, St. Michael, the Archangel.

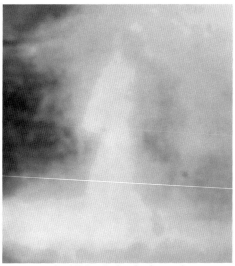

St. Michael, the Archangel

The news of the event spread like wildfire throughout the small village. Over the next twelve days the angel appeared to them several more times. As in Fátima, he was preparing them for the appearances of the Mother of God. Several weeks later, on Saturday, July 1st, the angel appeared again and spoke to them for the first time. He announced that the Blessed Virgin would appear to them the following day. This news spread even more quickly through the region than that of the angel. By Sunday, the town was packed with numerous people, both local and from out of town. Among them were several physicians and priests who had come to see for themselves what was occurring.

At six o'clock that evening the four girls went to the place where they originally saw the angel. The moment they saw Our Lady they simultaneously fell onto their knees in ecstasy. Two angels, one of whom was St. Michael, accompanied Mary. She was dressed similar to Our Lady of Mt. Carmel, much as she looked when she appeared in her last apparition in Fatima.

Conchita, the eldest child, described her appearance: "Our Lady comes wearing a white robe and blue cloak. She has a crown of golden stars; her feet are not visible. Her hands are slender with a scapular on her right wrist. The scapular is reddish. Her hair is long, wavy and dark brown, parted in the middle. Her face is long, her nose is long and slender and her mouth is dainty and very lovely; her lips are just a little bit thick. Her complexion is quite dark but lighter than the angel's.

Our Lady of Mt. Carmel

"Her voice is different from the angel's. It is a very beautiful voice, very unusual; I cannot explain it. There is no woman who is like Our Lady, either in voice or in any way at all. Sometimes she carries her Child Jesus in her arms. He is quite tiny, as tiny as a new-born baby. He has a round face and appears to have the same complexion as Our Lady, with a sweet little mouth. His blond hair is rather long; His hands are very small and He is dressed in a sort of sky-blue tunic. Our Lady seems to be about 18 years old."

The children told her about their tasks, how they were going to the meadows and "...she smiled at the little things we told her." Our Lady showed them how to treat her, "Like children who speak with their mother and tell her everything; Children who rejoice to see her when they have not seen her for a while."

On October 18, 1961, the children stated that Our Lady had given them a somber message: *"We must make many sacrifices, perform much penance, and visit the Blessed Sacrament frequently. But first, we must lead good lives. If we do not, a chastisement will befall us. The cup is already filling up and, if we do not change, a very great chastisement will come upon us."*

Mari Loli   Jacinta   Mary Cruz   Conchita

The message was written on paper by Conchita; then, signed by all four children. Then, four years later, on June 18, 1965, the children received a second message. St. Michael, the Archangel relayed it to the world 'because Our Lady said: *"It pained me to say it myself:*

"As my message of October 18, [1961] has not been complied with, and has not been made known to the world, I am advising you that this is the last one.

"Before, the cup was filling up. Now it is flowing over. Many cardinals, many bishops, and many priests are on the road to perdition and are taking many souls with them. Less and less importance is being given to the Eucharist. You should turn the wrath of God away from yourselves by your efforts. If you ask Him forgiveness with sincere hearts, He will pardon you.

"I, your mother, through the intercession of St. Michael the Archangel, ask you to amend your lives. You are now receiving the last warnings. I love you much and do not want your condemnation. Pray to us with sincerity and we will grant your requests. You should make more sacrifices. Think of the passion of Jesus."

Soon afterward, Our Lady advised them of three events that will occur in the future: first, there will be a worldwide *Warning*; the second event will be a *Miracle*; the third event will be a worldwide *Chastisement*! This chastisement is conditional; it can be mitigated or stopped completely, depending entirely on how we choose to respond to her messages!

Mari Loli   Conchita   Jacinta   Mary Cruz [1]

Before the miracle takes place, Our Lady said that all mankind will receive a warning from Heaven. Conchita said: "The warning comes directly from God and will be visible to the whole world, and from any place where anyone may happen to be. It will be like the revelation of our sins and it will be seen and felt by everyone, believer and unbeliever alike, irrespective of whatever religion they may belong to.

"It will be seen and felt in all parts of the world and by every person. It will happen in the sky; no one can prevent it from happening. It is like a momentary stopping of time around the world wherein people will see themselves as God sees them, and how they should amend their ways. We will even prefer to be dead rather than to pass through this warning."

---

[1] *by 1963, Mari Cruz no longer saw Our Lady but continued to hope she would appear again.*

The warning: "...will not, in itself, kill anyone; however some might die of fright. It will be a correction of our conscience. It will cause great fear and will make us reflect within ourselves on the consequences of our own personal sins. It will be like a warning of the punishment to come. In this way, the world will be offered a means of purification to prepare itself for the extraordinary grace of the great miracle."

She said that Our Lady has promised a miracle in Garabandal so that all may believe and obey the messages. Conchita observed: "As the punishment, which we deserve for the sins of the world is great, the miracle must also be a great one, for the world needs it."

"It will occur on a Thursday, at 8:30 in the evening, on the feast day of a saint devoted to the Eucharist, and will last for about one quarter of an hour. It will also coincide with a great event in the Church. The sick that come to Garabandal on that day will be cured and unbelievers will be converted. There will remain a permanent sign of the miracle at The Pines" – the place where Mary often appeared to Conchita alone.

This will be a proof of Our Lady's tremendous love for all her children. Conchita wrote: "The sign that will remain will be able to be seen, photographed and televised but will not be able to be touched. It will appear clearly that it is something not of this world, but of God." Conchita will publicly announce the date of the miracle eight days prior to its predicted date. Conchita added: "The Blessed Virgin will not allow me to reveal the nature of the miracle although I already know it. Neither can I reveal the date of it, which I know, until eight days before it is to happen."

Conchita wrote this about the chastisement: "I cannot reveal what kind of punishment it is except that it will be a result of the direct intervention of God, which makes it more terrible and fearful than anything we can imagine. It will be less painful for innocent babies to die a natural death than for those babies to die because of the punishment.

"All Catholics should go to confession before the punishment and the others should repent of their sins. When I saw it, I felt a great fear even though at the same time I was seeing Our Blessed Mother. The punishment, if it comes, will come after the miracle."

When Our Lady spoke to the children about the punishment, her face assumed a look of great sadness. They all stated: "We have never seen her look so serious. When she said the words, *'The cup is already filling up'* she spoke in a very low voice."

The punishment is conditional and will occur sometime after the miracle; it will encompass the whole world. During one of their ecstasies the girls were heard praying for the innocent children but they shed tears at the same time. Since that day they learned about the punishment they have developed a great spirit of sacrifice. They pray very much for sinners and for priests. They often say that if priests are not what they should be, many souls will be lost. Jacinta added: "The warning would come when conditions are at their worst." The date was not revealed to the children; however, Mari Loli does know the year.

On November 13, 1965, Conchita saw her for the last time. Our Lady asked: *"Do you know, Conchita, why I did not come personally on June 18th to give you the message for the world? Because it pained me to say it myself, but I have to say it to you for your own good and, if you fulfill it, for God's glory. I love you very much and I desire your salvation, to gather you all around God the Father, the Son and the Holy Spirit. Conchita, won't you respond to this?"* Conchita answered, "If I could be always seeing you, yes; but otherwise I can't because I am very bad." Our Lady replied: *"You do all you can and We will help you, as well as my daughters Loli, Jacinta and Mari Cruz."*

Conchita noted that Mary did not stay with her for long that day but she also said, *"This will be the last time you see me here, but I will always be with all my children."* She added, *"Conchita, why don't you go often to visit my Son in the Most Blessed Sacrament? Why do you let yourself be carried away by laziness and not go to visit Him Who is waiting for you day and night?"* Then, Conchita told Mary, "Oh, how happy I am when I see you. Why don't you take me with you right now?"

Our Lady answered: *"Remember what I told you on your saint's day. When you go before God you must show Him your hands filled with good works done by you for your brothers and for the glory of God. Now your hands are empty."* Conchita said, "I spent a happy moment with my mother from Heaven, my best friend, and with the Child Jesus. I have stopped seeing them, but not feeling them close."

"Again, they have sown in my soul great peace, joy, and a desire to conquer my defects so that I will be able to love, with all my strength, the hearts of Jesus and Mary who love us so much." Conchita added: "The Blessed Virgin Mary told me before that Jesus does not want to send the punishment in order to distress us but in order to help us and reproach us because we pay no attention to Him. And the warning will be sent in order to purify us for the miracle in which he will show us His great love, and in order that we may fulfill the message."

Conchita mentioned numerous things Our Lady had told her that would occur in the future. She stated that Communism [a form of atheistic Socialism] would engulf the entire world, including the United States. She also said that "murder would be commonplace throughout the world." She also affirmed that Mary told her: *"... after Pope Paul VI there would be two more popes and that would be the end of an era, but not the end of the world!"* When pressed about the meaning of this, Conchita said she did not know; Our Lady did not tell her.

At the time it was misunderstood by many that the last message, given in June, 1965, would be her last one for the world. That obviously was not the case as Mary would give additional messages at a later time in Akita, followed by the ongoing apparitions in Medjugorje.

In 1966, not long after the apparitions ended, Conchita went to Rome at the request of Cardinal Ottaviani, the Secretary of the Congregation for the Doctrine of the Faith. She was accompanied by her mother, Aniceta, and one priest. She met with Cardinal Ottaviani and other Vatican officials and was specifically questioned by the Holy Office. Later, accompanied by Cardinal Marcella, she was received in an audience with pope Paul VI,.

The bishops of Santander have stated the events could not be positively determined to be supernatural at this time; however, neither the bishops, nor the Church, have made a final decision about the events in Garabandal. It's rather curious that a little more than a year after Pope John XXIII decided in 1960 not to reveal the third part of the secret given to Lúcia at Fátima, Our Lady began this series of appearances in Spain with messages – similar to those in Fatima – warning the world of possible severe consequences.

In the early 1960s, Joey Lomangino went to Italy to visit St. Padre Pio and he asked if he thought Mary was appearing in Garabandal, Pio answered curtly: 'Certainly she is!' Later, Mother Teresa of Calcutta also endorsed her belief in the appearances of Our Lady in Garabandal.

In 1970, Alice and I drove to Long Island, New York, to visit Joey Lomangino in his home. To our surprise, Conchita was visiting at the same time. Joey expressed a desire to have Conchita visit the capital, so we suggested we could arrange a tour of the historical places. Inasmuch as we lived close to Washington and had both the time and room we invited to stay at our home in the country, near Annapolis, Maryland.

The following May, Conchita and her mother, Aniceta, and Joey Lomangino and his mother were our guests for about a week. I met them at Friendship Airport [now BWI] and drove them to our home. Turning into the rather lengthy curved driveway, our guests couldn't help but notice the numerous pink and white dogwood trees in full bloom on the front lawn. As I stopped the car for a better view, Conchita jumped out and, like an excited little child, ran over to one of the larger dogwood trees. She literally tore off some of the blossomed branches with her bare hands, No easy feat, that, for they were green!

We all watched in astonishment as she carried those branches to a site where a statue of Mary stood in front of an old pine grove; once there, she arranged the flowers neatly behind the statue, making a beautiful display for Mary. This was probably as close as she would come to being home again, near a place similar to the pines where Mary had appeared to her so often. Then, Conchita handed me a holy card on which she had written: "The Virgin speaks to you. Listen to her; her words are your salvation!"

Conchita was immediately adopted by our children and, in short order, learned to drive the tractor, not an easy task for a beginner. One must realize that the children in Garabandal, much like those worldwide who reside in out-of-the-way villages, are not as physically nor psychologically mature as our children.

Joey-Conchita-Msgr.

Fr. Nicola-Joey-Conchita

In the capital, we were guests of Msgr. William F. McDonough, Director of the *Basilica of the National Shrine of the Immaculate Conception*, and his able assistant, Fr. John J. Nicola, who also serves as the exorcist for the archdiocese. They were instrumental in arranging a tour of the places we wished to visit.

On the day prior to our guests' departure for New York, Msgr. McDonough, Fr. Nicola, and Fr. Victor B. Galeone concelebrated the Mass at our home with about forty guests in attendance. General permission had been previously granted from the surrounding three dioceses to allow priests to celebrate Mass at our home at any time. Fortunately, we were able to retain vestments at the house for the priests.

Several months later, Fr. Galeone served two periods from 1970–1975 and 1978–1984, as a missionary in Peru under the auspices of the Society of St. James, the Apostle, Following his return to the United States in 1984, he served as pastor of various parishes in Baltimore.

In 2001, Fr. Galeone was named bishop of the Diocese of St. Augustine, Florida by Pope John Paul II. During his tenure as bishop, he was quite outspoken in his obedience to Paul VI's teachings in *Humanae Vitae.* In 2011, after ten years of labor in that capacity, Bishop Galeone retired.

Conchita   Author   Fr. 'Vic'

In 1971, Fr. Joseph A. Pelletier, A.A,, a Mariologist, was a weekend guest in our home in southern Maryland to discuss several books he had written concerning Fatima and Garabandal. He would later write one about Medjugorje. We are truly blessed to have known so many of these faithful servants of the Lord.

I revisited Garabandal in 1972, this time with my spouse. We had a delightful conversation with Mari Loli and her father, Ceferino, the mayor of the small village. They remembered me from my visit the previous year, owing to the fact that, while eating a sandwich and soup they provided, I dropped a piece of bread. After retrieving and dusting it off prior to eating it, Mari Loli, the most outgoing of the four seers, immediately handed me a replacement piece. Yet, bread is not plentiful there.

During this second visit they kindly provided us with food and lodging, the latter being a bed in a rather large barn. The temperature was warmer than La Salette in 1970, but still bitter cold (sans heaters) at night; so cold, in fact, that it provided us with the weapons we needed for a snowball battle on a mountainside the day before. They were truly gracious hosts for the many strangers who visited there from around the world, much as the people who live in Medjugorje do to this day.

On July 27, 2007, the Spanish apostolic nunciature announced that Pope Benedict XVI named Msgr. Jiménez Zamora as the new bishop of Santander. Bishop Zamora had previously been the bishop of Osma-Soria for three years and appears open to the events in the village of Garabandal.

During an interview with *Garabandal International*, he was asked: "What is Garabandal?" He said: "There are clear signs that Our Lady is preparing the way for the prophesied events. The roads leading up to Garabandal are being widened. The road from Casio to Garabandal is being surveyed and pegged for widening and upgrading..."

Pope St. John Paul II   **Mari Loli**

Mari Loli died in Boston, Massachusetts on April 20, 2009. She left a signed statement about two visions the children had in 1962: on the 19th and, later, on the 23rd of June. The visions concerned the threatened punishment which Mari Loli describes quite vividly.

Loli wrote: "Although we continued to see the Blessed Virgin, we saw a great multitude of people who suffered greatly and screamed in anguish. The Virgin explained to us how this great punishment would come because there would come a moment a time in which the Church would seem to perish, as if it were finished, or disappearing. The Church would suffer a great trial! We asked the Virgin how this great punishment would be called and she said it was called Communism."

The punishment may well be a prelude to the chastisement, for Loli added: "Also, she made us see how the great chastisement for all humanity would come and how it comes directly from God. In a certain moment, not a single motor or machine will function. A terrible heat wave will come, and men will suffer a burning thirst. Desperately, they will look for water but, with the intense heat, it will evaporate. With this, there will enter into the people a desperation and they will attempt to kill each other; but, in those moments, their strength will fail and they will fall to the ground. God then will make them see that it is He who directly has permitted all this.

"Finally, we saw a multitude of people enveloped in flames; desperately they threw themselves into the seas and lakes but, upon entering the water, far from putting out the flames, the water was boiling and seemed to help the flames burn more. I asked the Blessed Virgin to take all our children with her. But she [Our Lady] said that when this happens, 'they will all be adults.'"

Epilogue, Garabandal

The apparitions that occurred in Garabandal from 1961-65 have been a source of both encouragement and doubt. On March 19, 1964, Conchita stated she received a message from Our Lady concerning the restoration of the eyesight of Joey Lomangino, a blind American whom she had befriended. Since the updated publication of this book in very early June, 2014, it came to the author's attention that Joey Lomangino died of a heart attack on June 18, 2014. His eyesight had not been restored.

This certainly brings into doubt the veracity of the other messages. The question now is whether all the messages given by Our Lady are also invalid, especially the two "for the world" received from her in 1961 and, again, in 1965, that were witnessed by all the children. Only one person can accurately address that now: it would be helpful if Conchita would make a public statement to help clarify this.

Obviously, there is no doubt Conchita was quite accurate when she stated in the early 1960s that "murder would be commonplace throughout the world." Who could have foreseen this horrendous problem we face today? Additionally, she affirmed that "Communism [atheistic Socialism] would engulf the entire world." We are only one of several nations who are still free; yet, given the current environment, one realizes we are not far from adopting some form of atheistic Socialism.

In 1971, a Monsignor in Baltimore advised me: "Regardless of whether Our Lady appeared in Garabandal, we know the messages are true!" His advice was based on his knowledge of the problems occurring in many seminaries where some basic teachings were glossed over. One must remember that Pope Paul VI's encyclical *Humanae Vitae* was not well received at that time by a number of both clergy and laity.

The rebellion after *Vatican II* became known as the *Spirit of Vatican II* (sans documents) and the media were having an absolute field day with their erroneous reporting of what they believed the Church should teach. To this day the media persists in its own viewpoint, garnered with sensationalism.

In all matters one is obliged to seek the truth. One must use reason in an attempt to understand the apparitions of Our Lady, always relying on the magisterium of the Church for guidance. As with all apparitions of Our Lady in the past, the final judgment of these matters is left to the Church who investigates and, after great diligence and patience, makes a statement concerning their final disposition. The Church is never in a hurry to make a final determination in these matters; however, when the Church does make a decision, it will be final.

It is important to recall that no one specific series of apparitions has any determination upon the accuracy of the other sites, either approved, or still under investigation. The mission of Our Lady does not rely upon the accreditation of any one series of her appearances. In any event, all the messages contained herein merely reaffirm and exhort us to do that which the Church has always taught. Since her appearances in Beauraing and Banneux, Mary has basically provided additional guidance and details about the future in order to help us understand the present day situation and the ensuing consequences.

So, the outcomes of the events in Garabandal remain unresolved at this time. They are interwoven into this story about Our Lady's mission as they show how these apparitions were perceived and experienced by the author. It is hoped this will serve as a guide to assist others in their search for understanding and truth.

CHAPTER 15

Our Lady of Akita, Japan

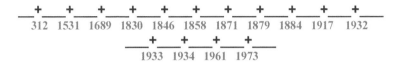

+	+	+	+	+	+	+	+	+	+	+
312	1531	1689	1830	1846	1858	1871	1879	1884	1917	1932

+	+	+	+
1933	1934	1961	1973

"My dear daughter...if men do not repent and better themselves, the Father will inflict a terrible punishment on all humanity. It will be a punishment greater than the deluge, such as no one has ever seen before."

Eight years after her appearances in Spain Our Lady appeared to Sr. Agnes Sasagawa, a nun living in the remote area of Yuzawadai, near the city of Akita, Japan. These events began on June 12, 1973 when Sr. Agnes noticed brilliant mysterious rays of light emanating from within the tabernacle. This sight was repeated over the next two days.

On July 6, as Sr. Agnes was praying in the chapel, she heard a voice coming from a statue of the Virgin Mary.. Sr. Agnes reported that the first message was: *"...Pray very much for the pope, bishops, and priests… Continue to pray very much...very much..."*

During that time, Our Lady asked her to recite a prayer of reparation adding that, eventually, her own deafness would be cured. On August 3, she received a second message: *"My daughter, my novice, do you love the Lord? If you love the Lord, listen to what I have to say to you. It is very important...You will convey it to your superior. Many men in this world afflict the Lord. I desire souls to console Him to soften the anger of the Heavenly Father. I wish, with my Son, for souls who will repair by their suffering and their poverty for the sinners and ingrates.*

"In order that the world might know His anger, the Heavenly Father is preparing to inflict a great chastisement on all mankind. With my Son I have intervened so many times to appease the wrath of the Father." "I have prevented the coming of calamities by offering Him the sufferings of the Son on the Cross, His Precious Blood and beloved souls who console Him, forming a cohort of victim souls."

"Prayer, penance and courageous sacrifices can soften the Father's anger. I desire this also from your community...that it love poverty, that it sanctify itself and pray in reparation for the ingratitude and outrages of so many men..."

Our Lady of Akita

A third message was received on the following October 13: *"My dear daughter, listen well to what I have to say to you. You will inform your superior. As I told you, if men do not repent and better themselves, the Father will inflict a terrible punishment on all humanity. It will be a punishment greater than the deluge, such as no one has ever seen before.*

"Fire will fall from the sky and will wipe out a great part of humanity, the good as well as the bad, sparing neither priests nor faithful. The survivors will find themselves so desolate that they will envy the dead. The only consolation which will remain for you will be the rosary and the Sign left by My Son. Each day recite the prayers of the rosary. With the rosary, pray for the Pope, the bishops and priests."

"The work of the devil will infiltrate even into the Church in such a way that one will see cardinals opposing cardinals, bishops against bishops. The priests who venerate me will be scorned and opposed by their confreres...churches and altars sacked; the Church will be full of those who accept compromises and the demon will press many priests and consecrated souls to leave the service of the Lord.

"The demon will be especially implacable against souls consecrated to God. The thought of the loss of so many souls is the cause of my sadness. If mankind's sins increase in number and gravity, there will be no longer pardon for them. With courage, speak to your superior. He will know how to encourage each one of you to pray and to accomplish works of reparation. It is Bishop Ito, who directs your community. Pray very much the prayers of the rosary. I alone am able still to save you from the calamities which approach. Those who place their confidence in me will be saved."

One and a half years later, on January 4, 1975, the statue of the Blessed Virgin began to weep. It continued to weep at intervals for the next 6 years and eight months, weeping over one-hundred times. The entire nation of Japan was able to view the tears of the statue of the Virgin Mary on national television.

Following eight years of intensive investigations and consultation with the Holy See, the messages of Our Lady of Akita were approved by the Bishop of the diocese on April 22, 1984, where a statue of the Madonna, according to the testimony of more than five-hundred witnesses – including the Buddhist mayor of the town – has shed blood, sweat and tears. On April 22, 1984, Bishop John Ito, of Niigata, Japan, who was an eyewitness to some of the events, stated: "As for the content of the messages received, it is no way contrary to Catholic doctrine or to good morals. When one thinks of the actual state of the world, the warning seems to correspond to it in many points."

He was likely referring to the dissention of so many Catholics who to this day continue to be in error, somehow believing their conscience to be the sole judgment in overruling the true teachings of the Church.

"Unfortunately, the reforms of Vatican II were being used as an excuse for innovation and modernism. Thousands of priests abandoned their vocation; innumerable religious abandoned their vows and were laicized. Most of the faithful were confused and totally distraught as they saw the authority of the papacy being undermined and reinterpreted by dissent and disobedience." [1]

Epilogue, Akita

In June, 1988, Bishop John Shojiro Ito of Niigata, Japan, went to the Vatican in Rome to consult with Joseph Cardinal Ratzinger [now, Pope Emeritus Benedict XVI] who formally approved Our Lady of Akita's appearances as worthy of belief.

---

[i] "Eternal City, The – Part II" – Courtesy EWTN
- I am personally aware of several Dominican nuns in my family who left the convent in San Rafael, California in the 1970s because the other nuns there were no longer praying. They decided they wanted to be part of the world, the world they left behind when they consecrated themselves totally to Christ. That convent was founded by my grandaunt, Sr. Marie Loretta Lilly, Ph.D. She was the first woman to obtain her doctorate in the State of Maryland.

CHAPTER 16

Our Lady of Medjugorje, Yugoslavia

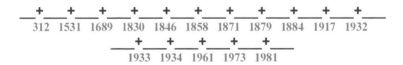

__+___+___+___+___+___+___+___+___+___+___+___
312 1531 1689 1830 1846 1858 1871 1879 1884 1917 1932

___+___+___+___+___+___
1933 1934 1961 1973 1981

"I am the Blessed Virgin Mary...I am your Mother, the Queen of Peace...I have come to tell the world that God exists...You must return to God...He has chosen each one of you to use you in His great plan for the salvation of mankind."

Eight years later Our Lady appeared to several children in Medjugorje, Yugoslavia, a small mountainous village in the region of Bosnia-Herzegovina. It was June 24, 1981, the feast day of St. John the Baptist. Late that afternoon, two teenagers, Ivanka Ivankovic, 15, and Mirjana Dragicevic, 16, decided to go for a walk.

As they passed Mount Podbrdo, a large hill behind her village, Ivanka noticed a light. Focusing her eyes she could barely make out a figure shining with light and standing just above the ground. It was a good distance away, about 200 yards, and as she continued to look, speechless, their conversation was all but forgotten as the figure seemed to form the shape of a young woman. Although not at all sure, she exclaimed to her friend: "Mirjana, look. There is Gospa!"

Mirjana thought Ivanka was joking so she didn't even bother to look where her friend was pointing. "Come on!" Mirjana said, mockingly, "You think Our Lady would appear to us?" Convinced, Ivanka said no more and they walked on toward home. Both were extremely frightened: Ivanka, by what she had seen and, Mirjana, by the look on Ivanka's face and her claim that she saw the Blessed Mother!

As they approached the village, they ran into Milka – the 12 year old sister of Marija Pavlovic – who asked for their help in getting her flock of sheep home. They agreed but this meant the girls would have to pass by the place where they had seen the figure shining with light. Arriving at the spot a little after 6 p.m., all three girls now clearly saw the figure.

I knew absolutely nothing about Mary's appearances in Medjugorje until 1985 when I moved permanently to the coastal area of South Carolina. One day, as I was leaving St. Michael's church in Murrells Inlet – a quaint fishing village south of Myrtle Beach – I happened upon the reprint of a newspaper article Wayne Weible had written on December 4, 1985, describing the appearances of Our Lady in Yugoslavia.

Several years later I had an opportunity to attend a presentation Wayne gave at a church in Georgetown, South Carolina. Accompanying him was Milka Pavlovic, the young girl who saw Our Lady on the first day. She described her experience: it seems that inasmuch as she had chores to do, her mother sent her older sister, Marija, 16, in her place on the following days. As a result, she never saw Our Lady again; however, she appeared to handle that loss quite well. Their young friend, Milka, would later disclose: "They wanted to sneak a smoke." Her statement will be clarified in an ensuing chapter.

I moved to central Florida a few years later and, by chance, met Wayne again near Disney World at the *Basilica of the National Shrine of Mary, Queen of the Universe*, a newly constructed shrine honoring Our Lady. At the end of his talk, an announcement was made that several people were planning to visit Medjugorje in May, 1990 to see for themselves what was occurring.

Inasmuch as Fr. Joseph Harte, Rector of the shrine, announced he was going to be the spiritual director for the trip, I decided to join them. I invited all my children to go with us; however my eldest daughter, Loretta Marie, was the only one whose schedule would permit it.

The trip was most interesting. We experienced many wonderful things both in Medjugorje and after our return. We gained an extremely refreshing insight into Our Lady's love and concern for each one of us. Here, I am obliged to note the peace one begins to feel about the second day of their visit to Medjugorje. Everyone I talked to stated they had a feeling of love for everyone else, followed by an inner peace they had not experienced at home. It was like a window or a doorway into Heaven. Several cried publicly when it was time to leave; they knew this extraordinary love was not necessarily what awaited them at home.

We were no different than those who preceded us; many of our rosaries turned to a golden color. Several of us watched in absolute fascination as the beads on the rosary that belonged to Mary Towneley began to blink just like Christmas tree lights. One bead would light up, then, go out and turn to a golden color, only to be followed by the next bead in turn until all the beads were a beautiful golden color.

Yugoslavia consists of six republics and two autonomous regions: Bosnia and Herzegovina, Croatia, Macedonia, Montenegro, Slovenia, and Serbia, which are now independent nations. The provinces of Vojvodina and Kosovo make up the rest of the country.

Unfortunately a terrible, brutal war engulfed Yugoslavia shortly after our return to the United States. It occurred during the process of their declaration of independence from the Soviet Union. Two of the driving factions were the religious differences between the Cath-  olic and Orthodox Christians, and Muslims; also, reparation due for the previous atrocities committed during the Nazi occupation.

The war lasted about five years and horrible things were done to the population, so severe that it was reminiscent of the horrendous *concentration camps* that existed in *World War II*. More than 200,000 people were killed. In addition to the wounded, we'll never know how many were displaced, some never to see their children or families again. The bombing and brutal slaying of the civilian population eventually became so intolerable that the United States intervened and a treaty was negotiated with NATO [North Atlantic Treaty Organization].

Thus the war was contained and formally ended when the leaders of Bosnia, Serbia and Croatia signed the Dayton Agreement on December 14, 1995. Medjugorje remains a place of peace and profound spirituality. Over thirty million people have visited there since and returned home safely and spiritually renewed.

I had the opportunity to visit there again in May, 1998. Touring a number of the surrounding areas in that country was quite distressing! Some of the buildings didn't exist, having been blown completely off the map.

Fortunately, despite the recent war throughout the area, only one bomb fell in Medjugorje: thankfully, it didn't explode. On the more pleasant side I found it refreshing that, in the village of Medjugorje itself, the peace I experienced during my first visit returned as before.

Earlier, while traveling on the bus from the airport to Medjugorje well after midnight, I had time to reflect on a favor I would like to receive from Our Lady. This is sometimes granted to those on a pilgrimage. I thought about Bernadette who, when asked if she wished to return to Lourdes in the hope of a cure of her illness, replied, "No, it is not for me!" So, taking a cue from her, I said quietly to myself: "No, nothing for me, thank you."

Yet, three days later, in Medjugorje, as I was returning from St. James' church to my residence, I was privileged to see a most unusual event involving the sun. It was a perfectly clear, cloudless day, about three o'clock in the afternoon. I was alone, yet I distinctly heard a voice to my right, strongly urging me to **"Look at the sun!"** I thought this a bit odd, considering I would have to turn away from where the voice emanated in order to see the sun on my left. Then, remembering my earlier decision on the bus, I said out loud to myself: "No, that's not for me!"

However, that command was repeated again, quite insistently this time: **"Look at the sun!"** At that point I could not refuse the command: turning to my left, I looked up into the sky directly at the sun which I could plainly see without blinking. I watched in absolute fascination as a color was slowly painted from right to left in the shape of an arc, directly above the sun. It was as if some invisible hand was using a huge roller brush, except neither hand nor brush could be seen.

The painted area was about two-thirds the size of the sun, the bottom of which was one-third of the diameter above the sun. It was the most gorgeous color of blue that I have ever seen. It was a shade darker than the sky and the only way I can describe that color is to say: I loved that color. I could not imagine that any color could be so beautiful. After about three seconds the blue disappeared. In the same manner this was followed by a striking hue of yellow; then, one of red. As soon as one color disappeared the next one was painted, one after the other in the same arc. It was just amazing! I haven't read of anyone reporting this specific phenomenon before. If you know of someone who has experienced it, I would certainly like to hear from them.

Mt. Krizevac (Cross Mountain)

It should be noted that I can stare at the sun here without difficulty and, to this day, can do so without damage to the retinae. In this area the sun is quite different than in Medjugorje for within several seconds, a grayish transparent disk literally jumps out in front of the sun to protect my eyes. I have no idea where this disk comes from; in fact, whenever I mention it to my ophthalmologist he just looks at me quizzically! Neither of us understands how this can occur.

A word of caution

You can cause serious, permanent damage to the retinae of your eyes if you attempt to do this! If you must look at the sun, never do it for more than a split second; then, try to read a license plate number or newspaper print. If there is a dark or blurred spot on the print, do not look at the sun again or you will do irreparable damage to your eyes.

I met a very courteous, young lady from Nova Scotia during my second visit to Medjugorje. The first thing she told me was to expect a feeling of love, which I would enjoy on about the second day. Most everyone experiences this and, true to form, there was a distinct change in how I felt emotionally.

I felt as though I was in love with everyone, much as one feels upon returning home after a strenuous visit abroad, only in this case their true home was in Medjugorje, a doorway into Heaven. This love for Mary, for God and for everyone permeated throughout the entire time there. Fr. Jozo, the pastor, clarified it when he said: "As Christians, we are taught to love God; when one goes to Medjugorje, one falls in love with Him!"

Mt. Podbrdo (Apparition Hill)

This, then, is the story of Medjugorje. Much of it is garnered from interviews with the children and from various web sites and books written in an attempt to describe what is actually occurring there. It is quite voluminous compared to other apparition sites. A number of the web sites permit reprinting the basic story. [i]

---

[i] The description of the events occurring during the first nine days begins here, as condensed from the website Medjugorje.org.

Early in the evening of June 24, 1981, Mirjana and Ivanka went to Vicka Ivankovic's house to invite her to join them for a walk. Because Vicka, aged 17, was resting, her mother said she would give her the message to join them later.

As soon as Vicka awoke she went out to find them and, on reaching the road, noticed they were waving with their hands, calling for her to come join them. When she got there, Mirjana said: "Look up there, the Madonna!" Vicka said: "What do you mean, the Madonna? What is the matter with you?"

Vicka did not look; she didn't even take the time to bother to look. Vicka was wearing slippers, but kicked them off and ran barefooted toward the village. On her way, she met Ivan Dravicevic, 16, and Ivan Ivankovic, 20. She said: "Ivan, the Madonna. They said that the Madonna has appeared up there. Let's go there, you and me. I'm afraid." Ivan said: "Of course we'll go, but why are you afraid?" Vicka thought: "He's not afraid."

When they got there, she turned toward Ivan to ask, "Do you see anything?" However, Ivan Dravicevic was gone; he had taken off on a dead run for home, losing his shoes in the process! So, she turned to Ivan Ivankovic: "Do you see anything?" He replied: "I see something completely white, turning." Milka was there and Vicka asked her if she saw anything. She said: "I see the Madonna." Vicka thought: "When I went up there the first time, I stood a little distance from them. I was afraid. But when I went the second time, I said to myself: If they are not running away, I will not run away either."

It was after 6:30 in the evening, raining a little and beginning to get dark. Vicka would later remark: "I saw it and what I saw was very white. I saw a gown, dark hair. All the time, she was covering and uncovering something she held in her left hand." Then, Vicka added: "I was not able to see what else she was doing, but it looked like she was showing something. Then, she called to us to come closer...but who was going to get any closer? We were saying to each other: 'She is calling us, but who is going to go?'"

Later, recounting their experiences to family and friends, Vicka noted, "There was real commotion. Some perhaps believed, some wondered, some explained it away as some kind of flying saucer and the like. Why, everything conceivable was said." Later, she added, "How could they be expected to believe us? In their place, I wouldn't have believed us either." Mirjana's experience was similar: "There was incredible light."

"The Blessed Mother held baby Jesus in Her arms, covering and uncovering Him as she called to us. It was overwhelming! We are from a small village, not like young people from America or Europe. We have never been anywhere away from home. Home, school, family: this is our life." When asked how she knew it was the Madonna, Mirjana replied, "My whole being knew without a doubt that this Lady of unexplainable beauty was the Mother of God. That is why I had such fear." In fact, during the first days of the apparitions, both Mirjana and Ivanka fainted many times. When asked why, Mirjana said, "I was quite overwhelmed to be in the holy presence of the Mother of God."

The next day, the children were expected to be up at dawn to help harvest the leaves from the large tobacco plants in their fields, so, they all went to bed. However, sleep did not come easily to those who had seen the vision. The children spent the next day working in the fields and, as they finished their work a little earlier than usual, four of them decided to see if Our Lady would return. They were Ivanka, Mirjana, Vicka and Ivan Dragicevic. Mirjana said, "I felt in my heart that I must go back. Interestingly, the others felt the same way too. We didn't plan it. We just all, about the same time, felt an immense desire to go back to that place."

Inasmuch as all four of the children felt drawn back to the spot, Vicka ran to get her friends, Marija, 16, and Jakov Colo, who was only 10. Marija had previously told Vicka, "If you see the Madonna, I would just like to be there. I do not have to see her." Jakov had also told Mirjana that: "He, too, would want to see her more than anything else in the world."

Mirjana stated they heard the Blessed Mother calling to them to come up the mountain, "She waved to us. We were at the foot of the hill. She was calling us to come to her. The Madonna called to us to go up on the hill, and we went. When you look up from the bottom of the hill, it looks close, but it is not. We ran quickly up the hill. It was not like walking on the ground. Nor did we look for the path. We simply ran toward her.

In five minutes we were on the hill, as if something had pulled us through the air. I was afraid. I also was barefoot, but no thorns had scratched me. When we were about seven feet away from the Madonna, we felt as if we were thrown to our knees. Jakov was thrown kneeling into a thorny bush, and I thought he would be injured, but he came out of it without a scratch."

Then I asked: "Marija, do you see the Madonna?" She said: "I see something white; it is getting clearer." Later, Marija saw her just like the rest of us.

The children say Our Lady looks about nineteen years old and is extremely beautiful with dark hair and blue eyes; she wears a silvery gray gown, a white veil and crown of stars. She appears in a glowing light, floating on a cloud, and is often accompanied by angels. They say it is impossible to truly describe her beauty; there is nothing so beautiful here on Earth. In complete awe the children asked the Lady who she was and why she had come to them. She replied,

"Dear children, I am the Blessed Virgin Mary...I am your Mother, the Queen of Peace...I love you...I come on a mission from God the Father...God has chosen each one of you to use you in a great plan for the salvation of mankind. I wish to be with you to reconcile the world through prayer, fasting, faith, conversion and peace."

Mirjana complained to Mary: "Dear Madonna, they will not believe us when we go home; they will tell us that we are crazy." Our Lady just smiled. We were on the hill for ten to fifteen minutes. Meanwhile, some people had come up to join us. When we were about to leave, the Madonna seemed to be hovering in the air, and we didn't know what to say. Then, she said to us: *"Go in God's peace."*

Our heads were all turned in the direction that she was leaving, all in the same direction. No one said anything, but everyone was frightened. Mirjana said: "When we were on the hill, praying with the Madonna on the second day, we prayed seven Our Fathers. We were praying because we did not know what else to do. We were crying a little and praying a little. She told us to pray seven Our Fathers, Hail Marys, Glory Bes, and the Credo."

Those who followed the six children up the hill that day were just dumbfounded. They could not believe the speed with which they saw the children climb the hill as they couldn't keep up with them. Mirjana's uncle, who was one of the adults present that day, stated: "It takes at least twelve minutes to get up there, yet they did it in two. It scared me to death." The apparition lasted almost 15 minutes and, coming down the hill, all the visionaries were weeping. They were both moved and frightened by their experience.

Marinko Ivankovic, 40, knew the children well, and knew them to be good girls. He was shaken by the story and decided that, if the children returned to the hill, he would keep a close watch on them. However, he arrived at the wrong time, and was there only to see the children, who were frightened and upset, coming down from the mountain. He said, "Ivanka was sobbing, terribly upset. I ran to her and asked what the matter was. She told me all that had passed between her and the apparition. I tried to tell her that if the vision had said her mother was well and happy, then, she should be laughing, not crying. But she was inconsolable."

Marinko felt that the parish priests should be informed and involved in these occurrences, especially if some evil power was at work here. However, to his dismay, the pastor, Fr. Jozo Zovko, was not in the village; the assistant pastor, Fr. Culvalo, wanted nothing to do with the matter. Marinko then took it upon himself to help and watch over the children. And, as he spoke to them, he began to believe their story.

The six children who went up the hill that day became the permanent group of visionaries. June the 25th then became the anniversary of the apparitions. At Mary's specific request that date was eventually named the *"Feast of Our Lady, Queen of Peace."*

Each child is asked to avidly pray and fast and to relate her messages to the world. They meet daily with pilgrims in Medjugorje, and in foreign lands, relating her impassioned call to peace, conversion and sacrifice, as she said: *"Children...convert, pray, fast, be reconciled."*

As of this writing, Our Lady has given all ten secrets to Mirjana, Ivanka and Jakov; Marija, Vicka, and Ivan have each received nine secrets. When all have received all the secrets, Our Lady will stop appearing in Medjugorje. Mary has chosen Mirjana to reveal the secrets. Ten days before each one will occur she will tell Father Petar Ljubicic, a Franciscan. After praying and fasting, he has the option of telling the secret to the world three days before it happens.

Our Lady also promised that a permanent sign would be left at the spot of her first apparition in Medjugorje. On the 25th of each month, Our Lady gives a message to Marija for the world. Maria writes the message down for the priest at St. James to translate so it can be relayed to the world.

Mirjana   Vicka   Ivanka   Jakov   Ivan   Marija

Over twenty-five million pilgrims of all denominations – including cardinals, bishops, priests, nuns, ministers and rabbis – have visited this tiny village. All have been moved by Mary's motherly love. She appears daily, offering hope and peace to her children in this deeply troubled world. Mirjana noted that Mary is planning to change the world: she did not come to destroy us; rather, to save us!

Our Lady said: *"I invite you to decide again to love God above all else. In this time, when due to the spirit of consumerism, one forgets what it means to love and to cherish true values. I invite you again, little children, to put God in the first place in your life. Do not let Satan attract you through material things but, little children, decide for God who is freedom and love."*

Thriftiness is essential to life in Medjugorje, even while tending the sheep in the 1980s and 1990s. At the same time a woman is watching them she works the bundle of sheep's wool into a ball of yarn, making sweaters and a myriad of other items. After Our Lady came, prayer increased, as did the fervor with which one prayed.

Marinko Ivankovic, already committed to supporting, defending, and protecting the children in any way he could, met them at the bottom of the hill the evening of the 26th; he had a bottle of holy water.

Holy water and blessed salt were commonly used to bless the houses to protect against the influence of evil in these Croatian Catholic homes. Vicka once said a favorite expression of her grandmother she had heard often when growing up: "He is fearful like the devil is of holy water!" Some of the older women told the visionaries to sprinkle the apparition with the water to see if it would flee.

Vicka   Jakov   Ivanka   Marija   Ivan

On the third day, there were several thousand people in attendance. At that time, Our Lady began to use a different means to attract the visionaries' attention. A very brilliant light would flash three times, announcing Mary's arrival. As soon as they see the light, the children began bounding up the mountain, telling Marinko exactly where they were headed so he could keep up with them. They were then followed by a multitude of children and adults. Vicka stated that, "We ran forward as though on wings. The place is all thorn and stone; it's awful steep, but we flew like birds. We just flew: we, and the people."

There was a great deal of excitement and fear among the people gathered for, whenever that light flashed, all those present were able to see it. This time, Our Lady led the visionaries much higher up the mountain than on the previous occasions, about 300 meters higher than previously [about four city blocks].

When they got there, the crowd saw the six children suddenly stop and, simultaneously, fall onto their knees in front of an old wooden cross.

Marinko stated, "I had taken the holy water from my house, to sprinkle it around the vision, in order to see what she is: either the Madonna or the devil. However, after we climbed up the hill, we knelt down and I gave the holy water for Vicka to sprinkle."

Vicka said: "I sprinkled her and, in full voice, said: 'If you are the Virgin, remain with us, if you are not, depart from us.' I came quite close and didn't spare the water." Vicka then stated that Our Lady smiled. "It seemed to me that she was pleased as she responded: *'I have come because there are many true believers here. I wish to be with you to convert and to reconcile the whole world.'"*

The children noticed that following the brilliant light, and after the third flash, they could all meet Our Lady at the same spot. Mirjana asked the Lady: "Who are you? *'I am the Blessed Virgin Mary.'* 'Why are you appearing to us; we are no better than others? *'I do not necessarily choose the best.'* Will you come back? *'Yes, to the same place as yesterday.'"* They asked her, "Is there life on other planets?" Our Lady responded: *"That is not for you to know now."*

Marija began descending alone and was half way down when she saw the Virgin again. Our Lady was crying and, behind her, there was a bare wooden cross. Mary said: *"Peace, Peace, Peace! Be reconciled! Only Peace. Make your peace with God and among yourselves. For that, it is necessary to believe, to pray, to fast, and to go to confession."*

Vicka related: "Marija said the Virgin was very sad, and that she spoke to her through tears. Marija was very frightened. She was unable to stand on her feet. We spotted her and helped her until she got her wits about her. And, slowly we managed to get home."

Marija said: "It was an overwhelming experience. I saw the Madonna weeping, and the sight drove me to commit myself totally to her request. She had come to inspire all of us to search for peace: peace in our own hearts; peace within our families; peace in the world."

On June 27, 1981, a series of new trials began for the six children and their families. That afternoon the police picked the children up for questioning and took them to the police station in nearby Citluk; however, the children never wavered in their testimony. They had seen the Virgin Mary up on Mount Podbrdo. In an attempt to have them labeled mentally unfit, they were sent to the doctor on duty to be examined. Ivan was the first to be called in; an entire hour passed before the doctor came out to call the next one.

By this time it was getting late in the afternoon and, due to Vicka's insistence, the doctor released them; he stated later that the children were normal, healthy and well balanced. It was now 6 p.m. and, by 6:30, the other five children were already at the foot of the hill, intent on ascending it. Mirjana, Ivanka, and Vicka began going up together, while Marija and Jakov waited down below, looking up towards the hill.

Suddenly, Marija saw a light, her face flushed to a scarlet hue and she said: 'Look! Look! Look!' Jakov said nothing, but together they ran ahead at what seemed to be a superhuman speed. Marija was wearing a white blouse and red skirt, so I could see her distinctly as she ran, almost seeming to fly. It was impossible to keep up with her. Reaching the top, Marija found herself standing in front of Our Lady, alone without the other visionaries. But, then, the Blessed Mother disappeared, leaving Marija with a puzzled look on her face. Jakov, who had not seen the light, joined the other three visionaries and Marija soon discovered them as well.

A Franciscan priest who was walking with them reported the following: "Like the clouds that enveloped Moses on Mt. Sinai, when he was given the Law, Podbrdo [Apparition Hill] is the spot God chose to send Our Lady for the first time to lead man back to the faith and back to the Ten Commandments, the spot He has chosen to leave a lasting sign which will prove to the world the truth of the apparitions."

It was not such an easy task for the visionaries to find each other on the hill as every day, the number of people present for the apparition increased. In fact, as the apparitions continued, the children were often separated from each other; however, when the light flashed announcing Our Lady's arrival, the six came together no matter where they were on the hill, led by the light. To the thousands on the hillside this gave clear validity to the children's testimony; otherwise, it would be impossible to find each other in such crowds that were gathered there.

That day on the mountain, the children asked Mary several questions. Jakov wanted to know what the Virgin expected of the Franciscans in Medjugorje. Our Lady responded: *"Have them persevere in the faith and protect the faith of the people."* The children asked Mary to leave a sign for the people; however, she told them: *"My angels, do not be afraid of injustices. They have always existed."* Also, the visionaries wanted to know: "How must we pray?" Our Lady responded: *"Continue to recite The Lord's Prayer, the Hail Mary, and the Glory Be seven times, but also add the Creed."*

This was an important apparition for those who were concerned that the children were making the whole story up. Father Joseph Pelletier, AA, author of *The Queen of Peace Visits Medjugorje*, spoke to this point: "The first sign was the way in which Our Lady appeared on this fourth day. It was completely different from the manner in which the apparition had occurred previously. It was so complicated and involved that it would seem to surpass the capacity of the young people to have thought it up by them. Marija broke away from Jakov and raced up the mountain alone. Our Lady appeared to her alone at a different place than before and, then, mysteriously disappeared.

"When Our Lady appeared, all five seers – along with the people – saw the light which immediately preceded Her arrival. During this apparition she appeared again to the five as they returned home and, finally, she appeared to Ivan alone, it was her sixth appearance in that single day. Many people felt that the pattern of what happened proved the apparitions were not under the control of the seers. In this regard, the apparition to the five seers on their way home was particularly impressive. Together, they all pulled away from the people who were supporting them and, together, they suddenly saw Our Lady."

Fr. Jozo Zovko

After several days of apparitions, Vicka's mother became so distraught that she sat outside Father Jozo's office as the children were being questioned. Father Tomislav Pervan was present in the waiting room with her and, in her anxiety, she was crying.

"Father, please try to get this crazy thing out of their minds. I cannot take it anymore! I have seven other children at home...and Grandma...and my husband is in Germany. And now all these police around the house and all that is happening and all this commotion around the house...and people gathering here. I cannot stand it. I cannot carry it anymore!" But Vicka just talked to her mother and me, and the pastor, and all who were present there, saying: "But mama, what can I say? I am seeing the Blessed Mother."

By June 30, 1981, as the number in the crowds continued to swell, the police became more and more concerned. The Communist government thought the people were moving the people toward a revolution. The local authorities were getting pressure from both Belgrade and Sarajevo to stop what they thought might lead to sedition. Their plan was to stop the gatherings on the hillside, so orders were sent out to the villagers to stop going up the mountain, and with those orders came threats! They forced some of the villagers to block everyone going up, stating that if they failed to do so their homes and fields would be confiscated.

In a Communist country the greatest threat to a family's existence is the loss of one's home and land. There is no welfare so you and your family starved. Therefore some villagers stood by with guns and pitchforks, blocking the entrance to the mountain; yet, others refused to allow threats to separate them from the apparitions of Our Lady. They were placed in a very difficult position by having to make a choice.

The Communists also hatched a plan to keep the children off the mountain. They arranged for two social workers known by the visionaries and their families, young women almost the same age as the older children, to take them on an afternoon excursion. The children considered it a relief to get away for a while, so all, except Ivan, agreed to go.

The two women then drove five of the seers through the local region. It eventually became apparent to them that they had been tricked. The social workers prevented the children from getting back in time in order to climb the hill in time for the apparition. When they saw the hill, the visionaries asked the women to stop the car; however, their request was ignored. Vicka stated, "We already realized while on the road that we made a mistake in going for the outing because it seemed to us that they just took us so that we might not be present for the Virgin.

They were somewhat reluctant to stop. They pretended not to hear us but, when we said we would jump out of the car if they didn't stop, they stopped. We then got out and went off the road a bit."

In an interview with Fr. Jozo later that evening, Ivanka told what happened next: "First, we prayed our usual prayers. Then, not thinking about what I was doing, I looked up the hill. I saw a light and the light was coming towards us. On the hillside where the people were, everything was bathed in that light. Those two social workers who drove them on the trip saw this also." I asked: "Do you see the light?" They said: "We see it."

"I looked at the light all the time. Then, we knelt and sang. Mirjana asked Our Lady if she was displeased that they had left the hill and gone to the other place; however, she said that she didn't mind. Mirjana said we asked Our Lady if she would mind if we do not go to the hill anymore and go to the church instead. Somehow, she seemed undecided when we asked her this. Even so, she said that she would not mind. Ivanka added that the apparitions would be at the same time."

The visionaries asked the two social workers to bring them to the parish office after the apparition because they were afraid to go to the hill after having disappointed the thousands who waited for them that evening. The police had warned them not to go back to the hill as well. The children said: "A large crowd gathered on Mt. Podbrdo. They waited for us and the Virgin, and neither we nor the Virgin were there."

The poor people! They wait and wait, but nothing. All kinds of rumors went around that we ran off somewhere, that they took us off to jail. It was then that they decided to go to Father Jozo who, upon learning they had not been on the mountain that night, began to question them individually until nearly nine o'clock that night.

Arriving at home they learned that their parents had been terribly upset, wondering what had happened to their children: if they had been taken by the police or if they had gotten into an accident. They imagined everything possible. News came to them late that night that Marinko had been arrested. Inasmuch as he was accused and suffering because of them, the children tried to find him but were unsuccessful. They protested his arrest at the police station, saying: "Arrest us if you want…but leave Marinko alone." The outcome of this very long, agonizing day was that the apparitions would begin taking place in the Church.

The government authorities stated they would be happy to have the crowds off the mountains, saying: "They can pray all day long, and all night too if they want, as long as they don't do it on the hill. The law makes no provision for worshiping on a hill." This statement was made by the Chairman of the League of Communists in Citluk.

Then, on July 1, 1981, a new threat was leveled at the children. The Secret Security police made an announcement to the villagers that the children were banned from both the hill and the Church. This pronouncement was made in a meeting held in the Medjugorje School after a summons went out to all the villagers. What if they refused? The parents were threatened that, if they did not cooperate, a rumor would be spread that the children are mentally unfit, then they would have no possibility of a future education.

Furthermore, they would face defamation of themselves and families. However, despite these threats, the parents deferred to their children. Someone came to Vicka's mother and said, "Zlota, let the children go no more to the church; let the children give that up. It is going to be difficult for you." Zlota answered, "I will see. I do not know. Who can order a child what to do?"

Shortly afterward, in the middle of the day, the police arrived and began to search for the children to try and stop them inasmuch as the two women had failed. They asked throughout the village where the children were. They wanted to remove them from the hill and from the people. The people responded in various ways: "in the fields, in the village, here, there." Even so, a police van pulled up the next day apparently with the same plan, which is to keep the children from going to the hill.

At first, the police officers were content to watch from their car but, as the time of the apparition got closer, they forced the children into the van. Fortunately, Jakov's mother was able to drag her son out before the doors closed; however, Marija, Vicka, and Ivanka remained in the van. The police drove them past the hill and the Church. Meanwhile, the trio was beating their fists on the windows and, finally, they stopped.

Yet, even in the midst of all this commotion, Our Lady appeared to the children. Marija said, "We felt quite strong. Our Lady helped us through. Somehow, the more problems we had, the better we coped. We spent all day talking to pilgrims, and every evening praying so, at most, we got two or three hours of sleep. Yet, in those days, we seemed to be living under a special grace."

The two social workers who had participated in the previous day's charade were greatly moved by what they had witnessed. They ended up resigning their position with the government; they had a change of heart and became believers. Fr. Jozo continued: "The two social workers who had experienced the events at Cerno resigned because of their own experience, [so] the police came to intervene directly."

The next day, trying to escape the oppression of the police, the six children, who knew they were being sought, slipped out of their homes and were running from the village through the vineyards, toward the church. In the process of escaping, they even changed their clothes in order to change their appearance. It was like playing a game of hide and go seek.

By July, 2ⁿᵈ, the police increased the daily harassment of the children, this time showing up near their homes around noontime. The children, realizing what the police meant to do, slipped out of their houses in an effort to elude them. Vicka told Fr. Bubalo: "We really didn't know where to hide."

"In the end we went towards the church, not by way of the road, but through our tobacco fields and vineyards again so that they wouldn't spot us. The church was locked. "Oh, God, where can we go now?"

Meanwhile, Fr. Jozo was alone in the church. He was in deep anguish over the situation in his parish and, at this moment, crying out to God to understand what he must do. He recalled: "I was in anguish because of all the events.

"It was at this time that something began to happen inside me, which led me to become more than just a listener to the children's reports. People from the government service were brought in to put a stop to the events. Those who were believers did not do it happily.

"While all this was going on, I was in the church praying, feeling great responsibility in front of God, as pastor. The people were asking questions and I had to say something to the people, to the priests and the sisters. In a way, I felt like Moses before the Red Sea.

"I knew that I could speak only to God. No man could have answered my need. I prayed, 'God, I know you talked to Abraham, to Moses and to others. Now there are thousands of people here these days. Tell me where the river is going. I do not know where the mouth of that river is, or what its source is.'"

"No one was in the church with me at that moment. And then, something happened that, for me, was important and decisive. It was both a turning point and a moment of revelation. While I was praying I heard a voice say, *'Come out and protect the children!'*"

"As I was leaving the church through the middle door, with my foot still in the air and the door handle in my hand, the children ran toward me from the left side of the church, escaping from the police. They told me, 'The police are chasing us. Hide us.'

"They had gathered around me and were crying. Ana, Vicka's sister, was with them sharing their fate. I embraced the children and took them to the rectory. I locked them in an unoccupied room of the house. Soon, the police came. They asked me, 'Did you see the children?' I answered: 'I did.'

Although the doors were locked, Fr. Jozo – responding to the voice he heard while praying – let the children in, just as the police came running past. "I left my Bible and breviary, genuflected and, with no further thought or delay, left the church."

"The police kept running very fast toward the village of Bijakovici to catch them. After the police left, I went to talk with the children. I asked them to stay in the rectory so they would not be caught. Shortly afterward, the Madonna came to them in the room. Later there were seven visions in that same room. The children wouldn't go up on the hill for the third day in a row, but the crowds of people still came."

Fr. Jozo brought the six children into the church and to the sanctuary behind the altar; from that day on, the people began to gather at the church to pray the rosary at 5 p.m, followed by the Mass at 6 p.m. The Our Father, Hail Mary, and Glory Be were recited seven times.

St. James Church

On the evening of July 11, 1981, people gathered in the church at about 5:00 pm and began to pray the rosary together. At a certain time during the rosary Fr. Jozo began to sing with great joy: *"How wonderful, wonderful, wonderful you are, Our Lady!"* It was as though he was personally singing to someone in the church.

At 6:00 pm, he began the celebration of Mass. During his homily, he spoke about Moses "leading the children of Israel out of Egypt and across the Red Sea, granting them signs throughout their forty year journey." He added, "Mary was the first believer who completely obeyed God and His call...Mary, as the first Christian, is here today with me, your priest, and with you as faithful Christians..."

He ended his homily with an invitation: "I beg you to start fasting, to fast tomorrow, to fast the day after tomorrow, taking only bread and water, so that God may reveal Himself to us and tell us what we are to do. There is no Heaven so closed that prayer, fasting, and penance may not find a way into it." [1]

Soon afterward, one of the Franciscans who spoke to Fr. Jozo following Mass announced to the crowd that, indeed, "Fr. Jozo had seen the Virgin during the rosary." Three other men, eye-witnesses, would later verify this event.

Fr. Jozo noted, "I wouldn't have believed the church could hold so many people. I was scarcely able to push my way through to the altar and when I got there and began to say Mass, I had no room to lift my arms to give a blessing." He added: "That mass of people responded to my request with great exclamation, full of faith, saying, 'We will.'" [1]

Later, he would add, "My motives in having Mass together with the apparitions, were based on the value of Mass...In that Mass, I wanted the people to cease being spectators and become participants in the events." Unfortunately, that sermon would cause serious repercussions for him!

---

[1] - Thus ends the description of the first nine days of Our Lady's appearances in Medjugorje. – courtesy of www. medjugorje.org.

During the ensuing days, the visionaries continued to be harassed by the police. This prevented them from being at the church every evening; yet, in spite of this, whenever the children were there, the apparition would usually occur during the recitation of the rosary just prior to Mass.

Fr. Jozo Zovko

In his first meeting with the visionaries, Fr. Jozo had questioned them about their knowledge of other apparitions. Mirjana stated, "I'd never heard of any other apparitions. I didn't know about Fátima or Lourdes. I suppose I'd never been interested in that kind of thing. In those days I only went to church when I had to."

Fr. Jozo then handed them a book entitled *The Apparitions of the Blessed Virgin.* They were fascinated when they read the story about Bernadette, the child who had seen Our Lady in Lourdes, France in 1858.

After the first nine days, Our Lady appeared to the children every day in Bosnia-Herzegovina – usually in the evening – with messages about the means to achieve peace: "in our hearts, in our homes, and in the world."

Those first days changed the direction of the children and how they view the world. Her overall messages are of peace in order to reconcile ourselves with each other and, especially, with God.

She says she has come to bring the world back to her Son. She advises us to pray, attend Mass frequently, go to confession at least once a month, fast on bread and water on Wednesdays and Fridays, and recite all fifteen decades of the rosary every day.

Mirjana, in ecstasy

We are still unable to fully grasp the magnitude of the messages received in Medjugorje. One day the children asked Our Lady how many more days she would appear. She answered: *"As long as you wish."* Another time, Marija and several of the seers asked Our Lady how long she was going to appear to them. Our Lady responded: *"Have I begun to bore you?"* They never asked her that again.

Note well, however, that there is a distinct change in the tone of Our Lady's messages. In Lourdes, she asked for *"Penance"*; at Fátima she asked for prayers and sacrifices: *"Pray for sinners for many souls go to Hell because there is no one to pray and offer sacrifices for them."* Now, in Medjugorje, she advises us: *"This time is for you; be converted now because, after the sign appears, there will be little time for anyone to convert."*

The *sign* will appear during the unfolding of the third secret. And, in what may likely be the climax of all these 185 years, she tells us for the first time that it will no longer be necessary for her to appear again, firmly stating on May 22, 1982: *"I have come to call the world to conversion for the last time. Later, I will never again appear on Earth [in this way]."*

The children are adults now. They are all married and busy raising their own families. Each of the children will ultimately receive ten secrets, each varying somewhat from the other seers. The visionaries say they will remain secret until an appointed time; however, they know the day the messages may be revealed. They concern future events, some of which are chastisements.

Mary told them that, as the third event transpires, a visible sign would be left at Mt. Podbrdo, the place of her first apparition, so that all will believe. Perhaps this visible sign will be similar to those predicted to occur in Akita and Garabandal. When all the visionaries have been given their ten secrets Our Lady stop appearing there.

Mirjana was especially chosen by Mary to reveal all ten of the secrets given to her as these pertain to the world. With Mary's approval, she has chosen Fr. Petar, a Franciscan priest, to announce them to the public. Ten days before each event is predicted to occur, the priest will receive a parchment from Mirjana which he will not be able to understand. However, after a number of days spent praying and fasting, he will be able to understand that specific secret.

Then, three days before each event is scheduled to occur, Fr. Petar may reveal that secret to the world. Whether he decides to do that or not is his choice! Each of the seers was given a specific mission: Jakov and Vicka's are for sick people; Ivan's is for the youth and priests; Ivanka's is for families; Marija's is for nuns and the souls in Purgatory; Mirjana's is for *unbelievers.* Our Lady continued to frequently mention the words: Believers and Unbelievers, stating at one point: *"All the problems in the world come from unbelievers!*

On May 12, 1998, in Medjugorje, I managed to videotape a half-hour interview with Mirjana. During it, Mirjana said she advised Fr. Petar of the scenario: "I'm going to tell him and he is supposed to let everybody know. So, he doesn't have [the] opportunity to choose whether to publish or not to publish the secrets. The secrets must be published!"

When asked for clarification about the means for revealing the secrets, she said: "I am supposed to let Fr. Petar know and three days before, Petar [knowing what] is going to be happening, will be published for the world. So, please, don't ask me anything else about the secrets because secrets are secret." Our Lady always says: *'Don't talk about the secrets: Pray!'"*

The following excerpt is from an article written by Fr. Petar: "Concerning the secrets, Mirjana herself states that she thinks the day of their fulfillment is nearing. And lately, Our Lady calls her to a specific program of how she should pray and live. God has announced to us that He will send signs of preliminary warning. He wishes to show clearly that He is forever Master of the world. God will send us some early signs and, then, He will give us a permanent sign.

"Mirjana says that when the signs appear many people will be converted: many who doubted until now and who deliberated about whether the event in Medjugorje came from God or from some other source. It will be clear to everyone who is open to the Spirit of God that God is indeed here and dwells among us."

1989   Fr. Petar   2000

"Concerning us specifically, of course we'd like to know when all of this will take place. I believe that curiosity can best be satisfied by fasting and prayer, and people who do so don't need to be afraid. Everything will turn out right. I don't know what misfortunes and catastrophes will come and, naturally, I don't know what will happen to us. I know only this: Without God's wisdom, nothing will happen to us.

"Everyone can receive what he needs to fulfill God's plan in his life. I believe that from this, we can conclude that God loves us today, too. I see positive proof of this in the fact that God is sending His Mother to us and that He has already given us many signs.

"There are many witnesses who have meditated about this and have been converted. They are the people who began to fast and pray. I believe these are signs and that they are more significant than physical signs. Material signs can be momentarily impressive, but the joy and happiness which one experiences in the soul remains and is not easily forgotten. That's the treasure we carry in our hearts."

"Shortly after Mirjana's visions ceased I was informed by the other visionaries that she had chosen me as the priest of her confidence. At that time I thought I was too far away from Medjugorje. I was a priest in another community and there was no indication that I would be moved to Medjugorje. Mirjana, who moved in the meantime to Sarajevo to continue her studies, told me that God will put everything in its place.

"Mirjana asked Our Lady whether she had acted correctly, and Our Lady told her that everything would happen at the proper time. Indeed, since the fall of 1985, I've been in Medjugorje for more than a year."

Mt. Podbrdo (Apparition Hill)

"Mirjana told me that Our Lady comes more often lately and that she hears her voice at a predetermined time. She said Our Lady is preparing her for the fulfillment of the secrets. Our Lady wants everything to develop in [a proper] order. She gave Mirjana something similar to paper, which contains information about the individual secrets. Ten days before, she'll know what will happen.

"Three days before a secret is revealed, it will be announced to the people so they'll know exactly what, where, how, what time, and for how long it will take place. The first two secrets will come as advance warnings and as proof that Our Lady was here in Medjugorje.

"The third secret will be a visible sign. This third secret is the same for all the visionaries. No one knows how many secrets are the same for all of them. As far as the visible sign is concerned, the exact information will be received three days in advance. All of us have to prepare for this with prayer and fasting."

On December 2, 1983, Fr. Vlasic, the pastor of St. James, sent a letter to Pope John Paul II, stating: "Mirjana had an apparition in 1982 wherein the Blessed Virgin told her: '...*You must realize that Satan exists. One day he appeared before the throne of God and asked permission to submit the Church to a period of trial. God gave him permission to try the Church for one century.*

"This century is under the power of the devil; but when the secrets confided to you come to pass, his power will be destroyed. Even now he is beginning to lose his power and has become aggressive. He is destroying marriages, creating divisions among priests, and is responsible for obsessions and murder. You must protect yourselves against these things through fasting and prayer, especially community prayer.'"

The Bible is replete with scripture concerning Our Lady and Satan: *"Therefore, rejoice, you heavens, and you who dwell in them. But woe to you, Earth and sea, for the Devil has come down to you in great fury, for he knows he has but a short time. Then the dragon [Satan] became angry with the woman and went off to wage war against the rest of her offspring, those who keep God's commandments and bear witness to Jesus"* (Rev. 12:10-12,17).

According to Marian theologians who have studied these apparitions, this message of Mirjana may shed light on the vision Pope Leo XIII had. It was after having an apocalyptic vision of the future of the Church that Leo XIII introduced the prayer to St. Michael, the Archangel, which priests and laity recited after Mass up until the close of the Second Vatican Council. They say that the century of trials foreseen by Leo XIII is about to end.

At the request of the Parish Office in Medjugorje, professional examinations were performed by scientists from Italy, France, and Slovenia. Their tests concluded: "The scientific tests permit us to ascertain that the visionaries are not manipulated, are not acting and that the state of ecstasy does not alter in any way their 'normal' daily behavior."

The Church has an obligation to care for all its members, whether residents or visitors, without giving approval of the apparitions. In June of 1986, in response to twelve Italian bishops seeking pastoral advice on whether people should make  pilgrimages to Medjugorje, Pope John Paul II said: *"Let the people go to Medjugorje if they convert, pray, confess, do penance and fast."*

In 1987, Alfred H. Kingon, the American Ambassador to the European Community under President Reagan, went to Medjugorje on a personal visit. Kingon was so impressed that he sent Reagan a personal two-and-a-half page summary. Then, at his request, Marija gave him a letter for President Reagan which he personally delivered to the White House:

"Dear President Reagan, The Blessed Mother appears every day in this small village of Medjugorje in Yugoslavia. She sends us a message of peace. We know that you do your best to improve the peace in the world, and we remember you every day in our prayers. We want you to know that you can count on our prayers and sacrifices. In this way, we want to help you in your difficult task.

Our Holy Mother said that, with prayers and fasting, even wars can be avoided. May this message help you and [may] Mary's daily appearances be a sign to you also that God loves His people. United in prayer, in the hearts of Jesus and Mary [The Queen of Peace], we express to you our love, and greet you with Peace. – Marija Pavlovic"

Gorbachev   **Reagan**

Reagan received Marija's letter shortly before meeting with Gorbachev for the 1987 Nuclear Arms Summit; Kingon stated that President Reagan was visibly moved when he read it, saying, "Now, with a new spirit, I am going to the meeting with Mr. Gorbachev." I distinctly recall the president entering that meeting with a broad grin on his face, waving a paper in his left hand, saying to a nearby television news team: "We have God on our side now!" This was just before his meeting with Gorbachev for the *Intermediate-Range Nuclear Forces Treaty* summit held in Washington.

It concerned a 1987 agreement between the United States and the Soviet Union, finalized and signed by U.S. President Ronald Reagan and General Secretary Mikhail Gorbachev on December 8, 1987, the feast of the Immaculate Conception. It was ratified by the United States Senate on May 27, 1988, becoming effective the following June 1st.

Kingon said that Reagan responded so favorably that he asked his secretary to contact Marija Pavlovic. Although she tried several times, the telephone service to the village was abysmal and Reagan was unable to reach her. Finally, on December 8, Kingon was able to connect with Marija by phone and told her how much the President appreciated her letter. Then, on Christmas Day, 1987, Marija received a picture from President Reagan with the message: "To Marija Pavlovic—with my heartfelt thanks and every good wish. God Bless You. Sincerely, Ronald Reagan."

At the request of Ambassador Kingon, Marija wrote a similar letter for Gorbachev, informing him of Our Lady's messages of peace from Medjugorje. Kingon added a condensed version of the events in Medjugorje into a one page letter; then, translated into Russian, they were presented to him in Moscow. Kingon stated: "There was no answer from Gorbachev, but it was indicated that he received it."

Kingon strongly believes there is "something of great import going on" in Medjugorje, stating it was his belief that "the whole world is going to change." Later, during a talk at the University of Notre Dame in 1992, Kingon stated: "Our Lady is now coming for all her children on Earth, in preparation for a major turning point in the affairs of men."

One of government's prime functions is to maintain law and order among its populace. Conflicts in religious matters such as occurred in Lourdes and Fátima between the government and the *believers* has always existed at the site of apparitions graced by Our Lady. This often produces anxiety on the people and, especially, the government.

This is obviously true within the Communist countries where there is always great concern about being overthrown by mob rule; hence, an outside gathering of more than a few people could be considered seditious.

Yet, in order to maintain peace with the citizens, religious freedom in Yugoslavia was permitted, albeit barely tolerated by the government. Religious gatherings were only allowed inside the church buildings; any type of public gatherings outdoors was closely monitored. This was the only exception permitted in any Soviet Communist nation!

In 1948, Josip Tito, the President of Yugoslavia, managed to negotiate an unusual treaty known as the *Tito-Stalin Split* while still remaining allied to the Soviet Union.

Joseph Stalin, the Premier of the Soviet Union, honored that treaty until his death in February, 1953, but he swore he would never again allow any country with such freedoms to exist within the Union of Socialist Soviet Republics.

On August 17, 1981, Fr. Jozo Zovko, the pastor of St. James' church, was arrested. He was charged with the crime of sedition, which could carry the death penalty. The sermon he gave on July 11, 1981 about Moses, and the enthusiastic response of the people, sounded subversive to the government. He was convicted of sedition four days later and sentenced to three-and-a-half years of hard labor. Thankfully, due to public notoriety, he was released after only one-and-a-half years.

I was fortunate to be with a small group that attended one of his rather guarded talks near Medjugorje after his release. He stated that every priest should have to endure some time in jail, claiming it humbles oneself. He also suggested that priests should spend much time in a confessional box, preferably in the heat of summer, sans air conditioning.

He was eventually sent to Austria and, in November, 2011, relocated in Croatia where he has all the faculties of a priest; however, he will not give interviews or talks in public about the apparitions or Mary's messages in Medjugorje until the Vatican Commission has finished its work.

Politics was not confined to the government alone; it existed within the three major religions of the area: Roman Catholic, Orthodox, and Islam, whose representatives often went against each other. Their history is full of atrocities committed by both sides during both the Nazi and Russian occupations.

Predictably, a few days after the apparitions began, the Communist government decided to persecute the children, believing that they were anti-socialist nationalists and hostile to the Communist Party. The police took the children by force to the Mostar mental facility, to a morgue, and to various other places intended to scare the children into confessing the staging of lies to subvert the government.

At one point, the police, believing Vicka was the leader of the children and the mastermind behind the hoax, even held a gun to her head. They also proceeded to harass the parents of the children as well, taking them into custody and ordering them to forbid their children from going to the church.

Additionally, there was some friction within the Catholic hierarchy. Bishop Pavao Žanić of the Diocese of Mostar, in whose district Medjugorje is located, visited Medjugorje numerous times in 1981. He was initially sympathetic to the apparitions and, on July 25, 1981, the same day he interviewed the children, stated in a homily during Mass:

"Six simple children like these would have told all in half an hour if anybody had been manipulating them. I assure you that none of the priests has done any such thing. The accusation is insulting and must be firmly rejected. Furthermore, I am convinced the children are not lying. They are saying what they most profoundly believe. Something has stirred in people's hearts. Confession, prayer, reconciliation between enemies: that is a most positive step forward."

Due to his positive stance about the apparitions, Žanić was then summoned to Sarajevo by the Communist State Police. During the interrogation about his involvement in Medjugorje, they threatened him with imprisonment – just as they did to Fr. Jozo – if he did not stop supporting the apparitions. Realizing the seriousness of this new dilemma, Žanić decided his own parish priests should resume control of the churches; hopefully, this would satisfy all parties involved.

So, then, the bishop told the Franciscans to vacate the premises as they were no longer needed! Yet, consider the residents' reactions. The Franciscans were greatly favored by the local population because they remained living with the people – serving them during both the Nazi and Russian occupations – whereas the parish priests vacated the area.

As a result two of the younger Franciscan priests, Fr. Ivica Vego and Fr. Ivan Prusina – finding themselves in a quandary – visited Medjugorje in early 1982. The local townspeople were sympathetic to the two priests and without thinking of the consequences encouraged them to approach the children to ask Our Lady for counsel. Apparently the Lady instructed them to relay the following message: "The Gospa [Our Lady] wants it said to the bishop that he has made a premature decision. Let him reflect again, and listen well to both parties. He must be just and patient. She says that both priests are not guilty." Once Žanić was informed of this he decided to rule unfavorably against the apparitions.

Bishop Žanić stated: "Our Lady could never disagree with what the bishop said!" According to the bishop, Our Lady basically said: *"Perhaps the bishop was hasty [harsh] in his decision!"*

As a result of Our Lady's response, and the earlier threats by the police in Sarajevo, Bishop Žanić developed a negative judgment about the veracity of Our Lady's appearances in Medjugorje. Thereafter, he concluded the apparitions had to be fraudulent, possibly a political move fostered by the Franciscans in order to remain in the parishes.

So, now, in the very place chosen by Our Lady to bring peace to the world – especially behind the *iron curtain* – a battle festered between certain elements within the Church. When Fr. Rene Laurentin, asked the bishop why he decided on this course of action, the bishop told him that this Lady "has been speaking against the bishop." Writing to bishop Žanić in 1984, Fr. Laurentin asked him why he willfully ignored the results of the scientific experiments performed on the children, which proved that they were neither hallucinating nor pathological.

Žanić responded: "The word hallucination is too flattering for what goes on in that apparition room. There are witnesses to testify that there are no ecstasies, no hallucinations, but simply parrot-like performances of a comic show. Therefore, I declare the word 'hallucination' too generous a description for such wicked play-acting. It will all blow up in your face sooner or later and, then, your precious encephalograms and cardiograms, and all your scientific apparatus will sink without trace."

After reading Bishop Žanić's December, 1984 unofficial decree, Hans Cardinal Urs von Balthasar responded with the following: "My Lord, what a sorry document you have sent throughout the world! I have been deeply pained to see the episcopal office degraded in this manner. Instead of biding your time – I you were recommended to do by higher authority – you fulminate and hurl thunderbolts like Jupiter. While you denigrate renowned people who are innocent, deserving of your respect and protection, you bring out accusations that have been refuted a hundred times over."

Later, in 1986, Bishop Žanić submitted a negative decision to Cardinal Ratzinger, then prefect of the Congregation for the Doctrine of the faith. However, instead of accepting the negative decision of the bishop, Cardinal Ratzinger dissolved the bishop's Commission. He then convened a new Commission of all the Yugoslavian Bishops in the region. Eventually, the standoff became so intolerable that the Vatican took the matter completely out of the hands of the local ordinary.

He asked the bishop to refrain from making any future public statements about the matter. According to Bishop Žanić, in 1986, Cardinal Ratzinger told him forthright: "No, you are going to dissolve your diocesan commission. The verdict is transferred to the Bishops Conference." On April 10, 1991, the Yugoslavian Episcopal Conference made a declaration regarding Medjugorje. Known as the *Declaration of the ex-Yugoslavian Bishops Conference,* the bishops therein stated the following: "There is no proof that the events in Medjugorje are supernatural." Importantly, however, they concluded that pilgrims can go to Medjugorje, and they are to be tended to in a pastoral manner.

The Yugoslavian Bishops Conference voted to classify Medjugorje in one of three ways; 1) certain of supernatural origin, 2) not yet certain of supernatural origin, 3) certain of no supernatural origin. The conference rejected the 3rd classification by a vote of 19 to 1, and after much deliberation between the 1st and 2nd classification, decided that Medjugorje cannot yet be confirmed supernatural, but also expresses its favorability to the apparitions.

"We, the bishops, after three years of examination by the Commission, have declared Medjugorje a place of prayer and a Marian sanctuary. This means that we are not opposed to people coming on pilgrimage to Medjugorje to venerate the Mother of God there, in conformity with the teaching and faith of the universal Church. As to the supernaturalism of the apparitions, we have declared: 'Up to this moment, we cannot affirm it. We leave it for later. The Church is not in a hurry.'"

In 1991, the new bishop, Peric, voiced his disagreement with the progress of the Yugoslavian Bishops Conference, stating; "My conviction and my position is not only 'non constat de supernaturalitate', but likewise, 'constat de non supernaturalitate' of the apparitions or revelations in Medjugorje." Cardinal Ratzinger [later, Pope Benedict XVI], prefect of the Congregation for the Doctrine of the Faith, quoted the Yugoslavian Bishops as stating the following; "We want to be concerned that this place, which has become a place of prayer and faith, remain and come to be even more in the most interior unity with the entire Church."

On July 20, 1992, in the midst of the Bosnian war, Fr. Jozo went to the Vatican where he met with John Paul II who reportedly told him: *"I am with you. Protect Medjugorje. Protect Our Lady's messages!"*

Finally, in 1993, Bishop Peric, the successor to Bishop Žanić, conceded to the findings of the Yugoslavian bishop's conference, stating: "Medjugorje is officially accepted as a place of prayer and pilgrimage."

In the same year, the two Franciscan priests who were unjustly expelled from the order in 1981 received a complete vindication from Rome. After the case was elevated to the Apostolic Signatura, the Tribunal responded definitively by declaring that Bishop Žanić's expulsion and laicization of those priests was hereby revoked. Both priests were then permitted to return to their community in good standing. Unfortunately, Ivica Vego was unable to continue his vocation as a priest for he had married in the interim.

In 1996, Dr. Joaquin Navarro-Valls, a Vatican spokesman, was asked about people going to Medjugorje: "Has the Vatican said no?" He answered: "No. You cannot say people cannot go there until it has been proven false. This has not been said, so anyone can go if they want. When Catholic faithful go anywhere, they are entitled to spiritual care, so the Church does not forbid priests to accompany lay-organized trips to Medjugorje in Bosnia-Herzegovina."

In 1998, the secretary of the Congregation for the Doctrine of the Faith responded in a letter of inquiry from Bishop Gilbert Aubry on the status of Medjugorje. He reiterates the Church's position by stating:

1) he defers all authority to the 1991 Bishop's Conference;
2) the bishop's opinion is merely his own opinion, and should not be considered the judgment of the Church;
3) private pilgrimages are permitted "so long as they are not regarded as an authentication of events still taking place and which still call for an examination by the Church."

On August 24, 2002, Pope John Paul II sent a letter of thanks to Fr. Jozo, "I grant from the heart a particular blessing to Father Jozo Zovko, OFM, and I invoke a new outpouring of graces and heavenly favors, and the continuous protection of the Blessed Virgin Mary." In the same year, the Pope elevated Sister Emmanuel's community to full recognition. She is the same woman who Bishop Žanić condemned and said that as she was not a nun, that she had no right to call herself, *Sister.*

By July, 2006, Vinko Cardinal Puljic, of Bosnia and Herzegovina, announced that the Congregation for the Doctrine of the Faith at the Vatican was establishing a Commission to carefully study the events in Medjugorje. In 2008, Cardinal Bertone of the Congregation of the Defense of the Faith wrote: "Bishop Peric's statement expresses a personal opinion of his own. It is not a definitive official judgment on the part of the Church." The Church defers to the Zadar statement [previously] issued on April 10, 1991 by the bishops of the former Yugoslavia.

The statement leaves the door open to further investigations of the affair. So the process of verification needs to move forward. Then, on April 13, 2010, the Holy See formed a new Commission to investigate the alleged apparitions in Medjugorje. The stated objective of this Commission is principally of a technical matter; to disseminate and publicize the details of the 1991 Yugoslavian Bishops Conference which, as we have also seen, had a positive view of the events.

On January, 20, 2014, the Holy See announced that the commission charged with investigating the alleged Marian apparitions in Medjugorje has completed its task, and will be submitting its findings to the Vatican's doctrine office.

Vatican spokesman, Fr. Federico Lombardi, confirmed on January, the 18th, that the international commission investigating the supposed apparitions had held its final meeting the prior day, and will submit its final report to the Congregation for the Doctrine of the Faith.

Presided over by Cardinal Camillo Ruini, emeritus vicar general of the Diocese of Rome, the commission was created by the Congregation for the Doctrine of the Faith in 2010, and was composed of an international panel of bishops, cardinals, theologians, and various experts who have undertaken a detailed study of the reports of the reported Marian apparitions. The commissions were established to further investigate "certain doctrinal and disciplinary aspects of the phenomenon of Medjugorje."

The Vatican commission completed its investigation of Medjugorje in 2014 and submitted its findings to the Congregation for the Doctrine of the Faith. The judgment awaits final approval from Pope Francis.

It is my understanding this is the first time that the Church has undertaken such a step. It would obviously appear they are quite open to the events and waiting to see what transpires. The Church is in no hurry to prematurely dismiss what may well turn out to be the greatest apparitions of Our Lady in the history of mankind! Yet, in fairness to Bishop Žanić, it must be understood that he has a genuine love for Our Lady and, at the same time, was trying to resolve the conflicts he had with the Franciscan priests and the children in Medjugorje. He is convinced he is going about it in the correct manner, yet, without all the facts, one cannot fault him for his approach in an attempt to clarify the matter. Actually, there are several contentious facts regarding what was said.

Now, I am well aware that the phrase noted earlier *"...to sneak a smoke"* may appear to be an odd way to begin the description of any apparition; yet, it has a sense of reality to it which we aren't often privy.

I included Milka's words: "...to sneak a smoke" because this incident would cause some concern during the later investigation of the validity of the apparitions. This was definitely confirmed during a transcript of the tape the local bishop eventually released. It stated: "The first one was Mirjana: 'We went to look for our sheep when at once...'

The associate pastor in the parish interrupted and told me [Žanić] that they actually went out to smoke, which they hid from their parents. 'Wait a minute, Mirjana, you're under oath. Did you go out to look for your sheep?' She put her hand over her mouth and added: 'Forgive me, we went out to smoke.'"

Not all those chosen by Our Lady lead saintly lives; after all, people are human and human beings make mistakes. Additionally, one must remember that not everything a visionary says is the absolute truth. They are quite normal people, often subject to misunderstanding and error in their remembrance of everything that transpired. There are times when the meanings of the words are lost: there could be a faulty translation and this may occur in a relatively short period of time.

We must also differentiate between the words of Our Lady and personal words of the seers. It is better to give credence to Mary's messages than personal ones. Regardless, some individuals just cannot bring themselves to believe in apparitions, even those of Our Lady of Lourdes; yet, the Church considers Bernadette's behavior to be the ideal in attempting to ascertain the veracity of other apparitions.

Unfortunately, ideals are not always the rule and we shall always have the skeptics among us. One should not easily discount that which Our Lady is telling us. If Mary is truly appearing there, no action by any of the detractors will change the eventual outcome.

This is not the first time we have been warned about our present day predicament. Our Lady will not rest until her message is made known throughout the world. She said to Ivanka: "No pain, no suffering is too great in order for my messages to reach each one of you."

Meanwhile, inasmuch as none of the messages in Medjugorje are contrary to Church teaching, we would do well to continue to listen to them and act accordingly. Surely, if these truly constitute Our Lady's last appearance on Earth, then, we should take an extraordinary amount of time to hear her out. There may well be no alternatives after this! And, regardless of the final outcome of the events in Medjugorje, whether it is approved or condemned, one must realize it would have little effect on the mission Mary is pursuing.

The Visionaries, in 1981:

Jakov Colo – 10

Ivanka Ivankovic-Elez – 15

Ivan Dragicevic – 16

Marija Pavlovic-Lunetti – 16

Mirjana Dragicevic-Soldo – 16

Vicka Ivankovic-Mijatovic – 17

One of the reasons Mary is taking so much time is to remind the faithful, and especially those who do not believe, what they must do in order to obtain eternal life in Heaven. Mary stated quite clearly that *"...those in Heaven know they have earned it."*

St. Paul, strongly advises us, *"...I drive my body and train it, for fear that, after having preached to others, I myself should be disqualified"* (1 Cor 9:27). How, then, can anyone assume they *are saved* until the final chapter of their life has played out on this Earth?

Mother Teresa stated: "I am grateful to Our Lady of Medjugorje. I know that many people go there and are converted. I thank God for leading us during these times this way."

"Dear children, you know that for your sake I have remained a long time so I might teach you how to make progress on the way of holiness. Therefore, dear children, pray without ceasing and live the messages which I am giving you for I am doing it with great love toward God and toward you. Thank you for having responded to my call." - January 1, 1987

"Dear children, I want you to comprehend that God has chosen each one of you, in order to use you in His great plan for the salvation of mankind. You are not able to comprehend how great your role is in God's design. Therefore, dear children, pray, so that in prayer you may be able to comprehend what God's plan is in your regard. I am with you in order that you may be able to bring it about in all its fullness." - January 25, 1987

"Dear children, Satan is very strong and, therefore, I ask you to dedicate your prayers to me so that those who are under his influence can be saved. Give witness by your life. Sacrifice your lives for the salvation of the world. I am with you, and I am grateful to you, but in Heaven you will receive the Father's reward which He has promised to you. Therefore, dear children, do not be afraid. If you pray, Satan cannot injure you even a little bit because you are God's children and He is watching over you. Pray and let the rosary always be in your hand as a sign to Satan that you belong to me. Thank you for having responded to my call." - February 25, 1988

"Dear children! Today I invite you to become missionaries of my messages, which I am giving here through this place that is dear to me. God has allowed me to stay this long with you and therefore, little children, I invite you to live with love the messages I give and to transmit them to the whole world, so that a river of love flows to people who are full of hatred and without peace. I invite you, little children, to become peace where there is no peace and light where there is darkness, so that each heart accepts the light and the way of salvation." - February 25, 1995

"Comprehend, little children, that you are today the salt of the Earth and the light of the world." - October 25, 1996

"Dear children! Today I call you to be my extended hands in this world that puts God in the last place. You, little children, put God in the first place in your life. God will bless you and give you strength to witness Him, the God of love and peace. I am with you and intercede for all of you. Little children, do not forget that I love you with a tender love." - February 25, 2005

"Dear children, as a mother, I am joyful to be among you because I desire to speak anew about the words of my Son and of His love. I hope that you will accept me with the heart, because the words of my Son and His love are the only light and hope in the darkness of today. This is the only truth and you who will accept and live it will have pure and humble hearts. My Son loves those who are pure and humble. Pure and humble hearts bring to life the words of my Son, they live them, they spread them and they make it possible for everyone to hear them.

"The words of my Son bring back life to those who listen to them. The words of my Son bring back love and hope. Therefore, my beloved apostles, my children, live the words of my Son. Love each other as He loved you. Love each other in His name, in memory of Him. The Church is advancing and growing because of those who listen to the words of my Son; because of those who love; because of those who suffer and endure in silence and in the hope of final redemption. Therefore, my beloved children, may the words of my Son and His love be the first and the last thought of your day. Thank you." - January 02, 2016

Epilogue, Medjugorje

Sr. Lúcia, the last survivor of the apparitions in Fatima, Portugal, wrote several books describing the events in great detail. In a similar manner, Mirjana Dragicevic-Soldo – one of the visionaries from Medjugorje – wrote a superb book about her experiences that began on June 24, 1981, and are ongoing. *My Heart Will Triumph* [1] is the story of Medjugorje as seen through Mirjana's own eyes: the same eyes that, according to her testimony, gaze upon the most revered woman in history.

Published on August 15, 2016, the Feast of the Assumption, it delves into both the exquisite pleasure and the extreme difficulties she encountered during the thirty-five years since the events in Medjugorje began. Mirjana was only 16 years old when she and five other children saw a mysterious young woman on Mt. Podbrdo, a remote hillside in the village of Medjugorje, a small village in Yugoslavia. The lady, who possessed a beauty and grace that seemed to come from beyond, identified herself as the Virgin Mary.

The apparitions that began on that late afternoon would dramatically change Mirjana's life and the lives of countless people around the world. The apparitions have continued for over 35 years and millions of pilgrims still travel to Medjugorje every year. Her claims, however, contradicted the atheistic ideologies of the Communist government and, at only sixteen years of age, she was branded an enemy of the state! Although they persecuted her severely, she never denied what she saw.

The messages given by Mary are a call for mankind to return to God. Mirjana said the Virgin has entrusted her with ten secrets that she will reveal to the world in her lifetime, secrets that foretell the future of the world. She hints at a timeline: *"At this moment we are living in a time of grace; after this will come the time of the secrets, and the time of her triumph!"*

No series of apparitions have continued as long as those in Medjugorje, nor have so many prophetic secrets been given. She implores us to: *"Look around you, and look at the signs of the times."* It is obvious that Our Lady truly wishes to help us while, at the same time, she implies that time is limited: *"I have come to call the world to conversion for the last time! Later, I will never again appear on Earth [in this way]."* [1]

[1.] My Heart Will Triumph by Dragicevic-Soldo, Mirjana, Cocoa, Fl, CatholicShop Publishing, 2016

CHAPTER 17

Revealed Secrets

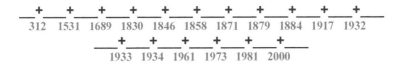

"...we saw an angel with a flaming sword in his left hand; flashing, it gave out flames that looked as though they would set the world on fire; but they died out in contact with the splendor that Our Lady radiated towards him from her right hand; pointing to the Earth with his right hand, the angel cried out in a loud voice: "Penance; Penance; Penance!"

On May 13, 2000, Francisco and Jacinta were beatified by Pope John Paul II in Fátima. This gave added credence to the horrific vision of Hell Our Lady showed to the three young children on July 13, 1917. Lúcia stated: "This vision lasted but an instant." It was so grotesque that the children stated: "How can we ever be grateful enough to our kind heavenly Mother who had already prepared us by promising, in the first apparition, to take us to Heaven? Otherwise, I think we would have died of fear and terror." Jacinta was only seven years old; yet, Our Lady did not spare her from that vision of Hell.

After this vision, Our Lady told them: *"You have seen Hell where the souls of poor sinners go. To save them, God wishes to establish in the world devotion to my Immaculate Heart. If what I say to you is done, many souls will be saved and there will be peace. The war is going to end; but if people do not cease offending God, a worse one will break out during the pontificate of Pius XI. To prevent this, I shall come to ask for the consecration of Russia to my Immaculate Heart, and the Communion of reparation on the First Saturdays. If my requests are heeded, Russia will be converted, and there will be peace; if not, she will spread her errors throughout the world, causing wars and persecutions of the Church. The good will be martyred; the Holy Father will have much to suffer; various nations will be annihilated"*

"In the end, my Immaculate Heart will triumph. The Holy Father will consecrate Russia to me, and she shall be converted, and a period of peace will be granted to the world."

Our Lady then told Lúcia: *"When you see a night illumined by an unknown light, know that this is the great sign given you by God that he is about to punish the world for its crimes, by means of war, famine, and persecutions of the Church and of the Holy Father."*

Mary sternly warned us that, *"...if people do not cease offending God..."* the world would be punished by means of wars, famines, and persecutions of the Church. Indeed, all too soon, the elements for these scenarios were being fulfilled and, by the end of 1918, anti-clerical Communism had marshaled its followers in two nations: Portugal and Russia.

In October 1918, one year after the miracle of the Sun was seen in Fátima, a young corporal fighting for the Germans in *World War I* was blinded in a mustard gas attack. He was sent to a military hospital where he eventually recovered his sight. By 1924, he had written a book entitled *Mein Kampf* which would list his desires for a world conquest by a *super race.* Thus began the meteoric ascent of Adolf Hitler in Germany. This would culminate in another war, that *"...worse one"* Our Lady warned about. It eventually became known as *World War II.*

On October 29, 1929, owing to an overinflated stock market, the *Wall Street Crash* occurred. It was the most devastating stock market crash in the history of the United States and signaled the beginning of the *Great Depression* that affected all Western industrialized countries. The economic depression that ensued engulfed the entire world. It didn't end in the United States until 1947, several years after *World War II* was over.

As if the depression wasn't difficult enough, over-farming of the prairies began. Whether through ignorance or greed, the plains were so overworked that the protection of the native grasses that grew there was decimated. Thus, when an extremely long dry spell occurred, the infamous *Dust Bowl* began. It ravaged mid-America. In 1932, fourteen dust storms were recorded on the Plains; in 1933, there were thirty-eight storms. By 1934, it was estimated that 100 million acres of farmland had lost most or all of the topsoil to the winds. In 1935, the entire month of April consisted of a series of dust storms which pummeled the Plains; however, nothing they had ever seen prepared them for the cloud that appeared on the horizon on the 14th.

The storm winds were clocked at 60 mph, reaching its apex on what is now referred to as *Black Sunday*. No one was spared from its ravages! Those who initially survived inhaled so much dust into their lungs that they were stricken with permanent lung diseases. Children had to be relocated away from their families in order to live, some never to see their parents or siblings again. There was nothing to come back to: no topsoil; no people; the *Oakies* had all moved westward, settling mostly in California. A movie *The Grapes of Wrath* chronicled this difficult time for the farming people of Oklahoma and surrounding states.

Then, in the evening of January 25-26, 1938, the prophetic sign Our Lady warned about in 1917 was fulfilled. I was only five-and-a-half years old at the time and can vividly remember standing in the street with my parents in Baltimore, Maryland until quite late, wondering at this ghostly phenomenon. We were entranced by the dancing, changing hues covering the entire sky.

Red Aurora Borealis

An *aurora borealis* had rarely been seen in that area before, and never that color. This aurora was seen over the whole of Europe, across the Atlantic to Bermuda and Southern California, and as far as Southern Australia. The color throughout Europe was of a distinct blood-red hue. Londoners actually thought their entire city was aflame. Many alarms were rung as the fire departments dashed about in all directions.

In England, a hook-and-ladder brigade was summoned to Windsor Castle to put out a nonexistent fire. In Bermuda, people thought that a ship at sea was on fire. Steamship agents took the precaution of checking with wireless stations to inquire if there had been any SOS calls. This phenomenon was also responsible for delaying express trains on the Manchester to Sheffield line: electrical disturbances hit the signaling apparatus. There was interference with short wave radio sets. Teletype systems at the local office of the Western Union were started without human intervention. In some quarters it was assumed the world was coming to an end.

I've seen many diverse night skies at sea but never any similar to that one. It wasn't until much later that I learned how unusual that aurora truly was. Astronomers in New England said the lights differed from previous aurorae. That difference was attributable to the intensity of the color and the direction of the beams, instead of appearing as usual in parallel lines.

It appeared as a low-altitude red aurora which only happens during intense geomagnetic storms. The immense arcs of crimson light – with shifting areas of green and blue – radiated from this brilliant auroral crown near its zenith. Normal aurorae are red on top with extremely red hues, and green on the bottom. However, in the all-red aurorae, the low-energy electrons strike the upper atmosphere. The red light is the ejection from atomic oxygen; however, when the electrons don't have enough energy to penetrate the lower altitudes of this planet, they cause ejection of the normal green hues.

Sr. Lúcia later confirmed that this was the *"...unknown light..."* Our Lady warned about in Fatima, on July 13, 1917, when she emphatically stated: *"When you see a night illumined by an unknown light, know that this is the great sign given you by God that he is about to punish the world for its crimes, by means of war, famine, and persecutions of the Church and of the Holy Father."*

Fifteen days later, on February 10, 1938, Adolf Hitler addressed the Reichstag about the Rearmament of Germany, thereby breaking The Treaty of Versailles that was signed on June 28, 1919. The war that followed was the worst in history! It was the first time civilians were deliberately bombed. The toll on humans was incalculable for it was impossible to keep records of all those who were injured. Finally, after enduring five years of horrific battles and millions of dead, the free world overcame the tremendous obstacles and won the war.

However, even in the early 1950s, most of the world continued to suffer, especially those whose infrastructure and governments had been completely destroyed. It invariably involved a struggle for control of the destiny of nations and the ensuing power. Many people wondered if the third part of the secret of Fátima contained a solution: after all, Sr. Lúcia said it could be revealed either after 1960, or upon her death, subject to which ever occurred first. Would it contain a solution for our troubles; perhaps a further chastisement; an apocalyptic struggle for survival? Only Sr. Lúcia and various popes knew for certain.

The Vatican states that the sealed envelope containing the secret was initially in the custody of the bishop of Leiria. The bishop of Leiria informed Sr. Lúcia of this; also, he advised her he had not read the contents of the envelope. On April 4, 1957, in order to ensure better protection for the secret, the envelope was placed in the Secret Archives of the Holy Office in Rome.

On August 17, 1959, with the agreement of Alfredo Cardinal Ottaviani, Prefect of the Congregation for the Doctrine of the Faith, the envelope containing the third part of the secret of Fátima was brought to Pope John XXIII by Fr. Pierre Paul Philippe, O.P. After some hesitation, His Holiness said, "We will wait. I shall pray. I shall let you know what I decide." In fact, what he decided to do was to return the sealed envelope to the Holy Office without revealing any information concerning the third part of that secret, the as yet undisclosed portion of the message.

Like many others who were aware of Our Lady of Fátima's efforts, I wrote to Alfredo Cardinal Ottaviani in the early 1960s, asking if he could reveal its contents. Cardinal Ottaviani sent a courteous response that His Holiness judged it better not to do that, stating quite clearly that, for reasons only the Church was privy to, "…It was a personal message for the Pope, and he alone could choose to reveal its contents."

In 1964, during the solemn closing ceremonies at the end of the third session of the Second Vatican Council, Pope Paul VI renewed Pius XII's consecration of the world to the Immaculate Heart of Mary. On March 27, 1965, Paul VI read the contents of the third part of the secret in that envelope but decided not to publish the text. Instead, he returned the envelope to the Archives of the Holy Office, determined it did not refer to his time. On May 13, 1965, as he had announced at the Second Vatican Council, Pope Paul VI presented the Golden Rose in Fátima through his Papal Legate, commending the whole Church to Our Lady of Fátima's care.

Two years later, on May 13, 1967, the fiftieth anniversary of the first Fátima apparition, the Holy Father went on another pilgrimage to the Shrine of Our Lady of Fátima. Paul VI died on August 6, 1978; the third part of the secret remained unrevealed to the public.

John Paul I was elected Pope on August 26, 1978; however, he died on September 29, 1978, only thirty-three days after his election. It is therefore unknown whether he had the opportunity to read the contents of the envelope.

Pope St. John Paul II exhibited his approval of Fátima many times, visiting there on the 13th of May in 1982, 1991 and 2000. During his homily at the Mass in Fátima on May 13, 1982, he said: "The appeal of the Lady of the Message of Fátima is so deeply rooted in the Gospel and the whole of Tradition that the Church feels that the Message imposes a commitment on Her. The Message is addressed to every human being...Because of the continuing increase of sin and the dangers, such as nuclear war now threatening humanity, the Message of Fátima is more urgent and relevant in our time than it was when Our Lady appeared 65 years ago.

"Today, John Paul II, successor of St. Peter, presents himself before the Mother of the Son of God in Her Shrine at Fátima. In what way does he come? He presents himself reading again with trepidation the motherly call to penance, to conversion, the ardent appeal of the Heart of Mary that resounded at Fátima 65 years ago. Yes, he reads it again with trepidation in his heart because he sees how many people and societies, how many Christians have gone in the opposite direction to the one indicated in the Message of Fátima. Sin has thus made itself firmly at home in the world, and denial of God has become widespread in the ideologies, ideas and plans of human beings."

John Paul II made the Feast day of Our Lady of Fátima universal by ordering it to be included in the Roman Missal. While he was recuperating from the assassination attempt in Rome on May 13, 1981 – a date which coincided with the 64th anniversary of the apparitions in 1917 – he requested the envelope containing the third part of the secret of Fátima.

On July 18, 1981, Franjo Cardinal Šeper – then Prefect of the Congregation for the Doctrine of the Faith – gave two envelopes to Archbishop Eduardo Martínez Somalo: one white envelope containing Sr. Lúcia's original text in Portuguese; the other, orange, with the Italian translation of the secret.

Pope John Paul II opened the envelope and read the contents. On the following 11th of August, Archbishop Martínez returned the two envelopes to the Archives of the Holy Office.

As is well known, John Paul II immediately thought of consecrating the world to the Immaculate Heart of Mary. He, himself, then composed a prayer for what he called an *Act of Entrustment.*

It is quite likely that the Holy Father had previously communicated this with Sr. Lúcia regarding the meaning of the final part of the secret because, on May 12, 1982, she wrote to the Holy Father giving an indication for his interpretation of the third part of the message [secret]: "The third part of the secret refers to Our Lady's words: *'If not [Russia] will spread her errors throughout the world, causing wars and persecutions of the Church. The good will be martyred; the Holy Father will have much to suffer; various nations will be annihilated.'*

"The third part of the secret is a symbolic revelation, referring to this part of the Message, conditioned by whether we accept or not what the Message itself asks of us: *'If my requests are heeded, Russia will be converted and there will be peace; if not, she will spread her errors throughout the world, etc.'* Since we did not heed this appeal of the Message, we see that it has been fulfilled, Russia has invaded the world with her errors.

"And if we have not yet seen the complete fulfillment of the final part of this prophecy, we are going towards it little by little with great strides. If we do not reject the path of sin, hatred, revenge, injustice, violations of the rights of the human person, immorality and violence, etc. And let us not say that it is God who is punishing us in this way; on the contrary, it is people themselves who are preparing their own punishment. In His kindness, God warns us and calls us to the right path, while respecting the freedom He has given us; hence people are responsible."

In order to respond more fully to the requests of Our Lady, during the Holy Year of the Redemption, the Holy Father desired to make the *Act of Entrustment* of May 7, 1981 more explicit. Although it had been repeated in Fátima on May 13, 1982, the Pope asked Sr. Lúcia if the consecration was done in accordance with Mary's request. However, she responded negatively with the following: "Our Lady clearly stated: *'God, asks the Holy Father, in union with all the bishops of the world, to make the consecration of Russia to My Immaculate Heart, promising to save it by this means.'*"

Finally, on March 25, 1984 in St. Peter's Square, while recalling the fiat uttered by Mary at the Annunciation, the Holy Father – in spiritual union with the Bishops of the world who had been convoked beforehand – entrusted all men and women and all peoples to the Immaculate Heart of Mary in terms which recalled the heartfelt words spoken in 1981, which began:

"O Mother of all men and women, and of all peoples, you who know all their sufferings and their hopes, you who have a mother's awareness of all the struggles between good and evil, between light and darkness, which afflict the modern world, accept the cry which we, moved by the Holy Spirit, address directly to your Heart.

"Embrace with the love of the Mother and Handmaid of the Lord, this human world of ours, which we entrust and consecrate to you, for we are full of concern for the earthly and eternal destiny of individuals and peoples. In a special way we entrust and consecrate to you those individuals and nations which particularly need to be thus entrusted and consecrated."

When His Holiness inquired of Lúcia if this consecration had been accepted by Heaven, she responded in the affirmative by way of a letter, dated November 8, 1989. In that correspondence, she personally confirmed that this solemn and universal act of consecration corresponded to what Mary wished, stating: "Yes, it has been done just as Our Lady asked, on 25 March 1984." We know for certain that Christ told Sr. Lúcia the Holy Father *"...will do it but it will be late. Nevertheless, the Immaculate Heart of Mary will save Russia. It has been entrusted to her."* [1]

"On April 27, 2000, a meeting took place in the Carmel in Coimbra, between Lúcia, Archbishop Bertone, Secretary of the Congregation for the Doctrine of the Faith, and the bishop of Leiria-Fátima. Sister Lúcia was lucid and at ease; she was very happy that the Holy Father was going to Fátima for the Beatification of Francisco and Jacinta, something she had looked forward to for a long time. The bishop of Leiria-Fátima read the autographed letter of the Holy Father, which explained the reasons for the visit. Sister Lúcia felt honored by this and reread the letter herself, contemplating it in her own hands. She said that she was prepared to answer all questions frankly.

"At this point, Archbishop Bertone presented two envelopes to her: the first containing the second, which held the third part of the secret of Fátima."

"Immediately, she said: 'This is my letter' and then, while reading it, said: 'This is my writing.' The original text, in Portuguese, was read and interpreted with the help of the bishop of Leiria-Fátima. Sister Lúcia agreed with the interpretation that the third part of the secret was a prophetic vision, similar to those in sacred history.

"She repeated her conviction that the vision of Fátima concerns above all the struggle of Communism (atheistic Socialism)ⁱ against the Church and against Christians, and describes the terrible sufferings of the victims of the faith in the twentieth century. When she was asked: 'Is the principal figure in the vision the pope?'

"Sister Lúcia replied at once that it was. She recalled that the three children were very sad about the suffering of the pope, and that Jacinta kept saying: 'Poor Holy Father, I am very sad for sinners!'"

Lúcia continued: "We did not know the name of the pope; Our Lady did not tell us the name of the pope; we did not know whether it was Benedict XV, or Pius XII, or Paul VI, or John Paul II, but it was the pope who was suffering and that made us suffer too.

"As regards the passage about the bishop dressed in white, that is, the Holy Father – the children immediately realized this during the vision – who is struck dead and falls to the ground. Sister Lúcia was in full agreement with the pope's claim in May 13, 1994, that: '...it was a mother's hand that guided the bullet's path and in his throes the pope halted at the threshold of death.'

"On June 17, 1944, before giving the sealed envelope containing the third part of the secret to the bishop of Leiria-Fátima, Sister Lúcia wrote on the outside envelope that it could be opened only after 1960, either by the Patriarch of Lisbon or the Bishop of Leiria. Archbishop Bertone therefore asked: 'Why only after 1960? Was it Our Lady who fixed that date?' Sister Lúcia replied: 'It was not Our Lady. I fixed the date because I had the intuition that before 1960 it would not be understood, but that only later would it be understood. Now it can be better understood. I wrote down what I saw; however it was not for me to interpret it, but for the pope.'

"Finally, mention was made of the unpublished manuscript *Os apelos da Mensagem de Fátima* which Sister Lúcia has prepared as a reply to the many letters that come from Marian devotees and from pilgrims. She was asked if she would be happy to have it published, and she replied: 'If the Holy Father agrees, then I am happy, otherwise I obey whatever the Holy Father decides.'"

The following pages are taken verbatim from the Vatican's web site: www.vatican. va/.../...message-Fátima_en.html:

"The action of God, the Lord of history, and the co-responsibility of man in the drama of his creative freedom, are the two pillars upon which human history is built. Our Lady, who appeared at Fátima, recalls these forgotten values. She reminds us that man's future is in God, and that we are active and responsible partners in creating that future."

"Sister Lúcia wants to present the text for ecclesiastical approval, and she hopes that what she has written will help to guide men and women of good will along the path that leads to God, the final goal of every human longing. The conversation ends with an exchange of rosaries. Sister Lúcia is given a rosary sent by the Holy Father, and she in turn offers a number of rosaries made by her. The meeting concludes with a blessing.

"Finally, on June 26, 2000 in Fátima, Pope John Paul II authorized the revelation of the third secret. With Sister Lúcia at his side, it was read to the millions tuned into the Beatification Mass for Jacinta and Francisco, the other two children to whom Our Lady appeared in 1917."

"After the two parts which I have already explained, at the left of Our Lady and a little above, we saw an angel with a flaming sword in his left hand; flashing, it gave out flames that looked as though they would set the world on fire; but, they died out in contact with the splendor that Our Lady radiated towards him from her right hand. Pointing to the Earth with his right hand, the Angel cried out in a loud voice: 'Penance; Penance; Penance!'

And we saw in an immense light that is God, something similar to how people appear in a mirror when they pass in front of it, a bishop, dressed in white; we had the impression that it was the Holy Father."

"Other bishops, priests, men and women religious going up a steep mountain, at the top of which there was a big Cross of rough-hewn trunks as of a cork-tree with the bark; before reaching there the Holy Father passed through a big city half in ruins and half trembling with halting step, afflicted with pain and sorrow, he prayed for the souls of the corpses he met on his way; having reached the top of the mountain, on his knees at the foot of the big Cross, he was killed by a group of soldiers who fired bullets and arrows at him."

"And in the same way there died one after another the other Bishops, Priests, men and women Religious, and various lay people of different ranks and positions. Beneath the two arms of the cross there were two Angels each with a crystal aspersorium in his hand, in which they gathered up the blood of the martyrs and with it sprinkled the souls that were making their way to God" (Tuy-3-1-1944).

"Fátima is undoubtedly the most prophetic of modern apparitions wherein most of the events have come to pass. The first and second parts of the message [secrets] refer especially to the frightening vision of Hell, devotion to the Immaculate Heart of Mary, World War II and, finally, the prediction of the immense damage that Russia would do to humanity by abandoning the Christian faith and embracing Communist totalitarianism,

"The decision of His Holiness, Pope John Paul II, to make public the third part of the secret of Fátima brings to an end a period of history marked by tragic human lust for power and evil, yet pervaded by the merciful love of God and the watchful care of the Mother of Jesus, and of the Church." [i]

The Church attributes the following scripture to Mary: *"A great sign appeared in the sky, a woman clothed with the sun, with the moon under her feet, and on her head was a crown of twelve stars"* (Rev 12:1) and, as such, has been given the grace from God to use as much power as she deems best to accomplish her specific mission!

Our Lady advised Jacinta: *"...the sin which sends most people to perdition is the sin of the flesh; that they should do without luxuries; that people should not remain obstinate in their sins as they had done up to then; that it was necessary to do much penance."*

On saying this, Our Lady was very sad." Because of this, Jacinta often exclaimed: "Oh, I am so sorry for Our Lady! I am so sorry for her!" Then, shortly before Jacinta's death on April 4, 1919, Our Lady told her: *"Certain fads [fashions] will be introduced that will offend Our Lord very much; Many marriages are not good; they do not please Our Lord and are not of God; Most people go to Hell because of sins of the flesh."*

Will we do that *"Penance; Penance; Penance"* the angel demanded: or just go on our merry way, choosing instead to wait and see? What will happen to us; to our children; to our country; to the world around us if we do not do perform that penance?

In 1917, during the miracle of the sun at Fátima, many of the witnesses fell onto their knees into the mud, crying out to Heaven: "Forgive me; don't let me die in my sins!" They truly believed that, for them, the world was coming to an end.

In 1931, Msgr. Eugenio Pacelli, who would become Pope Pius XII in 1939, stated: "I am worried by the Blessed Virgin's messages to Lucy of Fátima. This persistence of Mary about the dangers which menace the Church is a divine warning against the suicide of altering the faith, in Her liturgy, Her theology and Her soul. A day will come when the civilized world will deny its God, when the Church will doubt as Peter doubted. She will be tempted to believe that man has become God. In our churches Christians will search for the red lamp where God awaits them, like Mary Magdalene weeping before the empty tomb, they will ask, *'Where have they taken him?'* (Jn 20:13)."

August, 1945, saw the end of World War II - Peace at last!

Rising from the ashes of that tragedy a *cold war* developed between the U.S.S.R. and the free world, each side fully aware that a potential world war loomed on the horizon, a war from which literally no one would go unscathed! Beginning in the early 1960s, several events would occur that threatened to start a global thermonuclear war.

Each event was loaded with a nuclear hair-trigger and rested in the hands of one individual. He, alone, would make that decision, knowing full well that failure to follow orders would likely end in his being deemed a traitor to his government. Had he done exactly as he was instructed, my family would cease to exist; I would not be here to write this!

On October 18, 1961, Our Lady appeared in Spain to four children with a warning for the world: *"...The cup is already filling up and, if we do not change, a very great chastisement will come upon us."* Exactly one year later, in October, an event would occur!

In early 1962, owing to my installation of a multi-agency communications system for our Commission, our section was trained to trace nuclear radiation in the state of Maryland and vicinity. We were to measure the levels of radiation and transmit the data to the appropriate agencies. I was responsible for the city of Annapolis. We were informed that missiles were likely programed for the Baltimore–Washington–Annapolis triangle and, should an event occur, we would not survive.

It was only later, in 2000, after the third part of the secret of Fatima was revealed, that one could imagine how that triangle would resemble the *"big city, half in ruins"* that the pope was predicted to visit on his way to *"the big Cross [where] he was killed by a group of soldiers...and in the same way there died the other Bishops, Priests, and Religious."*

On October 22nd – due to the missile crisis developing in Cuba – President John Kennedy called for a naval quarantine [blockade] of the island. For the first time in history the Defense Readiness Condition [DEFCON] was raised from 4 to 3, thus coinciding with a chain of events that came within a hair's width of starting another *World War*. Realizing the gravity of the situation, associates working in Washington urged my family to join them at a mountain retreat in West Virginia for a long weekend. We declined owing to my commitment for Annapolis.

Earlier, on October 1st, four Soviet, F-class, diesel submarines slipped from their berths at a secret Arctic base on Kola Bay, a 35 mile Fjord of the Barents Sea near Murmansk. Captains Aleksei Dubivko, Valentin Savitsky, Nikolai Shumkov and Rurik Ketov were to maintain strict radio silence. Hence, they made a secret pact that, if either submarine was attacked by the U.S., they would all retaliate by firing their torpedoes.

Only Vasili Arkhipov, the Commander of the submarine fleet, aboard B-59, and the four captains knew that each submarine was equipped with a nuclear-tipped torpedo and authorization had been given for their immediate use if and when required! Each torpedo was capable of vaporizing everything within a ten mile radius, any of which would damage or sink a dozen U.S. warships. This would have called for retaliation by means of global thermonuclear war. Then, on the 26th, the DEFCON rating changed from 3 to 2. If it were to go to DEFCON 1, it would mean we were actually engaged in a total world war.

By the weekend of October 27-28, our ships commenced dropping depth charges, forcing the second of four submarines to surface. There being no need for radio silence now, the captains of all four submarines conferred and agreed.

They immediately loaded their nuclear-tipped torpedoes into the firing tubes and awaited Commander Arkhipov's order to give the final permission to fire. This was the proper order of command. Fortunately, Arkhipov overrode all four of the captains' decisions and decided against the use of the torpedoes. He determined it would serve no purpose other than to start World War III.

Ironically, shortly after their return to Russia, Rurik Ketov, the captain of submarine B-4 arrogantly declared: "If we captains had completed our mission there might be nuclear missile boats in Cuba today and we would have been honored as heroes. Instead, because all four of us chose not to fire our torpedoes and avoid starting a nuclear war we were later persecuted by our government as failures and traitors." Despite Ketov's comments, Commander Arkhipov was promoted to the rank of vice admiral and, in 2002, he was recognized at a seminar in Cuba as the man who "saved the world from nuclear annihilation."

In hopes of preventing a future catastrophic war a *hot line* was installed in the White House in August, 1963. Eventually, it would provide almost instant communications between Washington and Moscow.

Twenty years after Our Lady first appeared in Spain, she appeared in Yugoslavia – a country behind the iron curtain – and proclaimed: *"God has chosen each one of you to use you in a great plan for the salvation of mankind. I wish to be with you to reconcile the world through prayer, fasting, faith, conversion and peace."* It was June 24, 1981.

Two years later, in the fall of 1983, another event would occur. It was under President Ronald Reagan's watch. Operation *Able Archer* was a series of simulated, nuclear, first strikes against Russia. Amid the tension of repeated war games against the Soviet Union several of the Soviet leaders became convinced we were using the games as a cover for the real thing. Their military personnel were placed on full alert!

Shortly after midnight on September 26, 1983, Soviet Air Defense Forces' Lt. Col. Stanislaus Petrov settled into the commander's chair in a secret bunker just outside Moscow. Suddenly, the display on the computer screen showed that one intercontinental ballistic missile had been launched and was heading toward the Soviet Union; then another, and another, until there were five in total! His duty was to immediately notify his superior who would advise the Soviet Premier to retaliate.

Yet, Petrov reasoned: "It didn't make sense! Surely the U.S. would have fired all their missiles at once, not just five." Therefore, he determined it to be a false alarm.

Fifteen minutes later, when radar outposts confirmed there were no incoming missiles, he knew he had made the right decision! It was subsequently determined that the false blips were caused by a rare alignment of sunlight reflecting on the high-altitude clouds in conjunction with the satellites' improper orbits. Ironically, because Petrov did not heed his superiors and *go by the book*, he was reassigned to a less sensitive post and took early retirement.

Yet it was Petrov's cool thinking saved the world from a war too horrible to imagine. In 2004, Lt. Col. Petrov received a World Citizen Award. He was honored by the United Nations in 2006; then, in 2013, he was awarded the Dresden Peace Prize in Germany,

On December 26, 1957, in an interview with Father Augustin Fuentes, Lúcia said: "Father, the most holy Virgin is very sad because no one has paid any attention to her message, neither the good nor the bad. The good continue on their way, but without giving any importance to her message. Tell them, Father, that many times, the most holy Virgin told my cousins, Francisco and Jacinta, as well as myself, that *'Many nations will disappear from the face of the Earth.'"*

She added: "Russia will be the instrument of chastisement chosen by Heaven to punish the whole world if we do not beforehand obtain the conversion of that poor nation!" As we will see in the ensuing chapters, Our Lady tells us we *"should be prepared for the worst"*; we *"should not be afraid to die tomorrow."*

How we respond to Our Lady's pleas is a choice that will be put to each one of us. She is doing all she can for our conversion during this grace filled period. If we are true believers, we will accept death peaceably, knowing we will one day be in Heaven with God. We can be of help to others by our prayers and sacrifices.

The Bible refers to a future time when *"...a terrible calamity will come upon the Earth...There will be signs in the sun, the moon, and the stars, and on Earth nations will be in dismay, perplexed by the roaring of the sea and the waves. People will die of fright in anticipation of what is coming upon the world, for the powers of the heavens will be shaken...But, when these signs begin to happen, stand erect and raise your head because your redemption is at hand"* (Lk 21:23, 25-26, 28).

On March 17, 1990, Silvio Cardinal Oddi alluded to "dark times for the Church; grave confusions and troubling apostasies within Catholicism itself." As we shall see, Pope John Paul II, cognizant of this, closely followed the events in Medjugorje.

As pope, he was unable to go to Medjugorje but he still remained open to Our Lady's messages. In fact, he firmly believed in them, certain her appearance there was the answer to his prayers. Shortly before the events began he prayed for the intercession of Our Lady, pleading for her to appear in a Communist country where her voice could be heard: a place where the freedom of religion was actively prohibited.

In Medjugorje, on May 2, 2009, Our Lady strongly advised: *"Look around you, and look at the signs of the times!"* The need to do this will become quite apparent in the ensuing chapters.

Epilogue, Revealed Secrets

Joseph Cardinal Ratzinger was elected pope on April 19, 2005. It is quite likely he chose the name, Benedict XVI, owing to his great respect for Our Lady, and her immediate response at the height of World War I to the earnest pleas of his predecessor, Benedict XV.

On May 13, 2010, in Fatima, Pope Benedict XVI stressed: "We would be mistaken to think that Fátima's prophetic mission is complete. Here there takes on new life the plan of God:

"Mankind has succeeded in unleashing a cycle of death and terror, but failed in bringing it to an end. In sacred Scripture we often find that God seeks righteous men and women in order to save the city of man, and He does the same here, in Fatima, when Our Lady asks: *'Do you want to offer yourselves to God, to endure all the sufferings which He will send you, in an act of reparation for the sins by which He is offended and of supplication for the conversion of sinners?'*

"At a time when the human family was ready to sacrifice all that was most sacred on the altar of the petty and selfish interests of nations, races, ideologies, groups and individuals, our Blessed Mother came from Heaven offering to implant in the hearts of all those who trust in her the Love of God burning in her own heart. May the seven years [three months from now] which separate us from the centenary of the apparitions hasten the fulfillment of the prophecy of the triumph of the Immaculate Heart of Mary, to the glory of the Most Holy Trinity."

At Castel Gandolfo, Italy on Assumption Sunday, August 15, 2010, before the Marian prayer at noon, Benedict XVI highlighted Mary's historic role in the Church, inviting continued trust in the Mother of God and prayer for her aid on Earth. Pope Benedict XVI, referring to the words of one of his predecessors [Benedict XV], reminded us again: "Although Mary was assumed into Heaven, she 'has not abandoned her mission of intercession and salvation' on Earth.'" [1]

---

[1] My Heart Will Triumph by Dragicevic-Soldo, Mirjana, Cocoa, Fl, CatholicShop Publishing, 2016

CHAPTER 18

Future Events

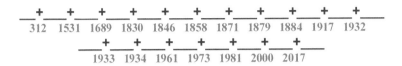

+	+	+	+	+	+	+	+	+	+	+
312	1531	1689	1830	1846	1858	1871	1879	1884	1917	1932

"You cannot imagine what is going to happen, nor what the Eternal Father will send to the Earth. That is why you must be converted! Renounce everything...I carry all these gifts to my Divine Son in order to obtain an alleviation of His justice against the sins of humanity."

O ur future depends to a great extent upon what we have learned from our history. How we respond to these heavenly interventions could well determine the outcome in our lifetime. Recall the story of our origins: *"In the beginning, God created man, male and female he made them, in his own image and likeness..."* (Gn 1:26-28), and our ancestors fall from grace (Gn 3:1-13). Because mankind broke that covenant, God sent man into a harsh world: *"Cursed be the ground because of you!...Thorns and thistles shall it bring forth to you...By the sweat of your face shall you get bread to eat, until you return to the ground from which you were taken; for you are dirt, and to dirt you shall return"* (Gn 3:17-19). However, God promised He would send a Redeemer, the Messiah.

Thousands of years later His only begotten Son, Jesus the Christ, was born of a woman, a virgin. St. John, the Evangelist, tells us in his gospel: *"In the beginning was the Word, and the Word was with God, and the Word was God...And the Word became flesh and made his dwelling among us"* (Jn 1:1,14). Christ would live, preach, suffer and die for us.

As this *"Word"* was dying on the cross He entrusted His mother to John, the beloved disciple: *"Woman, behold, your son"* (Jn 19:26); then, He told John: *"Behold, your mother"* (Jn 19:27). In so doing, He gave her to us.

Forty-three days later, just before ascending into Heaven, Christ founded His Church through which mankind could be saved: *"And so I say to you, you are Peter [Petros], and upon this rock [Petra], I will build my Church, and the gates of the netherworld shall not prevail against it. I will give you the keys to the kingdom of Heaven"* (Mt 16:18-19). St. John further clarified the Church's authority: *"Whose sins you forgive are forgiven them, and whose sins you retain are retained"* (Jn 20:23).

She reaffirmed this in 1531 when she appeared to Juan Diego in Guadalupe, in the Americas, reassuring us as a mother is wont to do: *"Am I not here with you who am your Mother? Are you not under my shadow and protection?"*

Still, over the course of two millennia, many continued to reject Christ. Month by month we notice the oftimes nonsensical media condoning evil by proclaiming its amoral values throughout the world. Gossip and greed have become an everyday proclamation of this so-called media, often destroying reputations, regardless of whether earned or not.

As the media gradually replaces the Bible, proclaiming itself as the conscience of the world, we note well how we are transforming ourselves into a world that sets its own rules. Yet, this goes firmly against the *Commandments* and *Statutes* that God gave us in order to survive and be fruitful. The Creator has no priority here!

Therefore, we should not be surprised when Our Lady reminds us: *"...wars are a punishment for sin"* and advises us that we may well be chastised once again in order to bring us back to our senses. Whether it is a direct act of God, causing a coronal mass ejection (CME) – or *terrorists,* unleashing an electromagnetic pulse (EMP) hundreds of miles above the Earth – the result will be equally devastating.

In 1830, Mary appeared in Paris, France, offering herself for us, thus marking the beginning of her final mission, for the salvation of the world. She would later term it, for "the salvation of the human race!" Eighty-seven years later, after enduring almost three years of horrors from *World War I* – the war which Pope Benedict XV termed: "the suicide of civilized Europe" – he pleaded for the intercession of the Mother of God.

During his public prayer on May 5, 1917, he invited the world to join him in a novena [nine days of prayers] beseeching Mary for peace and a quick end to the war. On the ninth day of the novena, in a direct response to those pleas, Our Lady appeared to three children in Fatima, Portugal. It was May 13, 1917.

On July 13th, two months after her first appearance in Fatima and immediately after showing the children that horrific vision of Hell, Mary told them: *"The war is going to end: but if people do not cease offending God, a worse one will break out during the Pontificate of Pius XI. When you see a night illumined by an unknown light, know that this is the great sign given you by God that he is about to punish the world for its crimes, by means of war, famine, and persecutions of the Church and of the Holy Father...The good will be martyred; the Holy Father will have much to suffer; various nations will be annihilated..."*

We didn't do as she asked and on January 25-26, 1938, that *"unknown light"* was seen throughout the world. The war she warned would occur *"...if people do not cease offending God"* actually began on March 12, 1938 when German troops entered Austria. Sr. Lúcia confirmed this later: "The annexation of Austria gave occasion for the war." Pope Pius XI died the following year on February 10, 1939, thus the prophecy Our Lady foretold concerning him was fulfilled during his reign. Then, Germany took the Czech region of Sudetenland and invaded Poland on September 1, 1939. The United States entered the war on December 7, 1941, the eve of the Feast of the Immaculate Conception; it ended on August 14, 1945, the eve of the Feast of the Assumption.

Coincidences? Perhaps; perhaps not! *World War II* ended with Japan's formal surrender on August 15, 1945, V-J Day. It was first announced here on August 14, 1945 by President Harry Truman; it was the headline in *The Baltimore Sun* newspaper. August 14th was my thirteenth birthday and, with my father's permission, I shot holes in the paper with my rifle. Unfortunately, children younger than I were forced to fight in the front lines on the battlefields of Europe!

We celebrate that victory in movies and books; yet, we don't seem to be able to comprehend what actually caused the war. If, as Our Lady said, *"wars are a punishment for sin,"* what did we do between 1918 and 1938 to cause *World War II* and the eventual global spreading of Communism [atheistic Socialism]? Had we learned from history and heeded her requests that war and the spread of Communism need not have happened. Archbishop Fulton J. Sheen, who had witnessed so much heartache, often reminded us, "...until we return to God, we will continue to shed the blood of our youth on the battlefields of the world!"

In 1934, Christ told St. Faustina to make an entry in her diary. Write this: *"Before I come as the Just Judge, I am coming first as the King of Mercy."*

"Before the day of justice arrives, there will be given to people a sign in the heavens of this sort: All light in the heavens will be extinguished, and there will be great darkness over the whole Earth. Then the sign of the cross will be seen in the sky and from the openings, where the hands and the feet of the Savior were nailed, will come forth great lights which will light up the Earth for a period of time" (Diary, 42).

The lights from the wounds of Christ described by St. Faustina may well be similar to the ones predicted to appear at both Garabandal and Medjugorje. When they occur, it would necessarily be the cause for the conversion of the Jews, who *"will look on Him whom they have pierced"* (Jn 19:37); the Muslim, who do not believe Christ actually died on the cross; the unbeliever who either does not know Christ, or else denies Him. This could usher in the *"...era of peace"* that Our Lady promised at Fátima. What a gift of love this would be for the whole world.

Earlier, whether from ignorance or refusal, King Louis XIV didn't place the requested sign on his standards and shields. This resulted in grave problems for his great, great, grandson, Louis XVI. So, it should come as no surprise that God would enable a similar event to help a confused world that has seemingly lost its way. St. John advises us: *"The hour is coming when everyone who kills you will think he is offering worship to God. They will do this because they have not known either the Father or me"* (Jn 16:2-3). God knows the condition in the world is beyond man's control; hence, it will require His direct intervention – a Divine Plan!

Within the last century the numerous appearances of Christ and Our Lady point to a Sign that all will see in the heavens. John Paul II stated quite frankly that he awaits the promised *sign* which would bring about a new era - if not in his lifetime, perhaps a later pope!

The Eternal City, a two hour documentary about the Vatican and the popes throughout history clearly states: "In the year since the assassination attempt there is growing evidence of a different kind of attack directed at the pope and his authority, not only from political adversaries in the secular world but - in a more sinister way - from a conspiracy within the highest echelons of the Church itself, which seeks to reshape the papacy for its own multinational agenda.

"John Paul II, like the faithful Old Testament watchman, Habakkuk, his eyes set firmly on the horizon, waits for the promised *Sign* which will usher in the end of our times, and for the second Pentecost which will bring about a spiritual renewal of a Godless world. He foresees the time is short and the struggle will be intense."

Is this the same *sign* noted in the Bible: *"I will pour out on the house of David and on the inhabitants of Jerusalem a spirit of grace and petition; and they will look on him whom they have thrust through, and they will mourn for him as one mourns for an only son, and they will grieve over him as one grieves over a first-born. On that day the mourning in Jerusalem shall be as great as the mourning of Hadadrimmon in the plain of Megiddo"* (Zec 12:10-11).

"And then the sign of the Son of Man will appear in Heaven, and all the tribes of the Earth will mourn, and they will see the Son of Man coming upon the clouds of Heaven with power and great glory. And he will send out his angels with a trumpet blast, and they will gather his elect from the four winds, from one end of the heavens to the other" (Mt 22:30-31).

In Garabandal, Our Lady said that there will still be some who will not believe even after the permanent Sign is left. Mary told Conchita that, "during this miracle, those who are ill among the onlookers will be cured and the unbelievers among them will be converted. This miracle will be the proof of the tender love of God and Our Lady for the world. And, after the miracle, God will permit a Sign to remain to remind us of it; that it will be visible to all those who are in the village and surrounding mountains; that the sick who are present will be cured and the incredulous will believe. It will be the greatest miracle that Jesus has performed for the world. There won't be the slightest doubt that it comes from God and that it is for the good of mankind. A Sign of the miracle, which will be possible to film or televise, will remain forever at the *Pines.*" Jesus told Conchita that this will occur in order *"...to convert the whole world...thus everyone will love Our Hearts."*

This would fulfill the request made in Fatima. Here, we do well to recall the prophetic words of Pope Paul VI who stated on June 30, 1972, "The smoke of Satan has entered the very heart of the Church!"

In Medjugorje on April 25, 1983, Our Lady said: *"Be converted! It will be too late when the Sign comes. Beforehand, several warnings will be given to the world. Have people become converted. I need your prayers and your penance."*

After the third secret is fulfilled and the *"Sign"* is seen by all, we will be *"either, for God, or against Him."* There will be no more straddling fences. She added, *"The only weapons that will remain will be the rosary and the Sign that the Eternal Father will leave."*

Jesus reminds us: *"I know your works; I know that you are neither cold nor hot. I wish you were either cold or hot. So, because you are lukewarm, neither hot nor cold, I will spit you out of my mouth"* (Rev 3:15-16). Finally, after the chastisement by fire that Our Lady predicted in Akita in 1965, and *"...various nations will be annihilated..."* as foretold in 1917 in Fátima, *"...an era of peace..."* will be ushered in.

In A.D. 30, John the Baptist, declared, *"I am the voice of one crying out in the desert, 'Make straight the way of the Lord'"* (Jn 1:23). On March 25, 1936, in a similar manner, Our Lady told Sr. Faustina: *"...I gave the Savior to the world, as for you, you have to speak to the world about His great mercy and prepare the world for the Second Coming of Him who will come, not as a merciful Savior, but as a just Judge. Oh, how terrible is that day"* (Diary 635).

Consider the changes that have occurred in our lifestyle since the 1960s and the effect it is having on our children. Respectful behavior in public has almost disappeared. Many of our youth sport tattoos and wear clothes with holes in them. Their torn garments don't fit while providing a *just off the boat* look. Many join gangs so they can appear tough and have a sense of belonging. Drugged with the temptations of the flesh they often react with anger and violence.

Many have no one to guide them and don't know which way to go. Parents often enable this behavior by their absence; others are often too busy working two jobs in order to make ends meet. And, too often, parents do not have the courage to correct them. These children have no idea what awaits them!

It is important to recall here that, on June 13, 1929, Our Lady called for the consecration of Russia to her Immaculate Heart, *"...promising to save it by this means. There are so many souls whom the Justice of God condemns for sin."* In a letter dated May 28, 1936, Sr. Lúcia reveals an intimate conversation she had with Our Lord. She wished to know if the consecration had to be performed specifically by the Holy Father. Christ told her, *"The Holy Father, pray much for the Holy Father. He will do it, but it will be late. Nevertheless, the Immaculate Heart of Mary will save Russia. It has been entrusted to her."*

In 1982, in a direct response to her request, Pope John Paul II called for the consecration of Russia to her Immaculate Heart. He then sought Sr. Lúcia's understanding as to whether the consecration fully satisfied Heaven's requests. She advised him that it did not as it was not done in union with all the bishops in the world and Our Lady specifically requested this.

Then, on March 24, 1984, John Paul II arranged another consecration, this time in union with all the bishops throughout the world. On August 29, 1989, owing to some confusion about the Consecration, Sr. Lúcia wrote that it was accepted by Heaven. Yet, we would do well to recall the words Christ told Sr. Lúcia in Rianjo, Spain in August, 1931: *"They have not chosen to heed My request...Like the King [Louis XVI] of France, they will regret it, but it will be late. Russia will already have spread her errors throughout the world, provoking wars and persecutions against the Church; the Holy Father will have much to suffer."*

Earlier, I noted Christ requested St. Margaret Mary to ask four special favors from King Louis XIV, of France. We know for a certainty that he did not fulfill them. Finally, 106 years later, his great-great-great grandson, [King] Louis XVI, complied with the first request: the consecration to the Sacred Heart of Jesus. He promised to fulfill the other requests at his next opportunity but, unfortunately, he was locked in the temple prison and could not fulfill them. For Divine Providence it *"...was now late"* and on July 21st, 1793, he was led to the infamous guillotine.

His wife, Marie-Antoinette, joined him shortly thereafter. Ironically, the phrase the crowd wrongly attributed to her: "Qu'ils mangent de la brioche" [let them eat cake] refers to a type of bread. It was later attributed to Jean Rousseau, a political philosopher who first stated it in a letter written 18 years before Marie-Antoinette was born.

Yet, there is great hope for the future! The problem is getting there with a minimum of bruises. Today, a majority of people think that God could never permit us to suffer, thinking, 'He's too nice; after all, He is love, isn't He?' Do you remember the equation about love vs. just punishment? Certainly the love portion of the equation is quite true; however, I would suggest they, along with modern theologians, look carefully at the punishment meted out to Amelia, Lúcia's eighteen year old friend from Fátima. When Lúcia asked Our Lady if she was in Heaven, Mary responded: *"She will be in Purgatory until the end of the world."* Many people have difficulty accepting that depth of punishment given to Amelia.

In Medjugorje, Mary doesn't hesitate to remind us how difficult Purgatory is, telling Marija: *"One hour in Purgatory is more painful than the longest, hardest life on Earth."* Yet, Amelia had none of the temptations so prevalent in our big cities of today. There were no movies, radio or television, not even a telephone. Some questioned Lúcia, stating it seemed so cruel! Now, lest someone think Amelia must have been a very sinful teenager to deserve this extreme punishment, Lúcia reminds us: "One can go to Hell for all eternity just for missing Mass on Sunday." Have we forgotten three of the *Ten Commandments: "Remember to keep holy the Sabbath day; Thou shall not commit adultery; Thou shall no [murder] kill"* (Ex 20:13)? Additionally, anyone who procures or participates in an abortion will incur an automatic excommunication from the Church! *"Formal cooperation in an abortion constitutes a grave offense. The Church attaches the canonical penalty of excommunication to this crime against human life"* (CCC n. 2272).

This condemnation would necessarily apply to anyone who assists in an abortion in any manner such as driving the car to the abortuary, making the appointment, etc. Certainly, the gravity of the offense would depend upon the circumstances and the individual's awareness of the Church's teaching on this matter. Infractions of any of these *Commandments* are tantamount to committing a mortal sin which causes death to the soul and, if not forgiven, may condemn one's soul to Hell for all eternity. And, let's be perfectly clear here: the Church teaches it is just as serious a sin to be a participant in an act of fornication as it is to participate in an adulterous or homosexual one. Are those who endorse or participate in some of these abhorrent behaviors unlike a new brand of Adam and Eve, choosing to taste the forbidden fruit again? If one's conscience differs from Church doctrine, the burden falls upon that person to reform their conscience.

Each of us has a serious obligation to be certain our conscience is honestly enlightened and correctly formed. Obviously, this means that any moral decision one makes must be in conformity with the teaching of the Magisterium of the Church: ergo, one cannot say that because one disagrees in conscience with the Church, one is excused from doing what the Church teaches and incurs no penalty! Have we not yet learned from history what happens to societies when they digress into moral turpitude? Do we think that the destruction of the ancient cities of Sodom and Gomorrah were just happen-chance? We must be truthful here: if our most brilliant minds cannot even determine when life begins, then, surely, we are all in serious trouble.

God established a community of the people of God to prepare mankind for the coming of the Messiah. His *Commandments* and *Statutes* give us the beginning of the Divine [Eternal] Law, which is the source of all laws. *Divine law* consists of the Old Covenant in the *Old Testament*, given to Moses on Mount Sinai, containing the *Ten Commandments* and 613 *Statutes*.

The former contains ten moral precepts: the first three, called Ceremonial, are for the worship of God; the remaining seven, known as Juridical, determine how we are to behave with our neighbors. Divine Law is also made up of the New Covenant of the New Testament, stated so eloquently in the Beatitudes given by Christ during the Sermon on the Mount.

A law is an instrument given by God or enacted by man to instruct and guide the people of a nation. These laws represent the values that a society chooses to embrace and display to the world and, inasmuch as we all have different ideas about life, they also prohibit harmful behavior with each other. The object of all laws must be for a right purpose and the circumstances must be according to human reason. Good laws must absolutely respect the *Rights* that are ordained by our Creator. Man's laws, such as our *Constitution* and *Bill of Rights,* merely guarantee those rights given to us by our Creator! We understand it by examining our nature which expresses the dignity of the person and determines the basis for our fundamental rights and duties.

There is no conflict between the law and freedom if the law is an ordinance of reason made for the common good by one who has the authority to do so and, then, is able to enact it. Therefore, in order to remain free from a tyrannical person or government, good laws are absolutely necessary. However, problems arise when governments enact laws that interfere and conflict with man, especially those laws that reject God's law outright. Inasmuch as man does not create nature, man must respect God's natural law; yet, when we forget that Heaven is the goal, we become mired in misunderstanding and difficulty.

"The Natural [Moral] Law is written and engraved in the soul of each and every man because it is human reason ordaining him to do good and forbidding him to sin..." (CCC n. 1778-1780). It is called natural because it consists of the laws of nature that are necessary to fulfill a human being because of one's nature.

It is present in the heart of each person and established by reason. It is universal in its precepts and its authority extends to all people. The natural moral law is significant because the first time we go against it, we know it immediately; we feel it deeply within us! Then, all manner of evil things occur: acts of murder, theft, fornication, adultery, homosexuality, alcoholism, drug abuse, etc.

Have we forgotten our basic moral values, opting instead only for love and the pleasure that ensues, which is only one side of the equation? Have we become so pampered that we imagine we have the right to choose to believe whatever we wish and that will be the truth, that it will be acceptable to our Creator?

Let us recall the prophet Isaiah's warning: *"Woe to those who call evil good, and good evil...For they have spurned the law of the Lord of Hosts...Therefore the wrath of the Lord blazes against his people, he raised his hand to strike them"* (Is 5:20; 24:25). In *Mere Christianity*, C. S. Lewis advised us: "There is nothing indulgent about the Moral Law. It is as hard as nails. It tells you to do the straight thing and it does not seem to care how painful, or dangerous, or difficult it is to do."

Then, of course, there are the laws of Nature, many of which govern gravity: "What goes up must come down; A body in rest tends to stay at rest, and a body in motion tends to stay in motion, unless the body is compelled to change its state."

However, Our Lady tells us that even this law may be mitigated. Do you remember the words that formed on the banner in Pont Main in 1871? Following that, a little over a century later in Medjugorje, she reminded us: *"You have forgotten that, through prayer and fasting, you can avert wars and suspend the laws of nature!"*

Oh, really? Yes! Do you not remember what Christ said, *"Amen, I say to you, if you have faith the size of a mustard seed, you will say to this mountain, 'Move from here to there, and it will move'"* (Mt 17:20). And, another time, *"Peter got out of the boat and began to walk on the water...he became frightened, and, beginning to sink, he cried out, 'Lord, save me!' Jesus said to him. 'O you of little faith, why did you doubt?'"* (Mt 14:29-31).

There are also specific laws in respect to marriage, a legal contract binding upon both the man and the woman for their lifetime. Since the beginning of time, all laws have defined marriage as a union between one man and one woman, blessed and honored by our Creator. Marriage is a sacrament, one of seven sacraments of the Church.

We learn much of our history from scripture: *"God created man in his image; in the divine image he created him; male and female he created them. God blessed them, saying, 'Be fertile and multiply, fill the Earth and subdue it'"* (Gn 1:27-28). Men and women, being profoundly different in their nature, have unique biological and emotional qualities.

Together, in harmony, the two provide the balanced family environment necessary for the healthy development of their offspring. The ensuing union is pleasing to Him only within the confines of His *Commandments* and *Statutes*; otherwise, it is a sin.

People marry because they wish to proclaim their love for each other by sharing that love as helpmates, assisting each other to reach their ultimate goal: Heaven! Yet, many have forgotten that the primary purpose of their physical union in marriage is to produce and raise children in a permanent and stable environment for the happiness and security of the children. The physical and psychological pleasure the parents receive is truly rewarding, but only secondary to the primary purpose of marriage. This uniting of a man and a woman as husband and wife also requires them to remain together, acting as helpmates to each other on their journey through life "...until death do us part."

Unfortunately, during an earlier period in history, Moses permitted divorce! However, Christ rebuked this, saying: *"Because of the hardness of your hearts Moses allowed you to divorce your wives, but from the beginning it was not so (Mt 19:8); Have you not read that from the beginning the Creator made them male and female...and the two will become one flesh? Therefore, what God has joined together, no human being must separate (Mt 19:4-6); Whoever divorces his wife and marries another commits adultery against her; and if she divorces her husband and marries another, she commits adultery"* (Mk 10:11).

The married woman receives the honored title. Mrs., a title of respect prefixed to her name. Unfortunately, the *feminist movement* opted for M's. that includes all females – young and old, single, married, or divorced – thereby demeaning a wife's respectful title. Marriages were traditionally performed in a formal setting, usually a church. Many marriages are now performed in public buildings as is commonly done in most Communist countries.

Here, we would do well to again heed those words of Our Lady, given to Jacinta in 1919: *"Many marriages are not good; they do not please Our Lord and are not of God...Most people go to Hell because of sins of the flesh."*

There is an adage: "Tell me who your friends are and I will tell you who you are!" Parents are well aware of the harm bad example does to their children. It is also contagious, yet many simply will not accept that what they do have any effect or influence on their children, or their neighbors. Was it not the moral corruption from within that eventually caused the collapse of most of the previous great societies? Are we not on the same path?

The Romans are an example of a *great society* that just couldn't seem to get enough gore; it had to be increased daily in order to keep the good citizens going back to the coliseum. In our times the trash and the outright anger prevalent in so many television shows and movies are quite acceptable now. In many cases what used to be termed immoral is now deemed worthwhile, even good!

This manner of thought has contaminated many of the most educated in our universities; it also reaches into the highest levels of government. One has only to glance at the news to see what the result of this type of thinking is doing to many today. Our Lady named abortion as one of the worst sins, along with immorality and pride. The greatest societal disease so prevalent in the world today is "freedom without responsibility!"

Today, as in the past, there are people who are unable to comprehend that the family is the basic building block of society. Ask any believer, whether Christian, Jew, or Muslim, what would happen to their societies without good, strong families. Although we often argue with each other, we know that adultery and other mortal [deadly] sins destroy the values a family requires in order to survive and flourish in a society.

Think about this a moment: At the present time, basic religious rights in the world are under attack by many governments. And, if traditional marriage falls, what will happen to the institution that declared it to be a sacrament? Would it not follow that the culture and civilizations these religions spawned will also be destroyed?

If we are unable to comprehend these things from history, then, we will continue on our merry way right over the edge toward the bottom of an abyss from which there is no return! We would do well to remember that this lifetime is only a *snap* of one's fingers compared to all eternity! *"Seventy is the sum of our years, or eighty if we are strong, and most of them are fruitless toil, for they pass quickly and we drift away"* (Ps 90:10). In 1961, Our Lady stated: *"The cup is already filling up and if we do not change a very great chastisement will come upon us"*; in 1965 she added: *"Now it is flowing over!"*

In January, 2011, the Illinois legislature passed a law enabling Civil Unions in that State. It became effective on June 1, 2011. The archbishop of Chicago, Francis Cardinal George, then stated: "I expect to die in bed, my successor will die in prison, and his successor will die a martyr in the public square. His successor will pick up the shards of a ruined society and slowly rebuild civilization as the Church has done so often in human history." Later, he wrote: "Neither Church, nor State, invented marriage, and neither can change its nature!" And, on October 21st, he added: "The world divorced from the God Who created and redeemed it inevitably comes to a bad end..."

In the latter 1960s, Our Lady told Conchita in Garabandal: *"After His Holiness Pope Paul VI, there will only be two more popes before the end of the present period, which is not the end of the world."* Conchita later clarified this, saying: "The Blessed Virgin told me so but I do not know what that means."

This being the case, that era ended with the death of Pope John Paul II in April, 2005. Yet, regardless of whether we are able to grasp this, we are now living in that new era! No one is certain what the future holds except for the fact that things will most markedly and surely be changed. By 1973, in Akita, Our Lady stated quite firmly: *"...fire will fall from the sky and will wipe out a great part of humanity; the good as well as the bad, sparing neither priest nor faithful."* Toward the end of her life, Sr. Lúcia said: "Tell them, Father, the punishment is imminent." Our Lady told her that for some, it's good; for others, bad! Mary told the children that, after the third secret occurs, *"I will never again appear on Earth [in this way]."*

In Medjugorje, Our Lady pleads: *"I pray to my Son not to punish the world. I beseech you, be converted. You cannot imagine what is going to happen nor what the Eternal Father will send to the Earth. That is why you must be converted!"* She further advises: *"Renounce everything. Sacrifice yourselves for those who need your help." "Express my gratitude to all those who pray and fast. I carry all these gifts to my Divine Son in order to obtain an alleviation of His justice against the sins of humanity. Persevere and help me that the world may be converted."* On August 15, 1985, she said to Mirjana: *"My angel, pray for unbelievers. People will tear their hair, brother will plead with brother, he will curse his past life lived without God. They will repent, but it will be too late! Now is the time for conversion. I have been exhorting you for the past four years. Pray for them. Invite everyone to pray the rosary."*

These are strong words, truly not for the faint-hearted! In fact, one of the requests of Our Lady to Mirjana is: *"Pray for unbelievers."* Now, Mirjana tells us: "God is at the end of His patience" and, later, "God cannot take it anymore!" Retribution is inevitable! Do we not understand the implications here? Having gone this far I don't think we will get out of our current predicament easily, with just a little rap on our fingers. Fortunately, we have her promise that *"...in the end my Immaculate Heart will triumph...and a period of peace will be granted to the world."* The difficulty is going from these present times to that promised, *"...end"* with as little pain as possible.

Presently, in Medjugorje, Mary reminds us that, after the ten predicted events have been accomplished, we will not see her again. This would appear to mean that it will not be necessary for her to appear again. Our Lady has pleaded with us over the past 185 years, but we paid little notice. The graces given at Fátima have been literally trampled into the dust. Meanwhile, we try to understand the future by looking at what was said in the past.

In an attempt to grasp the significance of these past events and how they may affect us in the future, recall what Our Lady told Lúcia in 1917: *"When you see a night illumined by an unknown light, know that this is the great sign given you by God that he is about to punish the world for its crimes..."* Sr. Lúcia said that this strange light occurred on January 25-26, 1938 and, although the media wrote it off with a scientific explanation as an aurora borealis, she stated: "...if they studied it further they would find it was not a true aurora!"

We know Mary told the children in Medjugorje that there would be ten events that will occur on the Earth during the lifetime of the seers; each one will be more severe than the previous one. Ivan, who knows what some consist of, stated that: "The tenth one is altogether bad!" Mirjana cries whenever she thinks about it and pleads with Mary: "Does it have to be that way?" Each time, Our Lady responds: *"Yes!"*

Here, too, one must not forget the warning about the need for *"Penance; Penance; Penance"* so eloquently stated by the angel in the third part of the secret of Fátima! This, of course, does not address what the chastisements will consist of for they are known only to the children. Perhaps history may be helpful in revealing how this could possibly occur. Earlier, I mentioned the effect the motion of the sun had on the people at Fátima. The sun was used as a direct warning to all the people of the Earth and may logically be included in future chastisements.

I offer you a potential scenario of how God could use the sun once more to inflict a punishment on mankind, literally bringing him to his knees! A little over a year after Our Lady's final appearance to Bernadette in Lourdes, Richard Carrington, a British astronomer of the Royal Astronomical Society, documented a rare occurrence in the heavens, eventually publishing a tome entitled *Observations of the Spots on the Sun.* He would later be recognized internationally as the British authority on sunspots, What he discovered and documented on the night of September 1, 1859, was a massive super solar flare lasting over five minutes.

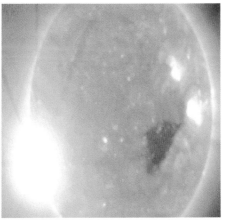

Super Solar Flare - NASA

Normally those types of ejections cause the ghostly lights later seen in the sky above the Earth, known as aurorae borealis, or northern lights. A truly massive one can heat up to over three million degrees Fahreheit and contain the power of about one billion hydrogen bombs. It pushes the ejection into space at a fantastic speed of about four million miles per hour and, if perchance it is aimed directly toward the Earth, it would arrive here sometime between eighteen to thirty-six hours later. We would see it as a giant halo of gas rushing toward us.

There have been five major Coronal Mass Ejections (CME) since that time. NASA and the ESA (European Space Agency) take them quite seriously and have already placed five satellites in orbit, giving NOAA the prime responsibility of monitoring the sun on a twenty-four hour basis. Inasmuch as the resulting solar winds could be potentially harmful to our planet, NOAA, in Boulder, Colorado would immediately pass that data to the appropriate agencies whenever harmful ones are found.

Solar flares result in the release of radiation across the spectrum, with the potential to damage human tissue by mutation of the DNA in the cells. Too much exposure will cause permanent damage to the cells, possibly leading to death.

The energetic particles from a super solar flare (CME) would be especially dangerous to an astronaut. If they are walking in space, they are told to immediately return to the space capsule and place everything bulky between them and the sun so as to minimize any exposure to the radiation.

CME & Earth's Magnetic Field

As of 2008, over 39 of these astronauts have developed some type of eye cataract within five years of their exposure. Airline crews and passengers are also at risk, although less so, depending on the strength of the storm and the distance the airplane is flying above the Earth's magnetic field. Satellites also are quite vulnerable and can be rendered permanently non-functional.

Fortunately for us, our entire solar system has a magnetic shield around it. The core of the Earth acts much like a bar magnet, producing its own magnetic shield that protects us from that radiation. The nearer one gets to the poles the weaker that shield is, due to the way it is formed in nature.

At the poles it is quite normal to see those ghostly greenish-blue lights on a nightly basis; however, when the storms are exceptionally strong, the lights may appear with a distinct reddish hue.

If a super-size solar storm comes directly toward us you would see a gaseous halo of light followed by a bright blood-red sky that would seem as though the entire heavens were on fire. The sight of it would be quite unnerving and, if the ejection is strong enough to penetrate our magnetic shield, it could destroy our technology by burning out many, if not all, of the nation's satellites and electrical grid transformers. The result could be the complete collapse of all our electrical and social systems.

If that happens there will be no television, no phones; you will not be able to refrigerate and cook your food nor heat and cool your home. And, on top of that, it could take up to ten years to completely repair. So, forget about your job; it would most likely be gone! An event such as this has the potential to threaten the extinction of billions of our population, perhaps causing the largest and most devastating disaster that could occur on the Earth.

Red Aurora Borealis

Lest you think this is fantasy you should be aware that the ejection in 1859 was so strong that, in burning through the Earth's magnetic field, it set many of the telegraph stations in North America on fire. Fortunately, there were no electrical grids to be concerned about then. However, on March 13, 1989, a severe geomagnetic storm struck the Earth, blacking out Québec's power grid, causing its second massive one in 11 months. That CME produced an aurora borealis seen as far south as Texas.

If you have ever visited small out of the way villages in Europe you would be familiar with how life functions without a steady source of electricity. It's not easy. Many areas in this country didn't have electricity until the turn of the twenty-first century. When we built our "total electric" country home in Southern Maryland in 1964, the local electric company had to install four standard-size poles and several blocks of wiring in order to reach the house.

Late one stormy evening, we watched as a lightning bolt hit the transformer on the pole nearest the house. During the ensuing explosion, the top of the sealed transformer flew off and the liquid carcinogenic contents spilled over quite an area. It required three massive vehicles, a comparable work crew, and many hours to repair that mess in a muddy field at three o'clock in the morning. Now, that was only one transformer; imagine all of them going at the same time, and who knows what else might need replacing!

So, our world is not as stable as you may think. This planet is hurtling through space at the rate of one-half million (574,585) miles per hour; at the same time it turns on a wobbly orbit at the rate of one thousand [1041.7] miles per hour. Our planet is the only one that contains life as we know it and it is well protected by the Creator of the entire universe; we just happened to come aboard at a certain time in its history!

So, it is not unreasonable to assume that God would use the sun, in a manner similar to that in Fátima, as a means of bringing us to our knees once again! Didn't the angel in the third part of the secret repeatedly call for: *"Penance; Penance; Penance?"* And, wasn't it Our Lady who delayed the angel from sending that fiery chastisement to the Earth? We must never forget: God does as He wills. He is the Creator, and we are His creatures, subject to His *Commandments* and *Statutes*!

During this same period of time, Our Lady appeared to other people in nations throughout the world. They are not included here inasmuch as they generally do not add anything new. Yet, there is one worth noting because of its Muslim heritage. A series of Marian apparitions began on April 2, 1968 in the Zeitoun district of Cairo, Egypt.
. They were similar to her appearance in Knock, Ireland, during which nothing was said; there was only silence. Mary was seen by numerous people, most of whom were Muslim, Islam being the predominant religion in Egypt. She was sometimes seen vaguely, although quite clearly, smiling, bowing and waving an olive branch. She was also seen praying and kneeling before the cross on the dome.

Many of the witnesses were absolutely spellbound and remained rooted to the ground as they prayed the rosary and sang Christian hymns. The Muslims began to chant from the Qur'an: "Mary, God has chosen Thee...He has chosen Thee above all women" (Qur'an: [003: 042] . [003:042]). Many of those who went home to rest for a while found her still there on their return; yet, others who had been watching intently and hopefully, saw nothing!

Our Lady of Zeitoun *(news photo)*

The Muslims began to chant from the Qur'an: "Mary, God has chosen Thee...He has chosen Thee above all women" (Qur'an: [003: 042] . [003:042]). Many of those who went home to rest for a while found her still there on their return; yet, others who had been watching intently and hopefully, saw nothing!

The apparitions, often lasting throughout the night, were photographed, televised and witnessed by millions. They were written about in many of the international secular and religious presses. They were seen by both religious and political dignitaries, including the president of Egypt, Abdul Nasser, a self-proclaimed Marxist. They were investigated thoroughly by government officials who were initially convinced it was a fake.

The workmen from the garage all gave similar testimonies, confirming their earlier statements when they were questioned about them. Fr. Costantin, pastor of the local church, agreed fully with what was said. Rev. Dr. Ibrahim Said, head of all Protestant Evangelical Ministries in Egypt at the time of the apparitions, affirmed that the apparitions were true as stated.

Catholic nuns from the Sacré-Coeur (Sacred Heart) order also witnessed the apparitions and sent a detailed report to the Vatican. Then, In the evening of Sunday, April 28, 1968, an envoy from the Vatican arrived and, after witnessing the apparitions, sent a report to Pope Paul VI. Cardinal Stephanos, the local Catholic Patriarch, did further investigations, submitting them to the pope in May, 1968.

He stated that the apparitions of Our Lady at Zeitoun were true beyond any doubt, and they were seen by many of his trustworthy Coptic Catholic children. The apparitions were accepted by the Roman Catholic Church; Pope Paul VI approved them as a valid visitation of the Mother of God.

Each of these appearances of Mary is a complete story in itself. She pleads with us to pray for sinners and for ourselves, to do penance and make sacrifices for the conversion of sinners. Changing our ways if we are to survive poses a real problem for some; yet, all her prophesies and warnings have come true in the past. Are we so foolish as to think they will not occur in the future?

Our Lady has warned us so many times – for almost two centuries now – that we must change, or else; we must be converted, or else; we must be full of love and kindness for our neighbor, not just on Sunday, or else; she reminds us that, first of all, we must love God with all our heart, our mind and our strength, or else! Perhaps this is why she cries during so many of her appearances, so few actually listen to her.

The Church teaches that all new revelation ended with the death of the apostles. One does not have to believe in the apparitions of Our Lady: "...it is not required for salvation." However, our belief, or lack of it, has no effect upon the certainty of their occurring, nor upon the things that she tells us during her recent appearances. In any event, Our Lady teaches nothing new; she simply gives us more detail, a clearer understanding of the future and how we may mitigate some of them.

The so-called unapproved messages are similar to the approved ones, except that they contain additional information with much more certainty and finality. The fact that the events noted in Garabandal and Medjugorje have not yet been approved does not mean we shouldn't do what Mary asks, as long as they do not contradict the Church's teachings. We must remember that the apparitions of Our Lady at Fátima were not approved until thirteen years after 70,000 people – with many skeptics among them – witnessed the only miracle in history that was foretold to occur at a specific time.

Conchita said that Mary told her the warning and the miracle are being sent in order to help us to avoid the chastisement. Yet, in her letter of August 17, 1971, Conchita mentioned that, at this time, the chastisement is practically inevitable, stating quite clearly: "However, it will not be possible to avoid the Chastisement because we have now lost even the sense of sin. We have now reached such an extreme that God cannot now avoid sending the Chastisement. We need it for our own good. Those who survive the Chastisement will change very much and, then, we will live for God until the end of time, which will also arrive."

In an attempt to describe what the warning will consist of, Conchita stated that the warning will be something like *"two planets that almost collide, but not quite!"* There has also been a fair amount of speculation concerning the permanent Sign that will remain at *The Pines* after the Miracle occurs. Conchita said that it may be likened to a pillar, or a post, which you will be able to see and photograph; however, if you attempt to touch it, it will seem to not be there. It will astound the scientific world who will be hard pressed to explain it.

There is great concern now regarding the apostasy sweeping throughout the Church, and the world in general. One has only to read the newspapers or watch the news on television to see how religion is held in such great disdain. Is it possible that the death of the *"...bishop, dressed in white...Other bishops, priests, men and women religious"* refer to the loss of the voice of the authority of the Pope, and the Church, insofar as the world is concerned?

Many think the public disclosure of the third secret of Fátima brings to an end a period of history marked by tragic lust for power and evil; however, I assure you, it did not! The requests of Our Lady for penance, prayer and sacrifices are more urgent now if we are to avert some of the consequences that are predicted to occur! On May 13, 1981, as Pope John Paul II lay in a hospital bed recovering from wounds inflicted by an assassin, he emphasized: *"Fatima is more important now then in 1917."*

On May 5, 1917, Pope Benedict XV called for a public novena [nine days of prayer] pleading for Our Lady's intersection to bring an end to the devastation of World War I. In response to his plea, and the many prayers offered by the people, she appeared to three small children in Fatima, Portugal. The date was May 13, 1917.

Similarly, when Pope John Paul II heard that Mary appeared in a small village in a Communist country in 1981, he believed Medjugorje was the answer to his prayer.

In July, 1987, Mirjana was invited to visit Rome. During the morning general assembly she was blessed by John Paul II. Later that evening, when she returned to her residence, she received a personal invitation for a private audience with the Pope on July 23, 1987.

Early the next morning Mirjana arrived at Castel Gandolfo. There, in a private conversation in the garden, John Paul II told her: *"I know all about Medjugorje!"* During a relaxed conversation he asked what it was like when Our Lady appeared. Then, he told her: *"Take good care of Medjugorje. Medjugorje is the hope of the entire world."* [1]

The time frame mandates these events must occur during the lifetime of either seer. Conchita was only 12 years of age when Our Lady first appeared to her, and is 67 years old now. She stated that all the children in Garabandal would be adults by that time the warning occurs. Conchita is permitted to announce the date of the Miracle eight days prior to its occurrence.

Mirjana was 15 years of age when Mary first appeared to her. In the ensuing years she was advised by Our Lady that the situation in the world was beyond man's ability to control; hence, the need for God's direct intervention into the affairs of mankind. Mirjana is 53 years of age now and, although she has recently stated that should she die prior to the fulfillment of the events, the secrets can be read by Fr. Petar. She noted they are written down on a piece of parchment to remind her, or in case of her death, they can be read by Fr. Petar.

Our Lady is attempting to reach many people throughout the world, especially through those who visit her shrines, requesting that they change their lives through conversion, fasting and prayer. Our concern should be to truly heed the importance of her messages. The great number and length of her latest appearances reinforce the urgency of the times in which we are living.

Will we change our lives and heed that which our heavenly mother advises us to do in order to bring about the fulfillment of her promise: *"In the end, my Immaculate Heart will triumph...a period of peace will be granted to the world!"*

On May 13, 2000, during the Beatification of Francisco and Jacinta in Fatima, John Paul II further reminded his audience of Francisco's comment: "We were burning in that Light which is God and we were not consumed. What is God like? It is impossible to say. In fact, we will never be able to tell people. God: a Light that burns without consuming.

"Moses had such an experience when he saw God in the burning bush. In her motherly concern, the Blessed Virgin came here to Fatima to ask men and women to '...*not offend the Lord our God anymore, because He is already too much offended.*' It is a mother's sorrow that compels her to speak, for the destiny of her children is at stake."

Additional information concerning the messages necessitated the addition of another chapter. Entitled, *The Decisive Battle*, it contains notes Sr. Lúcia sent long after the miracle occurred in Fatima on October 13, 1917. The chapter also contains the latest information about the secrets that are finally explained in some detail. It is a compilation of specific points gleaned from the various books and more specifically, interviews with the visionaries.

Epilogue, Future Events

Fr. Jozo Zovko was the pastor in Medjugorje when the apparitions began. He had a vision of Our Lady just before Mass on August 17, 1981. On July 20, 1992, in the midst of the Bosnian war, Fr. Jozo went to the Vatican where he met with John Paul II who reportedly told him: *"I am with you. Protect Medjugorje. Protect Our Lady's messages!"* [1]

On August 24, 2002, John Paul II sent a letter of thanks to Fr. Jozo, *"I grant from the heart a particular blessing to Father Jozo Zovko, OFM, and I invoke a new outpouring of graces and heavenly favors, and the continuous protection of the Blessed Virgin Mary."*

Fortunately, we are living in a time of great *"Gratia et Misericordia"* [grace and mercy]; a time allocated to comprehend and live all the messages Our Lady presents to the world. They serve to remind us of those things we seem to have forgotten - truths the Church continues to teach throughout the ages. Therefore, it is very important to focus on the overall mission of Our Lady instead of any one specific apparition, lest one loses sight of her original intent: ***"the salvation of the human race!"***

One is advised to read about the secrets in a wholesome manner. They are, after all, a part of the original messages which Our Lady did not hesitate to give to the seers. Here one should recall the vision of Hell Our Lady gave to the seers in Fatima. As difficult as they were for the children then, Mary did not hesitate to show what awaits those who reject God.

In her appearances during the past 187 years she has hinted about her overall mission at each site by leaving open the option of future appearances. Now, however, she tells us these will be her last apparitions on the Earth!

The messages given by Mary are a call for mankind to return to God. Mary implores us: *"Look around you, and look at the signs of the times!"* She emphasizes: *"I have come to call the world to conversion for the last time. I will never again appear on Earth [in this way]!"*

Mirjana said the Virgin has entrusted her with ten messages that she will reveal to the world in her lifetime, secrets that foretell the future of the world.

---

[1] - *My Heart Will Triumph* by Mirjana Dragicevic-Soldo, (Cocoa, FL 32922 : CatholicShop Publishing, 2016).

CHAPTER 19

The Decisive Battle

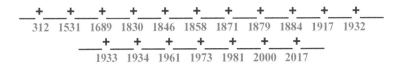

+	+	+	+	+	+	+	+	+	+	+
312	1531	1689	1830	1846	1858	1871	1879	1884	1917	1932

+	+	+	+	+	+	+
1933	1934	1961	1973	1981	2000	2017

"It was also allowed to make war against the holy ones and conquer them, and it was granted authority over every tribe, people, tongue and nation" (Rev 13:7).

O ur Lady is in the final stages of her mission on Earth, fulfilling God's plan for *the salvation of mankind.* She tells Mirjana Soldo: *" I have come to call the world to conversion for the last time. Later, I will not appear any more on this Earth [in this way]!"* *"What I have started in Fatima, I will complete in Medjugorje. My Heart will triumph!"* [1]

In late 1957, Sr. Lúcia dos Santos, noted: *"The Virgin was now engaged in a decisive battle with the devil. He saw that his time was growing short...At the end of this decisive battle people will be "either of God, or the evil one!"* [2]

Twenty-six years later, in 1983/4, Sr. Lúcia sent a letter to Carlo Cardinal Caffarra in response to several questions he had posed: *"Father, a time will come when the decisive battle between the kingdom of Christ and Satan will be over marriage and the family. And those who will work for the good of the family will experience persecution and tribulation."* [3]

In May, 2017, during one of his final talks to the Rome Life Forum, Cardinal Caffarra said: "Satan is hurling at God 'the ultimate and terrible challenge' to show he is capable of constructing an 'anti-creation' that mankind will be deceived into thinking is better than what God has created." He told the conference that his talk was "based on these words of Sr. Lúcia and therefore, on the conviction that what she said in those days, are being fulfilled in these days of ours." [4]

Three months later, in August, Raymond Cardinal Burke - referring to today's apocalyptic *"signs of the times"* - acknowledged his understanding of that letter from Sr. Lúcia. He said: "Thus, I really do believe that we are in this decisive battle. It is one of the reasons why – in my own little way – I am doing whatever I can to defend the truth about marriage and the family."

He also noted: "Our Lady used 'apostasy' in her Message of Fátima and this, in fact, is what is going on...The Church is being torn asunder right now by confusion and division." [5]

In an interview shortly before his death on September 6, 2017, Cardinal Caffarra said: "Only a blind man could deny there is great confusion, uncertainty and insecurity in the Church!"

The Eternal City, a documentary about the Vatican and the popes throughout history, notes: *"Pope John Paul II is waiting for the promised sign which will usher in the end of our times, and for the second Pentecost, which will bring about a spiritual renewal of a Godless world. He foresees the time is short and the struggle will be intense."* [6]

In his opening address in November, 2013 to the USCCB fall meeting in Baltimore, the Apostolic Nuncio, Archbishop Carlo Vigano, reminded the bishops of the prophetic warning of Karol Wojtyla in 1976, two years before he was elected pope: *"We are now standing in the face of the greatest historical confrontation humanity has ever experienced. I do not think that the wide circle of the American Society or the whole wide circle of the Christian Community realizes this fully.*

"We are now facing the final confrontation between the Church and the anti-church; between the Gospel and the anti-gospel; between Christ and the antichrist. The confrontation lies within the plans of divine Providence. It is, therefore, in God's Plan and it must be a trial which the Church must take up and face courageously." [7]

More than a century earlier, on October 13, 1884, Pope Leo XIII had a vision wherein he also heard God granting Satan a period of one century to carry out his plan to destroy the Church. It began about 1917 and will end when the first secret in Medjugorje has been accomplished.

On July 30, 1987, Our Lady said: *"Dear children, this is the reason for my presence among you for such a long time – to lead you on the path of Jesus. I want to save you and, through you, to save the whole world. Many people now live without faith; some don't even want to hear about Jesus, but they still want peace and satisfaction! Children, here is the reason why I need your prayer. **Prayer is the only way to save the human race!**"*

The mission entrusted to Mary began on the 18/19th of July, 1830, in Paris, France. She appeared to Sr. Catherine Labouré, a nun in the Sisters of Charity convent at 140 Rue du Bac, warning of the dangers to France. Within eight days the revolutionaries had completely overthrown the government!

Four months later, on November 27th, Mary appeared to Catherine again. Showing her an oval frame with gold lettering she told her, *"Have a Medal struck after this model. All who wear it will receive great graces; they should wear it around the neck. Graces will abound for persons who wear it with confidence."*

On the reverse side of the medal, Mary's heart is shown pierced by a sword, recalling the prophesy of Simeon: *"(and you yourself a sword will pierce) so that the thoughts of many hearts may be revealed"* (Lk 2:35). However, the position of the two hearts, adjacent to each other, was not clarified for another century.

Then, in 1936, Christ told Lúcia: *"I want My whole Church to acknowledge that consecration as a triumph of the Immaculate Heart of Mary so that, later on, it will put the devotion to the Immaculate Heart beside the devotion to My Sacred Heart."* Earlier, on June 13, 1917, Our Lady had appeared to Sr. Lúcia and told her: *"Jesus wishes to make use of you to make me known and loved. He wishes to establish in the world devotion to my Immaculate Heart."*

Mary has appeared in various places throughout Europe since 1830. The messages she presented were generally for penance and sacrifices, especially for the conversion of sinners. Then, on July 13, 1917, a noticeable change occurred. The children in Fatima were shown a horrific vision of Hell, and the threat of another war – one that would encompass the entire world. These were followed by her appearances in Spain in 1961, and Japan in 1973, both with the threat of great confusion in the Church and severe chastisements *"worse than the flood!"*

Our Lady's appearances culminated in 1981 when she began a final series of apparitions and messages to six children in Medjugorje, Yugoslavia. She is currently presenting each visionary with ten secrets; some similar; others quite different. The contents of the messages are generally unknown to each other; however, all agree the third secret refers to a permanent Sign from God as proof of His existence.

There will be three warnings given to the world. These warnings will be in the form of events on Earth. Our Lady has entrusted Mirjana with ten secrets that specifically pertain to the world. They will occur within her lifetime, and she will be a witness to them.

Mirjana said, "Our Lady told me that it is necessary to pray a great deal until the first secret is revealed. In addition to that it is necessary to make sacrifices as much as possible; to help others as much as it is within our abilities; to fast, especially now before the first secret." We are advised to begin our conversion now for the time remaining is short.

Ten days before each of the warnings, she will advise Fr. Petar Ljubicic – the priest she chose [and Mary confirmed] for this task – who will then pray and fast with Mirjana for seven days. Then, three days before each warning is to occur, Fr. Petar will announce to the world what, where, and when the event will take place.

After the first admonition, the others will follow in a rather short time. Thus, people will have some time for conversion. That time will be a period of great grace and conversion.

According to Mirjana, the events predicted by the Blessed Virgin are near. As a result Mirjana proclaims to the world: "Hurry, be converted; open your hearts to God." She hints at a timeline: "At this moment, according to Our Lady, we are living in a time of grace; after this will come the time of the secrets, and the time of her triumph. [8]

"Our Lady said that people should prepare themselves spiritually; they should be ready, and should not panic, and they should be reconciled in their souls. I mean they should be ready for it. They should be ready to die tomorrow. They should accept God so that they are not afraid since they have God in them and they can accept everything." [9]

On April 25, 1983, Our Lady said: *"Be converted! It will be too late when the Sign comes. Beforehand, several warnings will be given to the world. I need your prayers and your penance. I pray to my Son not to punish the world. I beseech you, be converted. You cannot imagine what is going to happen, nor what the Eternal Father will send to the Earth! That is why you must be converted!"*

She further advises: *"Renounce everything, sacrifice yourselves for those who need your help. Express my gratitude to all those who pray and fast. I carry all these gifts to my Divine Son in order to obtain an alleviation of His justice against the sins of humanity. Persevere and help me that the world may be converted."*

On August 15, 1985, Our Lady said to Mirjana: *"My angel, pray for unbelievers. People will tear their hair; brother will plead with brother; he will curse his past life lived without God. They will repent, but it will be too late! Now is the time for conversion."*

Mirjana said, "They have no idea what awaits them and that is why, as their Mother, she is in deep anguish for them! That is why the Blessed Virgin continues to encourage prayer and fasting: *'You have forgotten that with prayer and fasting you can ward off wars, suspend natural laws.'"*

Ivan Dragicevic stated: "One day when the time comes, when some things get revealed, you will understand why the apparitions are such a long time and why every day. Later on, we will understand some things; our eyes will be opened when we see physical changes that are going to happen in the world. This is so important to understand. The time in front of us is the time of great responsibility."

At times there is an ominous sadness in Our Lady's expression as she discloses the secrets to Mirjana, who finds them most difficult to accept; hence, the reason Mary often repeats them to her, especially the latter more serious ones. As we await the time of the unfolding of the secrets, let us put into practice all of Our Lady's messages.

A morbid curiosity about the secrets accomplishes little and can actually detract from the messages Our Lady presents to help us. Yet one must be made aware of the predicted events; they are a part of the messages. Perhaps some think it cruel to present them to children; however, one must recall that Jacinta, in Fatima, was only seven years old when Our Lady showed her the horrific vision of Hell.

Our Lady will stop appearing in Medjugorje when each visionary has received all ten secrets. What is known about the ten secrets is listed below. The information was obtained from several sources [Visionaries' interviews] and is presented as accurately as possible. The fourth through the seventh secrets contain no verifiable information.

The First Secret
The first occurrence will be something that people hear about, very far [away]. It will be something that everyone, everywhere, will immediately hear about. People would not race to the place where the first one occurs because surely no one wishes to watch disasters, distress, and misfortune. Mirjana said people in Medjugorje will know immediately that it is in connection with the secrets.

Mirjana indicated that the first of ten messages [secrets] she was given by the Virgin Mary involves not a global miracle, but a severe regional event. She said the first secret needs nothing to precede it and will abundantly speak for itself. There is little doubt that what she has been told is serious. She said: "The first two secrets are not all that severe and harsh. What I mean is, yes, they are severe, but not as much as the remaining ones."

On October 25, 1985, Mirjana was shown the first secret during a vision – like pictures projected on slides. She said, "'It shook me the most. Let me just say that it won't be good at all. It won't be pleasant. If the people saw the first secret as it was shown to me yesterday, all of them would most certainly be shaken enough to take a new and different look at themselves, and everything around them. I now know things that are not particularly pleasant. I believe that if everyone knew about these same things, each one of these people would be shocked to their senses and would view our world in a completely different light."

Mirjana offers some consolation when she tells us, "The first secret will break the power of Satan; and, that is why he is so aggressive now!" Then, with a knowing smile, she adds: "To the people of this world who pray, it will be a gift!" [10]

The Second Secret

Mirjana: "The first two secrets are not all that severe and harsh. What I mean is, yes, they are severe, but not as much as the remaining ones."

Fr. Petar Ljubicic: "Are [the secrets] perhaps of a notable, distinct character, or more of a spiritual nature?"

Mirjana: "It will be visible. It is necessary in order to shake up the world a little. It will make the world pause and think."

Fr. Petar: "A catastrophe?"

Mirjana: "No, it will not be anything as huge as that. **That will come later!** It will be something that will give the world something to think about seriously, allow it to see that she was indeed here, and to see and realize that there is God, that He exists." [11]

The Third Secret

This secret concerns a great Sign which Our Lady will leave at the place of her first appearance on Apparition Hill [Mt. Podbrdo]. The children know what the Sign will be and at least four of them know the date.

It will be a permanent, visible Sign. Our Lady said: *"Hasten your conversion. Do not wait for the Sign that has been announced. For unbelievers it will be too late to be converted. For you who believe, this is an opportunity to be converted and to deepen your faith."* [12]

After the visible Sign appears, those who are still alive will have little time for conversion. For that reason, the Blessed Virgin invites us to urgent conversion and reconciliation. The permanent Sign will lead to many healings and conversions before all the secrets are fulfilled.

After the third secret is fulfilled and the Sign is seen by all, we will be either for God, or against Him. There will be no more straddling fences. Our Lady added, *"The only weapons that will remain will be the rosary and the Sign that the Eternal Father will leave."*

The Fourth Secret
There are no verifiable comments.

The Fifth Secret
There are no verifiable comments.

The Sixth Secret
There are no verifiable comments.

The Seventh Secret
There are no verifiable comments.

The following comments are suggested for the eighth, ninth and tenth secrets. These three chastisements are speculative and they are, as yet, unfulfilled. They are severe chastisements, clearly described in the stories of three independent sources – Portugal, Spain, and Japan – two of whom are approved; one is under investigation by the Church. Interestingly, they all involve some type of heat, or fire!

The Eighth Secret
Ivan said the eighth secret is very difficult. Mirjana, noting the eighth secret is worse than the previous seven, prayed often with others for it to be mitigated. One day Our Lady told her she had succeeded in mitigating the secret; but, added: *"By the grace of God, it has been softened, but you must never ask such things again because God's will must be done!"* [13]

This chastisement – an approved apparition – was given to the visionaries in Fatima, Portugal, in 1917: "After the two parts which I have already explained, at the left of Our Lady and a little above, we saw an angel with a flaming sword in his left hand; flashing, it gave out flames that looked as though they would set the world on fire; but, they died out in contact with the splendor that Our Lady radiated towards him from her right hand. Pointing to the Earth with his right hand, the Angel then cried out in a loud voice: *'Penance; Penance; Penance!'*" [14]

The Ninth Secret

The ninth secret is serious. Ivan noted that, while the eighth secret is very difficult, "The ninth and tenth are altogether bad." Mirjana added: "Our Lady said people should prepare themselves spiritually, they should not panic. They should be ready for it. They should be ready to die tomorrow!" It concerns a chastisement for the sins of the world. Punishment is inevitable for we cannot expect the whole world to be converted. This punishment cannot be mitigated at all. [15]

This chastisement – an apparition currently under study by the Vatican – was given to the seers in Garabandal, Spain, in 1962. One of the visionaries, Mari Loli Mazon, died in Boston, Massachusetts on April 20, 2009. She purposely left a signed statement concerning two visions all four children had in 1962, on the 19th and the 23rd of June. The visions concerned the threatened punishment which she describes quite vividly.

"The Virgin explained to us how this great punishment would occur because there would come a moment in time in which the Church would seem to perish, as if it were finished, or disappearing. Finally, we saw a multitude of people enveloped in flames; desperately they threw themselves into the seas and lakes but, upon entering the water, far from putting out the flames, the water was boiling and seemed to help the flames burn more." [16]

The Tenth Secret

Ivan noted that, whereas the eighth secret is very difficult, "The ninth and tenth are altogether bad." Mirjana added: "Our Lady said people should prepare themselves spiritually, they should not panic. They should be ready for it. They should be ready to die tomorrow!"

This chastisement – an approved apparition – was given to Sr. Agnes, a visionary in Akita, Japan on October 13, 1973. Our Lady told Sr. Agnes, *"If men do not repent and better themselves, the Father will inflict a terrible punishment on all humanity. It will be a punishment greater than the deluge, such as no one has ever seen before."*

"Fire will fall from the sky and will wipe out a great part of humanity, the good as well as the bad, sparing neither priests nor faithful. The survivors will find themselves so desolate that they will envy the dead. The only consolation which will remain for you will be the rosary and the Sign left by my Son." [17]

All three chastisements have one thing in common: Fire! Will it be a type of fire that burns but does not consume? Again, it must be stressed that these three events are speculative at this time! In any event, no one would wish to endure the chastisements Mirjana indicates!

In Medjugorje, Mirjana noted: "Much of the world has strayed far from a life centered around God and family. The answers we need to redirect our life can be found by reading Scripture and living Our Lady's messages. I don't think anyone could argue, regardless of religious orientation, that today's world is[n't] in a state of crisis. All one has to do is read the newspaper or watch television to see how eroded the morals of our world have become. It is shocking to see and hear the examples of terrorism, inhumanity, cruelty, violence, abuse, drugs, war, crime, etc."

When God intervenes directly in the affairs of mankind we can expect some portions to be of a trying nature. Let us accept them with gratitude for God who dearly loves each one of us. One should find comfort in the fact that the visionaries have all chosen to marry and raise a family. Surely, this breathes hope in all who will be directly affected by those ten events.

This, then, is a message of love, and hope, for a world in crisis; a message that, with love and trust in God, peace will eventually be given to the world! We have the promise Our Lady gave to the children in Fatima in 1917: *"In the end my Immaculate Heart will triumph!"*

As we include Our Lady's messages into our daily lives, we await the unfolding of the *great plan*, including the revelation of the ten messages that are termed secrets. Each secret will be publicly announced to the world several days before the specific event occurs. This will also serve as proof that God exists, and that Our Lady definitely appeared there.

At a predetermined date in time, following the fulfillment of the tenth secret, we will enter into a new era, a time wherein we will see the Triumph of the Immaculate Heart of Mary acknowledged and proclaimed throughout the world, thereby fulfilling Our Lady's promise to the visionaries in Fatima, in 1917.

Meanwhile, we await the *Sign* John Paul II anticipated; a Sign similar to that seen by St. Paul, Constantine, and St. Faustina – predicted to be seen at many of the sites where Mary appeared over the last century. It will give us the assurance that God truly exists and afford us the courage we will surely need in order to get through those difficult times. Pope St. John Paul II stated quite often: "Be not afraid!" If, and when, those prophesized events occur, let us respond as Christ advised: *"But when these signs begin to happen, stand erect and raise your heads because your redemption is at hand"* (Lk 21:28). *"Come, you who are blessed of My Father, inherit the kingdom prepared for you from the foundation of the world"* (Mt 25:34).

"Then I saw a new Heaven and a new Earth. The former Heaven and the former Earth had passed away, and the sea was no more. I also saw the holy city, a new Jerusalem, coming down out of Heaven from God, prepared as a bride adorned for her husband.

"I heard a loud voice from the throne saying, 'Behold, God's dwelling is with the human race. He will dwell with them and they will be his people and God himself will always be with them [as their God]. He will wipe every tear from their eyes, and there will be no more death or mourning, wailing or pain, [for] the old order has passed away. The victor shall inherit these gifts, and I shall be his God, and he will be my son'" (Rev 21:1-4, 7).

Endnotes for Chapter 19, The Decisive Battle

1 - My Heart Will Triumph by Soldo, Mirjana, Cocoa, Fl, CatholicShop Publishing, 2016, 145
2 - Encountering Mary by S. Swartz, Princeton, University Press, First Avon books, 1992, 210
3 - The Wanderer, August 10, 2017, 1a
4 - National Catholic Register, September 6, 2017, Edw. Pentin, 219-220
5- The Wanderer, August 10, 2017, 7a
6 - The Eternal City, a 2-hour documentary about the Vatican and the popes, EWTN, Part II
7 - Apostolic Nuncio, Archbishop Vigano, opening address, USCCB, Baltimore, Nov 11, 2013
8 - My Heart Will Triumph by Soldo, Mirjana, Cocoa, Fl, CatholicShop Publishing, 2016, 327
9 - Mary, Queen of Peace by Faricy, R., SJ, & Rooney, L., SSND (Dublin, Veritas), 61-62
10 - The Visions of the Children by Connell, J.T., (New York, St. Martins Press), 61
11 - Mary, Queen of Peace by Faricy, R., SJ, & Rooney, L., SSND (Dublin, Veritas), 49-79
12 - Ibid., 42
13 - Ibid., 61
14 - http://w2.vatican.va/content/vatican/en,html
15 - Mary, Queen of Peace by Faricy, R., SJ, & Rooney, L., SSND (Dublin, Veritas), 61
16 - The Salvation of the World by Tall. Jr., G. B. (Murrells Inlet, San Michel's Alcove 29576), 130
17 – Ibid., 134

PART IV

Finale

I n his book, *Joyful Good News for Young & Old,* Bishop Victor Galeone quoted Venerable Archbishop Fulton J. Sheen: "God, Who made the sun, also made the moon. The moon does not take away from the brilliance of the sun. The moon would be only a burnt-out cinder floating in the immensity of space, were it not for the sun. All its light is reflected from the sun.

"The Blessed Mother reflects her Divine Son; without Him, she is nothing. With Him, she is the Mother of Men. On dark nights we are grateful for the moon; when we see it shining, we know there must be a sun. So in this dark night of the world when men turn their backs on Him Who is the Light of the World, we look to Mary to guide their feet while we await the sunrise." [1]

Who is this *"...woman, clothed with the sun, with the moon under her feet, and on her head a crown of twelve stars..."* (Rev. 12:1). She is the same woman who said, *"I am the handmaid of the Lord..."* (Lk 1:38) and, in 1858, told St. Bernadette: *"I am the Immaculate Conception!"*

Is Mary actually capable of comprehending pain, even shedding physical tears as a result? Is it possible for a heavenly being to display similar emotions one undergoes while living on Earth? Recall the statement St. John Paul II made at Fatima on May 13, 2000: "Little Jacinta personally felt and personally experienced Our Lady's anguish, offering herself heroically as a victim for sinners."

In his book, *Consoling the Heart of Jesus,* Fr. Michael Gaitley has masterfully treated the issue of how we human beings still cause sorrow to Christ and His Mother because of our sins and our lack of faith. [2]

Earlier, referring to Our Lady of La Salette in France, Pope Pius IX reminded us: "In this place, Mary, the loving Mother appeared manifesting her pain for the moral evil caused by humanity. Her tears help us to understand the seriousness of sin and the rejection of God..."

The outcome of these events will be determined to a great extent by how we respond to her requests. Will we accomplish the penance Our Lady has requested? And, the angel's: *"Penance; Penance; Penance!"*

We are living in a transitional time, a period between the end of one era and the beginning of another. Often accompanied with uncertainty and social instability, this time is also replete with grace and mercy.

Our Lady said this time of grace is given to comprehend and live the messages she presents to the world. To further that end she has entrusted Mirjana – a visionary in Medjugorje – with ten messages that she is to reveal to the world: secrets that foretell the "future of the world." In May, 2009, Mary advised: *"Look around you, and look at the signs of the times"* – to which Mirjana clarified, "Our Lady is preparing us for everything that is going to take place in the world." She hints at a timeline: "At this moment, according to Our Lady, we are living in a time of grace. After this will come the time of the secrets, and the time of her triumph."

Our Lady is doing all she can to help us during this time of grace; however, the time remaining is obviously limited. Therefore, she encourages our assistance, reminding us: *"Without your prayers, my dear children, I cannot help you to understand what my Lord has given me to give you."* Then, she told Mirjana, *"I have come to call the world to conversion for the last time. I will never again appear on Earth [in this way]!"*

As we merge Our Lady's words into our daily lives, we await the unfolding of the great plan that, additionally, contains the revelation of the ten messages, termed secrets. Each one will be publicly announced to the world several days before the specific event occurs. This will also serve as proof of Mary's appearances.

We wait in anticipation, then, for the triumph of the Immaculate Heart of Mary – a proclamation to be celebrated throughout the world – thereby fulfilling Our Lady's promise to the children in Fatima, Portugal, in 1917: *"In the end my Immaculate Heart will triumph!"*

---

[1] - *Joyful Good News for Young & Old* by Galeone, V.B., Bishop, (Houston, TX: Magnificat Institute Press, 2014), p. 74

[2] - *Consoling the Heart of Jesus* by Gaitley, M.E., (Stockbridge, MA: Marian Press, 2010).

CHAPTER 20

The Immaculate Conception

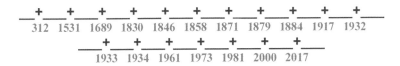

+	+	+	+	+	+	+	+	+	+	+
312	1531	1689	1830	1846	1858	1871	1879	1884	1917	1932

+	+	+	+	+	+	+
1933	1934	1961	1973	1981	2000	2017

"She lifted up her eyes to Heaven, joined her hands as though in prayer that were held out and open towards the ground, and said to me: Que soy era Immaculada Councepciou."'

Since the beginning of creation, when the stars and their satellites began to form, one planet would stand out from all the others. It became known as the blue planet. There, a little over 2,000 years ago, a woman was born, especially selected by God, distinct from all other woman and chosen to be the Immaculate Mother of the Redeemer *"...comparing her with Eve"* (CCC n. 968-143).

This woman responded affirmatively to the Annunciation by the Archangel Gabriel: *"Behold, I am the handmaid of the Lord. May it be done to me according to your word"* (Lk 1:38). She was destined to be honored above every other woman for she was endowed: *"Most blessed are you among women and blessed is the fruit of your womb"* (Lk 1:42). We often refer to her as the Blessed Virgin Mary, the *"woman clothed with the sun, with the moon under her feet, and on her head a crown of twelve stars"* (Rev 12:1). She occasionally appears to children – usually young girls – sometimes surrounded by stars. At other times, she appears wearing a crown of twelve stars that often sparkle like diamonds. In 1858, she appeared to Bernadette Soubirouis, in Lourdes, France, and stated so eloquently and humbly, *"I am the Immaculate Conception!"*

Bernadette had no way of knowing that four years earlier, on December 8, 1854, the Dogma of the Immaculate Conception had been proclaimed by Pope Pius IX: *"The most Blessed Virgin Mary was, from the first moment of her conception, by a singular grace and privilege of almighty God and by virtue of the merits of Jesus Christ, Savior of the human race, preserved immune from all stain of original sin"* (CCC n. 491).

Adam and Eve were uniquely created: *"The first man was from the Earth, a man of dust..."* (CCC n. 504). *"The Lord God...took out one of [Adam's] ribs...The man called his wife Eve, because she became the mother of all the living"* (Gen 2:21,3:20). Their disobedience to the Creator in the Garden of Eden is known as *Original Sin*. The Church clearly defines it: *"Man, tempted by the devil, let his trust in his Creator die in his heart and, abusing his freedom, disobeyed God's command. This is what man's first sin consisted of. All subsequent sin would be disobedience toward God and lack of trust in his goodness"* (CCC n. 397).

Yet, Mary, although conceived in the womb, was nonetheless immaculately conceived (free from Original Sin) and remained without sin throughout her life. A virgin, both before and after giving birth, Mary retained her *"...real and perpetual virginity even in the act of giving birth to the Son of God made man"* (CCC n. 499).

Betrothed to Joseph in her youth she was chosen to be the Mother of the Savior, *"Jesus is conceived by the Holy Spirit in the Virgin Mary's womb because he is the new Adam..."* (CCC n. 504). *"From the first formulations of her faith, the Church has confessed that Jesus was conceived solely by the power of the Holy Spirit in the womb of the Virgin Mary...without human seed"* (CCC n. 496). Hence, we are assured of being correct when we bestow upon her the title, *Blessed Virgin Mary, Mother of God!*

This woman, now resplendent in the heavens and honored by the Creator, knew almost unimaginable suffering. Shortly after the birth of Jesus they had to flee into Egypt to escape from King Herod who jealously demanded the death of her Son. Joseph, her spouse, died while Jesus was still a young man and soon thereafter she was a witness to the entire horrendous scene of her Son's crucifixion and death on an ignominious cross.

While dying on the cross He entrusted her care to St. John, the young apostle who loved Christ more than the others. She understands our pain and anguish and is therefore able to empathize with our difficulties. In the same manner as she pleads with us, we in turn plead with her to obtain assistance, much as one might ask a good friend or a neighbor to secure a particular favor for us.

Is there anyone better able to intercede with God in hopes of gaining the assistance we need to overcome our difficulties? Is there anyone closer to God than the mother who bore Him and nourished Him throughout her life? This compassionate mother has received extraordinary graces from God during these latter days in order to obtain the conversion of many souls and the cures of thousands of people throughout the world.

Millions of people flock to the shrines dedicated to her throughout the world where they pray and give thanks for the many favors obtained through her intercession. One has only to read about the miraculous events that transpire so often in Lourdes, France to verify this. As our heavenly mother she gives us hope, joyful hope!

On July 13, 1917, Our Lady promised to *"perform a miracle for all to see and believe."* It was witnessed by more than 70,000 people who

traveled to Fátima on October 13, 1917 in order to see it. In Lisbon, *O Seculo,* the newspaper in Portugal, proclaimed it so loudly and clearly that even the skeptics had difficulty denying it! Yet there is more to this story about Mary, for God entrusted her with a specific mission, one that would finally culminate in this new era. The countdown to its fulfillment actually began in 1830, and upon her acceptance of this extraordinary mission she was endowed with an abundance of graces from the Eternal Father. She has pleaded for our help in the past and, now, even more so as this countdown nears completion. This is evidenced by her recent appearances throughout the world. Christ, her Son, has also appeared numerous times since 1917 to visionaries other than the children in Fatima.

We should not be reluctant to accept the words she has so generously uttered, often with tears, for they are always offered with great concern in her desire to help and guide us. She reminds us of those moral teachings of the Church, those we have forgotten, the things that are expected of us. Are we listening?

The Bible humbly recalls Mary's relationship with us: *"Behold, from now on will all generations call me blessed. The Mighty One has done great things for me..."* (Lk 1:48-49). And, so, throughout the world there are many shrines that honor Mary, the Mother of God. All the sites of the approved apparitions of Our Lady have shrines which recognize and honor her for all she has done over the years. They are most prominent in France, Portugal, England, Mexico, Ireland, and Belgium; some are quite magnificent in appearance. One of the most notable shrines is located in the United States, in Washington, D.C. known as the *Basilica of the National Shrine of the Immaculate Conception*.

Basilica of the National Shrine

In 1990, it was elevated to the rank of a minor basilica. It is the largest Roman Catholic church in the United States and one of the ten largest churches in the world. Dedicated to Our Lady, the shrine strives to serve people from all over the globe, a place where one may visit and pray for peace in their hearts, their homes and in the world. Within, one finds altars for the celebration of Holy Mass, and statues of Our Lady that were donated by funds and materials from many nations of the world. They represent the faith and the love we have for God, through His mother, Mary. Here we especially honor her. We do not worship her; we acknowledge her role as the Mother of God and all men, and her work for the salvation of mankind.

In 1846, the Massachusetts *Lowell Courier* spoke of a Catholic church 'to be built in Washington after the manner of the great cathedrals of the old world, with subscriptions from every Catholic Parish in America.'

On August 15, 1913, in a private audience with then Msgr. Thomas J. Shahan, Pope Pius X gave his apostolic blessing to begin the collection of funds to build this noble church. The first Mass was offered in the *National Shrine* on April 20 Easter Sunday, 1924. As construction continued, so did the celebration of Masses. By 1926, the lower *Crypt Church* was completed. The lower level of the National Shrine, which extends south, was completed by 1931. The death of Bishop Shahan in 1932, followed by the Depression and World War II, brought further construction to a halt.

I distinctly remember driving through the capital in my youth, wondering about the appearance of the *Crypt Church*. It was truly an odd sight for only the lower portion of the shrine was visible. Little did I imagine that I would one day be able to present one of my lectures there about the Blessed Virgin Mary.

The effort to build the superstructure, or *Great Upper Church*, was renewed during the Marian Year 1953-1954 by the Episcopal Committee for the National Shrine, Bishop John Noll, of Fort Wayne, Chairman. Catholics throughout the United States responded enthusiastically to the fund raising effort and, in 1955, the superstructure began to rise. With the completion of the *Great Upper Church*, the National Shrine was dedicated on November 20, 1959. The Basilica houses more than seventy chapels and oratories honoring Mary, donated by various Catholic immigrant groups and religious orders and communities.

I became active in the Spiritual Committee of the Shrine Guild in 1970 under the guidance of Msgr. William F. McDonough, the sixth director, and Fr. John J. Nicola, the associate director and was appointed chairman shortly thereafter. I first met Patrick Cardinal O'Boyle at the shrine where he led one of the three-hour *Prayers for Priests* vigils. Apart from the love God has shown me throughout my lifetime there is perhaps nothing more endearing to me personally then that which He has shown me through Mary, the Mother of God.

On October 7, 1979, John Paul II became the first reigning pope to visit the shrine. He was also the first pope to visit the White House. His visit was very inspiring to so many. My children were among the throngs of those who saw him. They'll never forget it!

On April 27, 2014, Pope Francis announced the canonization of John Paul II, who died in 2005. At the same time Pope John XXIII was also elevated to sainthood within the Roman Catholic Church.

Pope Benedict XVI also honored the shrine with his visit on April 16, 2008. Prior to his departure, the Pope presented "a Golden Rose for Our Mother Mary" to the *Basilica of the National Shrine of the Immaculate Conception* as a sign of his reverence, esteem and paternal affection.

In 2005, Msgr. Walter R. Rossi was named the 11th director and, at the same time, the second rector of the *Basilica of the National Shrine* where he serves at the discretion of the National Shrine Board of Trustees. The National Shrine welcomes nearly one million visitors annually. On feast days and special occasions, the Eternal Word Television Network (EWTN) broadcasts Masses from the National Shrine worldwide.

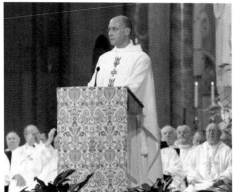

Msgr. Walter R. Rossi

"While we at the shrine are here to serve and assist our pilgrims as they seek to encounter the Lord through the guidance of the Blessed Virgin Mary, they, in turn, strengthen our faith through their witness."

– *Msgr. Walter R. Rossi, July, 2009.*

While studying to become a Carmelite in Florida in the early 1990s, one of the new lay Carmelite Communities in need of a chaplain approached Bishop Emeritus Thomas J. Grady of the Orlando, Florida Diocese to see if he would be able to assist them. As the fifth director of the National Shrine of the Immaculate Conception he eagerly took on the responsibility as chaplain for that Community. I had the privilege of being asked to serve at his initial Mass for the Community.

Bishop Grady recognized the need to minister to the tourist population in his area. In 1975, he named Fr. F. Joseph Harte (with whom I later traveled to Medjugorje) as the first rector of the new shrine to be built in central Florida. By 1979, plans were made for the construction of the shrine under the patronage of Mary, Queen of the Universe. On December 8, 1984, the feast of the Immaculate Conception, ground was broken for the first phase of construction and groundbreaking for the main church began on August 22, 1990, the feast of Mary's Queenship.

On September 11, 2002, a decade after my return to the South Carolina Lowcountry [coastal area], I happened upon an excellent article about Bishop Grady concerning his death on April 21, 2002. It was written by Dr. Geraldine M. Rohling, Archivist-Curator of the Basilica of the National Shrine of the Immaculate Conception: In October, 1956, Msgr. Grady began his tenure as the fifth director of the National Shrine...[he] was a key player in the construction of the Upper Church.

"In October, 1959, one month before the dedication of the Shrine, in an article for *The American Ecclesiastical Review*, Msgr. Grady wrote: 'As time passes...the meaning of the Shrine will become ever more profoundly true. As decades pass, the Shrine will age gracefully as a building. In time, the architecture will mingle with the symbol...It will be part of America. It will be caught up into stone, an expression of...love and trust...It will stand older than some of the states of the Union, holding communion both with its own past and also the people it newly embraces...[on] November 20, 1959, its doors will swing open and history will walk in.'" [1]

i "Bishop Thomas Grady, A Disciple of Mary, A Developer of Her National Shrine" by Dr. Geraldine M. Rohling, Archivist-Curator, Basilica of the National Shrine of the Immaculate Conception, Washington, DC 20017.

St. Louis de Montfort wrote much about Mary: "Since she is the dawn which precedes and discloses the Sun of Justice, Jesus Christ, she must be known and acknowledged so that Jesus may be known and acknowledged...As she was the way by which Jesus first came to us, she will again be the way by which he will come to us the second time, though not in the same manner.

"In these latter times Mary must shine forth more than ever in mercy, power and grace; in mercy, to bring back and welcome lovingly the poor sinners and wanderers who are to return to the Catholic Church; in power, to combat the enemies of God who will rise up menacingly to seduce and crush by promises and threats all those who oppose them; finally, she must shine forth in grace to inspire and support the valiant soldiers and loyal servants of Jesus Christ who are fighting for his cause.

"Lastly, Mary must become as terrible as an army in battle array to the devil and his followers, especially in these latter times. For Satan, knowing that he has little time - even less now than ever - to destroy souls, intensifies his efforts and his onslaughts every day. He will not hesitate to stir up savage persecutions and set treacherous snares for Mary's faithful servants and children whom he finds more difficult to overcome than others.

"It is chiefly in reference to these last wicked persecutions of the devil, daily increasing until the advent of the reign of anti-christ, that we should understand that first and well-known prophecy and curse of God uttered against the serpent in the garden of paradise. It is opportune to explain it here for the glory of the Blessed Virgin, the salvation of her children and the confusion of the devil. *'I will place enmities between you and the woman, between your race [seed] and her race [seed]; she will crush your head and you will lie in wait for her heel'* (Gn 3:15).

"What Lucifer lost by pride, Mary won by humility. What Eve ruined and lost by disobedience, Mary saved by obedience. By obeying the serpent, Eve ruined her children as well as herself and delivered them up to him. Mary, by her perfect fidelity to God, saved her children with herself and consecrated them to his divine majesty. Thus the most fearful enemy that God has set up against the devil is Mary, his holy Mother."

Additional information about St. Louis de Montfort will be noted in an ensuing chapter.

What was to be Mary's role in the salvation of the world 1800 years after leaving this blue planet? Why would God endow her with so many graces that even *"an angel with a flaming sword in his left hand; flashing, it gave out flames that looked as though they would set the world on fire"* would heed her? Why would Christ assure us that *"... the salvation of the world has been entrusted to her"* yet, at the same time, require man's assistance to accomplish it? It is through our understanding Mary and the love she displays for all her children that one will find the answers.

Her role became even more evident when many of the events she predicted – if mankind would not change – came to fruition: *"When you see a night illumined by an unknown light, know that this is the great sign given you by God that he is about to punish the world for its crimes, by means of war, famine, and persecutions of the Church and of the Holy Father...The good will be martyred; the Holy Father will have much to suffer; various nations will be annihilated."*

But God told us: *"I will not leave you orphans. I will come to you"* (Jn 14:18). On May 18,  1920, Karol Józef Wojtyla was born in Poland. In his youth he learned about the extreme difficulties misguided rulers inflict on their subjects. Determined to become a priest, he entered a secret seminary in 1942; later, he was named bishop, cardinal, and in 1978, elected pope. We know him today as Pope Saint John Paul II. A survivor of *World War II* ,and bent under the domination of both Nazi and Communist regimes, perhaps no cleric has had to endure more than he. Owing to the trauma of his youth he has accomplished during his lifetime what no man or government before him was able to effect: the unbloody overthrow of an atheistic government set on world domination, one that literally enslaved its population. He brought hope and courage throughout the world with his motto: "Be Not Afraid!"

World War I began on July 28, 1914 and, within three years, had ravished most of Europe. The carnage was so horrible that Pope Benedict XV pleaded for the intercession of the Mother of God. During his public prayer on May 5, 1917 he invited the world to perform a nine-day novena of prayer, asking Mary for peace and a quick end to the war. On the ninth day of the novena, in a direct response to those pleas, Our Lady made the first of six appearances to three children at the Cova da Ira, in Fatima, Portugal. It was May 13, 1917.

Two of the six Republics within Yugoslavia, Croatia and Bosnia, share a common border. On October 18, 1970, Croatian Catholics living in the United States and Canada donated a chapel to the Basilica of the National Shrine of the Immaculate Conception under the title *Mary, Queen of Peace.* Evidently she heard their pleas and, on August 6, 1981, less than 11 years later, she appeared to six children in Medjugorje (Bosnia), informing them that, indeed, *"I am the Queen of Peace."*

Earlier, in 1917, Our Lady appeared to three children with a "peace plan" from Heaven. We know from history that because the world did not adhere to that plan, great wars and strife followed exactly as Our Lady had predicted. Then, on May 22, 1982, Our Lady appeared again, this time with a final "peace plan" for the world, stating quite clearly: *"I have come to call the world to conversion for the last time! Later, I will never again appear on Earth [in this way]."* [1]

---

[1] – Mirjana said adding "in this way" onto the end of the above sentence will provide a better [more correct] translation. Vicka added: "For me the message that the Madonna has given is very clear: this is the last time that she will be present here on Earth in the way she has been present at Medjugorje – for such a long period of time."

CHAPTER 21

The Chair of Peter

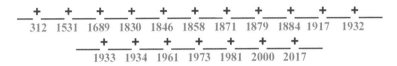

+	+	+	+	+	+	+	+	+	+	+
312	1531	1689	1830	1846	1858	1871	1879	1884	1917	1932

+	+	+	+	+	+	+
1933	1934	1961	1973	1981	2000	2017

"I am the way and the truth and the life. No one comes to the Father except through me. If you know me, you will also know my Father. From now on, you know him and have seen him" (Jn 14:6-7).

Quodam cathedra Petri, unus est, de coelo – *"One Chair of Peter, one true font of baptism."* The chair of a bishop is known as a cathedra; however, it refers only to the occupant, not the furniture. The bish-op of Rome is the pope and the ca-thedra in St. Peter's Basilica was once used by the popes. When the pope pronounces a dogma *Ex Cathedra [With Authority]* from the chair of Peter, it be-comes Church teach-ing and is infallible and binding upon all believers.

The Papal Seal

Pope John Paul II once recalled how, as a young seminarian, he "read and reread many times and with great spiritual profit" some writings of St. Louis-Marie de Montfort. Known as the *Apostle of the End Times,* St. Louis is also called a prophet of the *Age of Mary.* His classic document *True Devotion to Mary,* written eight years prior to his death in 1716, was thrown into a chest along with other documents. Later, about 1789, the chest was buried in a field to avoid destruction by the armies of the French Revolution.

Then, in 1842, just 12 years after Our Lady began her mission for the salvation of the world, his classic document was discovered and published. On page xxii, he wrote: "Thousands of souls perish because Mary is withheld from them." St. Louis also stated: "In these latter times Mary must shine forth more than ever in mercy, power and grace..."

Pope John Paul II expressed his personal consecration to Mary based on the spiritual approach of St. Louis-Marie de Montfort and the Mariology in his works. As a result, he made the consecration of de Montfort early in his life; it became a keystone of his vocation as a priest. As pope, John Paul II declared to Mary: "*Totus tuus ego sum!*" It became his apostolic motto. According to his apostolic letter *Rosarium Virginis Mariae,* he borrowed the motto from the Marian consecration prayer found in the same book. The complete text of the prayer translated from Latin is: "I belong entirely to you, and all that I have is yours. I take you for my all. O Mary, give me your heart." In *Crossing the Threshold of Hope,* the pontiff further explained the meaning of those words.

From 1143 to 1963, the papal tiara was solemnly placed on the pope's head during a papal coronation. The crossed keys symbolize the keys of Simon Peter. The keys are gold and silver to represent the power of loosing and binding. Each ring of the tiara signifies a specific state in our journey from this world to the next: the Church Militant are those on Earth; the Church Suffering are those in Purgatory; the Church Triumphant are those in Heaven. In an act of humility, Paul VI sold it and donated the proceeds to charity.

La Salette, like many of the apparitions of Mary, has its own apocalyptic depictions. Both children reluctantly penned their secrets for the edification of the Holy Father. The secrets of La Salette, given to Melanie and Maximum, were hand-carried to Rome by two priests who gave the sealed envelopes to Pope Pius IX on July 18, 1851. They told of the chastisements that would be visited upon a sinful world. Reading the contents, he said: "If we do not pray we shall all perish!"

What did the popes throughout history have to say regarding those apparitions and, specifically, those of Our Lady of La Salette?

Pius IX: "In this place, Mary, the loving Mother appeared manifesting her pain for the moral evil caused by humanity. Her tears help us to understand the seriousness of sin and the rejection of God, and at the same time it is a manifestation of the passionate fidelity that her Son has for each person, even though His redemptive love is marked by the wounds of treason and abandonment by man.

The Shrine of La Salette is of great authority and is destined to have a future. I love this devotion and shall be glad to see it spread."

Leo XIII: "With all my heart, I bless La Salette and everything that pertains to La Salette."

Pius X: gave his most copious blessings to La Salette.

Benedict XV: "The devotion of Our Lady of La Salette ought to spread, for it is a devotion that goes straight to the heart."

Pius XI: "Our Lady of La Salette is to you a kind Providence."

Pius XII: "It can be easily understood that your Religious Family should particularly take to heart the Centenary celebration of the blessed afternoon, the 19th of September, 1846, when the Madonna in Tears came to adjure her children to enter resolutely the path of conversion to her Divine Son, and of reparation for so many sins that offend the August and Eternal Majesty.

"Very willingly do we direct our desires and encouragement to the dear Missionaries of Our Lady of La Salette, in the easy confidence that the Most Holy Virgin will, in return, be glad to obtain for them a great abundance of graces and consolation for the fruitfulness of their ministry, now so varied and reaching to the most distant fields of the Apostolate."

John Paul II: "The message of La Salette was given to two young shepherds in a period of great suffering. People were scourged by famine...Indifference or hostility toward the Gospel message worsened. As she appeared, bearing upon her breast the likeness of her crucified Son, Our Lady showed herself to be associated to the work of salvation, experiencing compassion for her children. La Salette is a message of hope - a hope sustained by the intercession of her who is the Mother of all peoples...The arm of Mary's Son will not weigh upon, will not condemn, the people who walk humbly in the pathway of the Lord.

"Christ will take the outstretched hand into his own and lead to new life the sinner reconciled by the grace of the Cross. At La Salette, Mary clearly spoke of the constancy of her prayer for the world: she will never abandon the people created in the image and likeness of God, those to whom it has been given to become children of God. May she lead to her Son all the nations of the Earth."

Finally, we are at the end of this story. Yet, it is actually just the beginning, as we will see when these events begin to unfold. Mirjana has committed to memory the times of each event Our Lady gave her. She will release each one just prior to its occurrence. Life in this world will necessarily change as they unfold; eventually, the survivors will believe as they did in earlier times.

Since they began in 1830, and continued until the early 1970s, these prophetic future events were for the most part, conditional; that is they depended upon how well we responded to Our Lady's pleas. Obviously, since we paid little attention to her, we were told in 1973 in Akita, Japan, that these events will occur and they will change many lives.

They were confirmed again in 1981 and are now etched in stone; they cannot be stopped! Yes, some can be mitigated by our prayers, fasting, and sacrifices; but, as stated so clearly by Mirjana in Medjugorje: "God is at the end of His patience" and retribution is inevitable!

It is sincerely hoped that this book will be the source of encouragement for the present generation, and enlightenment for the next generation – especially those who know so little about Mary, their spiritual mother – and prepare them for the events coming upon us. The time is ever so much closer now! Vicka said the Madonna told her that we should prepare ourselves spiritually and be reconciled in our soul.

We should be prepared for the worst; we should not be afraid to die tomorrow! Our Lady is leaving no stone unturned; she is doing all she can for our conversion during this grace filled period. If we are true believers we will accept death peaceably, knowing we will one day be in Heaven with our Lord. We can be of help to others by our prayers and sacrifices. How we respond to Our Lady's pleas is a choice that will be put to each one of us!

In her Magnificat, Mary tells us with great humility, *"His mercy is from age to age to those who fear him"* (Lk 1:50). Holy Scripture reminds us, *"The fear of the Lord is the beginning of wisdom"* (Ps 111:10) and, *"This is the one whom I approve: the lowly and afflicted man who trembles at my word"* (Is 66:2). Can this holy fear of the Lord eventually help us to love our Creator? Certainly! If all else fails, this fear of the Lord does just that; if love is not there, holy fear of our Creator may be the one element God uses, at least initially, to save the souls of His children. We would do well to remember that Our Lady at Fátima did not hesitate to show the children that horrendous vision of Hell about which Lúcia, the eldest of the children, would later say:

"This vision lasted but an instant. How can we ever be grateful enough to our kind heavenly Mother who had already prepared us by promising, in the first apparition, to take us to Heaven? Otherwise, I think we would have died of fright."

Why else would Our Lady have shown that horrible vision and made it available to the public? It was so we could understand that the place called Hell exists, and is the eventual destination of all those who do not follow the laws and statutes of their Creator.

In a similar manner, do we not all live under systems of government wherein the alternative to being a good and productive citizen is to be either abandoned or placed in a cell for an extended period of time, sometimes for life? To prepare for those times – before each one of us is called to that fearful judgment – we are offered mercy by our Creator. Once the soul departs from the body, we are judged by a just Judge and mercy ceases to be a factor.

In the summer of 1934, Christ told St. Faustina, *"… before I come as the Just Judge, I am coming first as the King of Mercy. Before the day of justice arrives, there will be given to people a sign in the heavens…"* (Diary, 42). He also told St. Faustina that He wanted the image of the Divine Mercy to be *"…solemnly blessed on the first Sunday after Easter; that Sunday is to be the Feast of Mercy"* (Diary, 49). Since the year 2000, His Church has celebrated this feast day on the first Sunday after Easter: Mercy Sunday. It is a day on which all temporal punishment due to sins may be forgiven.

It begins first with our asking for forgiveness by our reception of the sacrament of *Penance,* as we should be free of any stain of sin. However one avails themselves of it, whether in a confessional box in church, or on our knees at home, we end it with a prayer: "O, my God, I am heartily sorry for having offended You, and I detest all my sins because I dread the loss of Heaven and the pains of Hell; but, most of all, because they offend You, my God, Who are all good and deserving of all my love. I firmly resolve, with the help of Your grace, to confess my sins, to do penance, and to amend my life. Amen!"

We know each one of us will eventually die! The Church offers us the sacrament of healing by *Anointing of the Sick* (Extreme Unction), often known as the Last Rites. Probably the greatest healing sacrament is Confession, of which there are three rites of Reconciliation. As a young man I well remember the Jesuits advising us to: "Get in the box at the back of the church before you get in the box in the front!""

However, before we reach that threshold we would do well to examine Vicka's description of the alternatives that await us: "One afternoon I was with Jakov at his home and Our Lady came, telling us that she was going to take us to show us Heaven, Hell, and Purgatory. Before we left we were wondering how long the journey was going to take, whether we would go up, or down, or how many days we would be traveling. But Our Lady just took Jakov's left hand and my right hand and we went up. We could see the walls just moving aside, giving us enough space to go through. It took us just a moment, and we found ourselves in Heaven.

"**Heaven** is one huge, endless space. There is a special kind of light that does not exist on Earth at all. We saw people dressed in gray, yellow, and pink gowns. They were walking, praying and singing together. We were able to see small angels circling around. There is a special kind of joy in Heaven. I have never experienced anything like that at any other time. Our Lady told us to see how overjoyed [are] the people who were in Heaven.

"**Purgatory** is also one huge space but we were not able to see people. We could only see darkness: an ashy color. We were able to feel the physical suffering of the people. They were shivering and struggling. Our Lady said we need to pray for those people so that they can get out of Purgatory.

"As for **Hell**, there is one huge fire in the middle. First, we were shown people in [their] normal condition, before they were caught by that fire. Then, as they are being caught by that fire, they become the shape of animals like they have never been humans before. As they are falling deeper into the fire, they yell against God even more. Our Lady says that for all those who are in Hell it was their choice, their decision to get there.

"Our Lady says for all those who are living here on Earth who are living against God's commands, even here they are living in a kind of Hell, so, when they are there they are continuing just the same life as before. Our Lady says that there are so many who live here on the Earth who believe that, when this life is finished, everything is finished; but, Our Lady says: *'If you think so, you are very wrong, because we are just passersby on the Earth.'*"

Four of the most famous opening lines ever written remain eye openers to this day. The first two, *"In the beginning..."* (Gn 1:1; Jn 1:1) come from both the Old and the New Testament of the Bible. The third is found in the novel *Paul Cliffordopen*: "It was a dark and stormy night!"

The fourth is taken from *A Tale of Two Cities*: "It was the best of times; it was the worst of times."

Three years after the end of *World War II*, General Omar Bradley, cautioned: "We have men of science, too few men of God. We have grasped the mystery of the atom and rejected the *Sermon on the Mount*. The world has achieved brilliance without conscience. Ours is a world of nuclear giants and ethical infants. We know more about war than we know about peace, more about killing than we know about living. If we continue to develop our technology without wisdom or prudence, our servant may prove to be our executioner." In a future time, what lies ahead for us

may well be written about in a similar manner; however, that will only be the beginning! Archbishop Sheen would later write: "Hate today is in the saddle of one of the four horses of the Apocalypse, and love is trampled beneath its thundering hooves." Suppose that in-

stead of the hatred, anger and betrayal that are so pervasively glorified throughout the media today, we would begin our days filled with love. A spiritual love that requires us to love our Creator above all things, in adherence to the *Commandments* He has given us; then, to love all our fellow man as ourselves. It would change the world!

In the movie, *Goodbye, Mr. Chips* – adapted from a novel by James Hilton – depicting an English boy's school just prior to World War II, their day begins with the school song:

> *"In the morning of my life I shall look to the sunrise.*
> *At a moment in my life when the world is new.*
> *And the blessing I shall ask is that God will grant me,*
> *To be brave and strong and true,*
> *And to fill the world with love my whole life through."*

> *"In the evening of my life I shall look to the sunset,*
> *At a moment in my life when the night is due.*
> *And the question I shall ask only I can answer.*
> *Was I brave and strong and true?*
> *Did I fill the world with love my whole life through?"*

That steep, narrow, rock strewn path we've been searching for is also paved with love! It is the only solution to the world's problems today. Without love there is nothing, only evil, about which Pope St. John Paul II noted earlier in his life: "The absence of love is nothingness...a place where evil exists." He added: "Evil destroys itself!"

Yet to acquire that love we must have faith: faith in a God Who freely bestows it on all His children. St. Bernadette of Lourdes saw and believed; however, without that luxury, we must believe through faith alone that which we cannot see. Faith, once found, is similar to everything else that lives. It must be nurtured, it must be fed and watered daily throughout life else it will wither on the vine and die. That spiritual nourishment is prayer: without it, the gift of faith will surely die!

 St. Augustine, a brilliant theologian and Doctor of the Church, stated: "Where your pleasure is, there is your treasure; where your treasure is, there is your heart; where your heart is, there is your happiness [love]; to fall in love with God is the greatest romance; to seek Him is the greatest adventure; to find Him is the greatest human achievement, as God is the source of all love and life!" "Our hearts are restless, Oh God, until they rest in You!"

Spiritual love affords us both the desire and the strength to perform that which the angel, appearing in the third secret of Fátima, demanded: *"Penance; Penance; Penance."* It is the same penance Our Lady has pleaded for in so many places where she has appeared throughout the world. We will need the nourishment derived from prayer, sacrifice and penance in order to carry our cross each day, for that is the only way we can accomplish the challenge from Christ: *"...If anyone wishes to come after me, he must deny himself and take up his cross daily and follow me"* (Lk 9:23). St. Matthew writes: *"Enter through the narrow gate; for the gate is wide and the road broad that leads to destruction, and those who enter through it are many. How narrow the gate and constricted the road that leads to life. And those who find it are few"* (Mt 7:13-14).

This will require both patience and perseverance on our part; yet, sooner then we can imagine, the day will come when we will hear these words from Christ: *"Come, you who are blessed by my Father. Inherit the kingdom prepared for you from the foundation of the world"* (Mt 25:34). And we will see the place that, *"...eye hath not seen, nor ear heard, neither hath it entered into the heart of man, what things God hath prepared for them that love him"* (1 Cor 2:9).

EPILOGUE

The first man of the cloth I met upon my arrival in South Carolina in the early 1980s was Rt. Rev. Edmund F. McCaffrey, O.S.B, the former Abbot of Belmont Abbey, in North Carolina. In 1976, he was the first pastor assigned to St. Michael's Catholic Church in Murrells Inlet, a small fishing village straddling the Horry/Georgetown County border south of Myrtle Beach. He has been an inspiration to many who had the privilege of hearing his interesting sermons at St. Michael's church. He also appeared quite often on the Eternal Word Television Network.

During his last sermon in the original St. Michael's church on the feast of the Assumption three years ago, he noted that he had recently returned from his final pilgrimage to Fátima, something he did annually for many years. How fitting it was to see this now older man of the cloth, who gave his first and last sermon in the old St. Michael's church, present at the dedication of the new building. He died in a Little Sisters of the Poor home in North Carolina, on November 13, 2016.

The original metal-clad building, having seen better days, was demolished recently and a much larger St. Michael's church was erected there under the able guidance of Rev. Raymond J. Carlo. It was officially consecrated on August 17, 2012, by Robert E. Guglielmone, bishop of the Diocese of Charleston.

Perpetual Eucharistic Adoration began on December 8, 2000 at St. Michael's under the sponsorship of Bishop Robert J. Baker and guided by the pastor, Msgr. Thomas R. Duffy. It will continue as before in a chapel in the new church set aside for Adoration of the Blessed Sacrament. Deacon Donald Efkin originally monitored the scheduling of parishioners to ensure at least two adorers are in attendance for each hour in order to provide a perpetual (24/365) presence. The prayer to St. Michael, the Archangel, is recited daily by both the priest and the parishioners at the end of Mass.

Near the close of the millennium I moved into a new home in Murrells Inlet. I had many neighbors who, if you had time to spare, were eager to relate their own stories. If you've ever visited the southern portion of the United States in the middle of summer one thing stands out: the temperature and humidity.

During one exceptionally hot summer I became quite interested in the tale of my neighbor, a retired farmer named Lyde, a native of Kingstree. He emphasized that, in his youth, he was required to sit outside the family farm all day in the sizzling hot sun selling, of all things, hot boiled peanuts. He was just ten years old at the time.

His wife would often join in our discussions, describing how they fanned themselves in an attempt to survive the horrendous heat. Long before air conditioning and electric fans, long before electricity there, one would use a newspaper or hat brim to rid their face of perspiration.

In those days, assorted, ornate folding fans were available in most areas of the country and one could always find free fans in the local churches, stored neatly in the pews or on the seats of the chairs. Oftentimes, the ladies in church fanned the air so briskly that you didn't need to retrieve yours.

Like so many others who fought in *World War II*, Lyde was in his late teens when he enlisted. By then, smoking had become a standard ration for the fighting men and the government supplied them with as many cigarettes as they could use. Unfortunately, it was only much later that the harmful effects of those *coffin nails* would be understood. Lyde was no exception; he eventually acquired a terminal case of emphysema that necessitated toting a bottle of oxygen just to hobble across the street.

Over time each breath became increasingly laborious, so much so that he was hospitalized. He died shortly afterward. He was a gentle soul; a fine southern Baptist who never forgot that he was a Christian first, and a veteran – nor that, as a child, he had to sell hot boiled peanuts during the *dog days* of summer.

In the fall of 2011, a friend told me about a shrine in Kingstree dedicated to Our Lady under the title *Our Lady of South Carolina*. Traveling to the shrine necessitated driving through the town of Kingstree itself. It remained much as Lyde described it: a typical sleepy, southern community – rather poor by today's standards – neither the people nor the dwellings have changed much over time.

Rev. Stanley Smolenski, SPMA – the founder of the shrine – was named director in 2006 by Bishop Robert J. Baker, of the diocese of Charleston, SC. Then, on May 27, 2007, Bishop Baker also received his profession to the eremitic state. Fr. Stan is a quiet, unassuming hermit who, although not living in a desert or on a mountaintop, is acutely aware that it can feel just as hot during the summertime in Kingstree, South Carolina.

An avid supporter of Mary's shrine, Bishop Baker was eventually anointed bishop of the Diocese of Birmingham on August 14. 2007. He can be seen quite often on the Eternal Word Television Network (EWTN), located in Irondale, Alabama.

Our Lady of South Carolina

The following month I was invited to visit Mepkin Abbey, a Trappist monastery located in Moncks Corner, South Carolina. The Abbey itself is situated on a very secluded sanctuary with well-maintained land, conducive to both meditation and strolling.

The monks there follow the *Rule of St. Benedict*, devoting their entire lives to prayer, spiritual study and work. Under the care of the Abbot, Stanislaus Gumula, O.C.S.O. and the monks, the abbey is open to visitors where a warm welcome is extended to people of all faiths. It is a rare gem where one may roam about the grounds in quiet contemplation.

The land was donated to the Church in 1949 by Henry and Clare Booth Luce. In 1944, several years after the death of her daughter, Ann, Claire became a Catholic. She attributed her conversion to Archbishop Fulton J. Sheen, whose cause for sainthood is currently under study by the Church. Claire was buried in the cemetery at the monastery.

In 2011, Bishop Victor Galeone took up permanent residence in Mep-kin Abbey after his retirement from the Diocese of St. Augustine. He now enjoys the quiet surroundings of the spacious grounds.

It is my hope that many who read this story, about the love their heavenly mother has for each one of us will find time in their hectic, day-to-day schedules to visit these places of prayer and meditation where one's soul may find refreshment and true peace, a peace that can only come from God.

It was in these humble surroundings that the seed sown in me so many years ago was nourished and led to the writing of this book about the love of a mother, her Son, and the Eternal Father who made it all possible. It was there that I found that I was able to comply with those requests of Our Lady for penance, prayer, and reparation for the conversion of sinners.

Both the abbey and the grounds are open to those who will adhere to the quiet times shared by all. One may wish to join the monks in prayer in their chapel and, perhaps, dine with them in silence in the refectory. The abbey is one of the most relaxing places one can find in a world so busy with just being busy.

MARIAN DOCTRINE AND DOGMA

The Church has defined Marian doctrine and dogma over the years regarding Mary's relationship with God and her role in human salvation:

1) The Divine Motherhood of Mary was proclaimed at the Council of Ephesus in 431.

2) The Immaculate Conception was proclaimed as an independent dogma by Pope Blessed Pius IX in his Apostolic Constitution *Ineffabilis Deus* (December 8, 1854). The solemn definition of Mary's Immaculate Conception is like the Divine Motherhood and Perpetual Virginity part of the Christological doctrine.

3) The Assumption was proclaimed as dogma by Pope Pius XII on November 1, 1950 in his Encyclical *Munificentissimus Deus.*

4) The Perpetual Virginity of Mary – although part and parcel of the faith of the early Church – was never defined as dogma. It wasn't necessary inasmuch as everyone accepted it. It remains much like the Assumption prior to 1950, believed and celebrated; however, as yet, it has no papal proclamation. The doctrine of perpetual virginity is distinct from the dogma of the Immaculate Conception of Mary which relates to the conception of the Virgin Mary without any stain of original sin.

5) The Mediatrix of All Graces has not been declared as doctrine/dogma of the Church, although it has been proposed by both the Church and the laity over several centuries. It is closely related to the Catholic teaching on Mary's cooperation in the redemption; the teaching that with, though, and under her Son, Mary is the mediatrix of all graces. This latter proposal is very clear and the Church accepts it fully.

In 1936, Christ emphatically declared to Sr. Lúcia: *"I want My whole Church to acknowledge that consecration as a triumph of the Immaculate Heart of Mary...and put the devotion to the Immaculate Heart beside the devotion to My Sacred Heart"* where they will be venerated by all. The declaration of Mary as the mediatrix of all graces would help fulfill that request.

Pope Saint Leo XIII was the first pope to fully embrace the concept of Mary as *Mediatrix of All Graces.* In his rosary encyclicals, he described the Virgin Mary as mediating all graces. In 1883, he wrote that nothing is as salvific and powerful as asking for the support of the Virgin, the mediator of peace with God and of heavenly graces. In his rosary encyclical *Octobri Mense,* he stated that Mary is administrator of graces on Earth, part of a new salvation order.

On November 21, 1964, during Vatican II, Paul VI promulgated *Lumen Gentium* (Light of the World), which states in part III, On the Blessed Virgin and the Church: There is but one Mediator as we know from the words of the apostle, *"For there is one God. There is also one mediator between God and the human race, Christ Jesus, himself human, who gave himself as redemption for all"* (1 Tm 2:5).

Therefore the Blessed Virgin is invoked by the Church under the titles of *Advocate, Auxiliatrix, Adjutrix,* and *Mediatrix.* This, however, is to be so understood that it neither takes away from nor adds anything to the dignity and efficaciousness of Christ the one Mediator. "...The Church does not hesitate to profess this subordinate role of Mary. It knows it through unfailing experience of it and commends it to the hearts of the faithful, so that encouraged by this maternal help they may the more intimately adhere to the Mediator and Redeemer."

However, while the phrase *of all graces* was excluded from the Vatican II statements, it did refer to previous encyclicals by several popes. In the encyclical Adiutricem, on September 5, 1895, Pope Leo XIII stated: "...Among her many other titles we find her hailed as "Our Lady, our Mediatrix, the Reparatrix of the whole world, the Dispenser of all heavenly gifts."

On February 2nd, 1904, in his encyclical *Ad Diem Illum Laetissiumum,* Pope Pius X wrote: "...And from this community of will and suffering between Christ and Mary she merited to become most worthily the Reparatrix of the lost world (*Eadmeri Mon. De Excellentia Virg. Mariae*) and *Dispensatrix* of all the gifts that Our Savior purchased for us by His Death and by His Blood."

"It cannot, of course, be denied that the dispensation of these treasures is the particular and peculiar right of Jesus Christ, for they are the exclusive fruit of His Death, who by His nature is the mediator between God and man. Nevertheless, by this companionship in sorrow and suffering already mentioned between the Mother and the Son, it has been allowed to the august Virgin to be the most powerful Mediatrix and advocate of the whole world with her Divine Son" (Pius IX: *Ineffabilis*).

Pope Benedict XV supported the mediatrix theology and authorized the Feast of *Mary, Mediatrix of all Graces.* When Pope John Paul II was asked to declare Our Lady as *Mediatrix of All Graces* as dogma, he replied: "Not now!" However, it is hoped that the time will eventually arrive. Perhaps this will occur at the conclusion of those predicted events in Garabandal and Medjugorje. Time alone will enlighten us.

Appendix

The rosary consists of 15 decades, although only 5 decades are normally recited at one time. It is divided into 15 beads on which the *"Our Father"* is recited, and 150 beads on which the Hail Mary is recited; each decade is followed by a Glory Be. There are also 15 mysteries; one is recited before each decade. The Our Father is unquestionably biblical. The Hail Mary is also biblical: *"Hail favored one! The Lord is with you"* (Lk 1:28). *"Most blessed are you among woman, and blessed is the fruit of your womb"* (Lk 1:42). "Holy Mary, Mother of God, pray for us sinners now, and at the hour of our death." is added, asking Mary to pray for us, not unlike requesting one's pastor or friend to pray for someone.

The Rosary Prayer

On July, 13, 1917, Immediately after showing the children the vision of Hell, Our Lady told them: *"When you pray the rosary, say after each mystery: 'O my Jesus, forgive us (our sins), save us from the fire(s) of Hell. Lead all souls to Heaven, especially those who are most in need (of Your mercy).'"* The formula of the prayer Mary gave to the children is quite specific and is now in common use throughout the world. However, it has been altered somewhat by individuals who added words that may well change the original meaning of the prayer. Our Lady did not include the words in (brackets) in her request. In fact, in all her writings and books, Sr. Lúcia very clearly spelled out the exact words of the Rosary Prayer that Our Lady taught her: [1]

Português

O'meu Jesus perdoai-nos, livrai-nos do fogo do inferno, levai as almin has todas para o leu, principalmente aquelas que mais precisarem.

[1] – p. 166, Fatima, in Lúcia's Own Words, by Sr. Lúcia, (Still RIver, MA 01467, Ravengate Press, August 13, 1995)

English

«O my Jesus! Forgive us, save us from the fire of hell. Lead all souls to heaven, especially those who are most in need.»

Perhaps some felt that adding those letters/words would provide additional emphasis; yet, it seems rather futile to add to, or take away from, the exact words spoken by a heavenly messenger, especially Our Lady. The added phrases [our sins] and [of Your mercy] may limit that which we are asking. We are certainly in need of more than forgiveness for our sins. Surely, in addition to His mercy, do we not also need wisdom, courage, strength, perseverance and, most of all, His love?

The Divine Comedy

As regards the pluralization of the phrase "fire(s) of Hell" – in 1300, when Dante Alighieri was only thirty-five years old, he wrote The Divine Comedy. It consists of three parts: first, Inferno, tells of the narrator's journey through what is Alighieri's concept of Hell which depicts nine circles of suffering located within the Earth. This is followed by Purgatorio [Purgatory] and Paradiso [Heaven].

While the plural fires of Hell are well enumerated in Dante's Inferno, it was actually a satirical work – likely not heavenly inspired – wherein Dante depicted specifically named members of the Church hierarchy whom he intensely disliked, stating they were going to Hell. The Church has never condemned anyone to Hell, nor stated any person other than Satan was a guest there. That judgment belongs exclusively to God.

The fiery pool was well described at both Fátima: "...a sea of fire. Plunged in this fire were demons..." and in Medjugorje: "There is one huge fire in the middle!" They both emphasize a single fire, not plural fires. A diligent search of the Bible indicates only one singular fire: "Anyone whose name was not found written in the book of life was thrown in the pool of fire" (Rev 20:15). While there were no indications of plural fires of Hell, there may well be different degrees of torment in that horrendous place.

Apparitions of Our Lady

Following an exhaustive study the decision of the ordinary [local bishop] will be one of the following: [1]

1) "constat de supernaturalitate" [established as supernatural]
   Determined as true and worthy of belief by the Church

Akita, Japan
Banneux, Belgium
Beauraing, Belgium
Cairo, Egypt
Fátima, Portugal
Guadalupe, Mexico
Knock, Ireland
La Salette, France
Lourdes, France
Paray-le-Monial, France
Pont Main, France
Rue du Bac, France
Rwanda, Africa

2) "non constat de supernaturalitate" [supernaturally is not established]
   Determined as uncertain and require further study by the Church

Garabandal, Spain
Medjugorje, Yugoslavia

3) "constat de non supernaturalitate" [established as not supernatural]
   Determined by the Church to be false and unworthy of belief

Bayside, New York, USA
Necedah, Wisconsin, USA
San Damiano, Italy

---

[1]- http://www.vatican.va/roman_curia/congregations/cfaith/documents/ /documents/rc_con_cfaith_doc_19780225_norme-apparizioni_en.html

The author resided for several months in most of the sites described herein; other sites have been carefully researched. It is not the author's concern whether you believe them or not for, once they begin to unfold, you will begin to understand what I have described herein. The statements within are factual. The words in italic are, for the most part, taken directly from the Bible, or are the actual words spoken by Our Lady at the various apparition sites. They are words she has repeated countless times to numerous generations, especially over the past 185 years.

Footnotes and endnotes are generally not included in this manuscript inasmuch as the average reader for whom this work is intended has neither the time nor the inclination to ascertain the veracity of said notes.

Recently, however, some footnotes have been added to clarify items that may br cause for concern. Should the reader require additional authentication of any of the writings concerning the apparitions herein, they may be found in the many books written about each specific apparition, or on various web sites such as these, several of whom contain the *Nihil Obstat* and *Imprimatur*.

Lourdes, France Official Site.
- https://en.Lourdes-France.org

Fátima, The Third Secret of
– www.vatican.va/roman_curia/congregations/cfaith/documents/

Medjugorje, St. James' Church Site
– www.medjugorje.hr/en/

Offences against the Sacred Heart of Jesus:

1) Outrages
2) Sacrileges
3) Indifferences

Offences against the Immaculate Heart of Mary:

1) Blasphemies
2) Ingratitude

CREDITS

"Bernadette" – www.catholic.org/photos

"Bishop Thomas Grady, A Disciple of Mary, A Developer of Her National Shrine" – Dr. Geraldine M. Rohling, Archivist-Curator, Basilica of the National Shrine of the Immaculate Conception, Washington, DC 20017.

"Both Servant and Free" – Mullady, Brian, O.P., S.T.D.: EWTN

"CCC" – Catechism of the Catholic Church – Benziger Publishing Company

"CCD" – Confraternity of Christian Doctrine, Washington, DC

"Conchita's Diary" – "Our Lady Comes to Garabandal" – Pelletier, Joseph A., A.A.

"Consoling the Heart of Jesus" – Gaitley, M.E., Msgr., Stockbridge, MA: Marian Press, 2010

"Cosmos Shows Love-Life And Love-Death Themes" – Sheen, Archbishop

"Diary of St. Faustina" – Divine Mercy in My Soul

"Eternal City, The – Part II" – Pope John Paul II, Courtesy EWTN

"EWTN" – The Eternal Word Television Network

"Fátima, In Lúcia's Own Words" – Lúcia, Sister

"Fátima, The Third Secret of" –
www.vatican.va/roman_curia/congregations/cfaith/documents/
www.vatican.va/roman_curia/congregations/cfaith/documents/rc_con_cfaith_doc_20000
626_message-Fátima_en.html

"Garabandal, Mari Loli's Messages" – www.garabandal.org

"Goodbye, Mr. Chips" – Hilton , James, novel

"Gorbachev" – www.gfna.net/

"ICEL" – The International Commission on English in the Liturgy

"Joyful Good News for Young & Old" – Galeone, V.B., Bishop, Houston, TX: Magnificat Institute Press, 2014

"La Salette (in the French Alps)" – Photo © Missionaries of La Salette.

"L'Osservatore Romano" – The Cathedral Foundation, Baltimore, Maryland

"Lourdes" – www.lourdes-france.org

"Medjugorje Apologia" – www.medjugorje-apologia.com

"Medjugorje Messages" – www.medjugorje.org

"Memoirs of Sister Lúcia" – Lúcia, Sister, I, p. 162

"Mont Saint-Michel" – http://upload/wikimedia.org/wikipedia/commons

"Moses on Mount Sinai" – Gérôme, Jean-Léon , French painter

"My Heart Will Triumph" – Dragicevic-Soldo, Mirjana, CatholicShop Publishing, 2016).

"O Seculo" – Lisbon newspaper

"Our Lady of Mt. Carmel" – Picture: http://suzannetony.wordpress.com/ 2012/08/14/our-lady's-messages-to-the-world/

"Papal Seal" – http://en.wikipedia.org/wiki/File:John_paul_2_coa.svg

"Pie XII Devant L'Historie" – Roche, Msgr., pp. 52-3

"Reagan" – www.reagan.utexas.edu/archives/textual/smof/kingon.htm

"Spirit of Medjugorje" – www.spiritofmedjugorje.org/beginnersguide.htm

"St. Joseph Edition: The New American Bible" – © 1970, including the Revised New Testament © 1986" – Confraternity of Christian Doctrine, Washington, DC, provided all Bible References unless otherwise specifically stated.

"USCCB" – United States Conference of Catholic Bishops

"Creative Common Org" – For any reuse or distribution of material from this book in electronic form, see the following sites:
  - http://creativecommons.org/licenses/by-sa/3.0/
  - http://creativecommons.org/licenses/by-sa/3.0/legalcode

SELECTED BIBLIOGRAPHY

"Words of wisdom" from the following authors/books have encouraged the author while writing THE SALVATION OF THE WORLD; *All Ages Will Call Me Blessed*. Acknowledgment, where possible, was extended to the authors.

TREASURE IN CLAY
Archbishop Fulton J. **Sheen**
www.catholicfreeshipping.com/Articles.asp?ID=268

JOYFUL GOOD NEWS; FOR YOUNG AND OLD
Bishop Victor B. **Galeone**
www.legatus.org/joyful-good-news-for-young-and-old/

THE LIFE OF CATHERINE LABOURE, 1806-1876
Fr. René **Laurentin**
www.amazon.com/Ren%C3%A9Laurentin/e/B001HCYRJU

THE QUEEN OF PEACE VISITS MEDJUGORJE
Fr. Joseph A. **Pelletier**, A.A.
www.assumption.us/news/books

CONSOLING THE HEART OF JESUS
Fr. Michael E. **Gaitley**, MIC
www.shopmercy.org/Books/ALL/dpt/101/157/NO/*1*

MY HEART WILL TRIUMPH
Mirjana Dragicevic-**Soldo**
www.myheartwilltriumph.com/

 THE BIBLE is one of the fundamental sources of information shared by all major faiths: Judaism, Christianity and Islam. First used by the Israelites who formed Scripture into the Old Testament called the Torah; then, Christians added the New Testament. Later, Islam incorporated part of each into the Qur'an.

As the Gospel is the *Good News,* and the Bible contains all the Gospels, so the initials for the Bible may easily be understood as:

Basic Instructions Before Leaving Earth

SUGGESTED CHAPTER BIBLIOGRAPHY

CHAPTER 1 – Constantine
- **Constantine the Emperor** – Potter, David

CHAPTER 2 – Guadalupe
- **Our Lady of Guadalupe** – Anderson, Carl

CHAPTER 3 – Paray-le-Monial
- **Autobiography of St. Margaret Mary**

CHAPTER 4 – Rue du Bac
- **Saint Catherine Labouré** – Dirvin, Joseph I.

CHAPTER 5 – La Salette
- **Light On the Mountain** – Kennedy, John S.

CHAPTER 6 – Lourdes
- **Lourdes** – Ruth Harris
- **Song of Bernadette** – Movie, 1943, Jennifer Jones, C. Bickford

CHAPTER 7 – Pont Main
- **Our Lady of Pontmain** (kindle) – Lord, Bob and Penny

CHAPTER 8 – Knock
- **A Woman Clothed With the Sun** – Delaney, John J.

CHAPTER 9 – Michael, the Archangel
- **Mont Saint-Michel** –

CHAPTER 10 – Fátima
- **Fatima, In Lúcia's Own Words; Calls** – Sr. Lúcia

CHAPTER 11 – Beauraing
- **A Woman Clothed With the Sun** – Delaney, John J.

CHAPTER 12 – Banneux
- **A Woman Clothed With the Sun** – Delaney, John J.

CHAPTER 13 – Divine Mercy
- **Diary of Saint Maria Faustina Kowalska**

CHAPTER 14 – Garabandal
- **Star On the Mountain** – Laffineur and Pelletier

CHAPTER 15 – Akita
- **Akita: The Tears and Message of Mary** – Teiji Yasuda

CHAPTER 16 – Medjugorje
- **My Heart Will Triumph** – Soldo, Mirjana
- **The Queen of Peace Visits Medjugorje** – Pelletier, J. A.
- **Medjugorje** – Laurentin, René

"For God so loved the world..." (Jn 3:16)

San Michel's Alcove

"An Online Religious Referral Bookstore"

Murrells Inlet, SC 20976

sanmichelsalcove.com

Sr. Lúcia, of Fatima, provides a wonderful description of God, and the role of His angels

"The angels in Heaven always behold the face of Eternal Light, and in it – as in an immense mirror before which everything passes – everything is present, everything remains as if carved in indelible characters: the past, the present and the future.

"Everything that exists and was created by God: Heaven and Hell, the Earth, the stars, the sun, the moon, worlds known and unknown, all animate and inanimate beings...absolutely everything, receives its being and life from the wish, the power, the knowledge and the wisdom of that Infinite Light which is God, the one and only Source from which is derived all life that exists, and of which every other light and life is no more than a tiny particle, a pale reflection, one of His sparks.

"The angels, in their role as messengers, are our guardians and protectors throughout our lifetime: Thus the angels in Heaven, gazing into this mirror of Light which is God, in Him, see all things, know all things, understand all things, through their complete union with God and their participation in His gifts."

An Invitation

If you enjoyed reading this book you might also enjoy free, digital, color copies of the updated book for leisurely reading on computers, tablets and smartphones. It displays nicely on Apple, iPhone, iPad, Kindle, Android and Microsoft.

Type: www.sanmichelsalcove.com in your internet browser, then, click the PDF Icon on either the Alcove or Contact Us page for leisurely reading in your browser. If you prefer, you may download the file and read it later on your computer, tablet or smartphone.

The website is multilingual and affords translations into 100+ other languages. Click on the *Select Language* button; then, read or download each page from the website for your leisurely perusal. The free, updated, digital, color copies of the book may be distributed to others but you may not sell it or any part thereof for profit.

A laminated, printed, full-color copy of the book is also available in English from the website. Contact:

www.sanmichelsalcove.com
michelsalcove@gmail.com